DATE DUE

DEMCO 38-296

STRATEGIES FOR BUSINESS IN MEXICO

STRATEGIES FOR BUSINESS IN MEXICO

Free Trade and the Emergence of North America, Inc.

Louis E.V. Nevaer

Q

QUORUM BOOKS
Westport, Connecticut • London

Library of Congress Cataloging-in-Publication Data

Nevaer, Louis E.V.
    Strategies for business in Mexico : free trade and the emergence
of North America, Inc. / by Louis E.V. Nevaer.
      p. cm.
    Includes bibliographical references and index.
    ISBN 0–89930–882–1 (alk. paper)
    1. Mexico—Economic conditions—1982– 2. Mexico—Commerce—United
States. 3. United States—Commerce—Mexico. 4. Free trade—Mexico.
5. National characteristics, Mexican. I. Title.
    HC135.N44   1995
    382′.0973072—dc20   95–6921

British Library Cataloguing in Publication Data is available.

Library of Congress Catalog Card Number: 95–6921
ISBN: 0–89930–882–1

First published in 1995

Quorum Books, 88 Post Road West, Westport, CT 06881
An imprint of Greenwood Publishing Group, Inc.

Printed in the United States of America

The paper used in this book complies with the
Permanent Paper Standard issued by the National
Information Standards Organization (Z39.48-1984).

10 9 8 7 6 5 4 3 2

Copyright Acknowledgments

Grateful acknowledgment is given for permission to quote from the following sources:

The Broken Spears by Miguel Leon-Portilla. Copyright © 1962, 1992 by Miguel Leon-Portilla. Reprinted by permission of Beacon Press.

The Labyrinth of Solitude: Life and Thought in Mexico. Copyright © 1961 by Octavio Paz. Reprinted by permission of Grove/Atlantic, Inc.

With grand admiration this book is for my mentor
JORGE CANTO CANTO
and for my doctor
GEORGE ANDREW BISHOPRIC, JR.

Contents

**Part III: Integrating the Mexican Economy into
           the Age of Free Trade**

Preface

As this goes to press, Mexico has finished negotiating an international loan package to guarantee financial liquidity for 1995. On December 20, 1994, the Mexican peso was sharply devalued, something the three-week-old Zedillo administration said would not happen just days before. The unexpected policy reversal, coupled with the confusing manner in which the devaluation was handled, has created a credibility, as well as financial, crisis for the new administration that will be in office until the year 2000.

This "crisis," however, stands to be a short-lived phenomenon. To be sure, the devaluation of the Mexican peso and the necessity for emergency loans from the International Monetary Fund and the G-7 nations are not to be dismissed lightly, but it bears keeping a perspective. The fundamentals of the Mexican economy remain sound, and this correction, while drastic, is healthy, for it brings a semblance of reality into the Mexican equation. The Mexican peso had continued to become overvalued vis-à-vis the American dollar, and the worsening balance of the trade deficit created liquidity problems for Mexico's central bank.

The abrupt free fall of the Mexican peso, however, shocked investors worldwide. To make matters more troubling, the Zedillo administration handled the devaluation in a clumsy and amateurish manner, fanning the flames of panic not seen since Harold Wilson devalued the British pound in 1967 in a similarly chaotic way. "Once again," a New York investment banker with significant Mexican exposure confided the last week in December 1994, "the international community is asked to step in and save the Mexicans from themselves."

But recall how Mexico was being praised exactly six months before this collapse. "It's getting sunny in Mexico again, and one way investors can bask in the warmth without heading south is through American depository receipts," the *New York Times* reported on July 30, 1994, with a definite certainty.

The unkind truth for many American investors is that Mexico had been oversold for most of 1994, often pushed by brokers who ensnare innocents by failing to disclose accurately the risks involved or to explain adequately the economic and political developments that affect the prospects of investments being offered. That American investors lost over $10 billion in December's debacle is undeniable, but, to a great extent, many have made much more, and the recent turn of events was precipitated by runaway greed instead of sound business or investment judgment. A correction of some kind, somewhere along the line, is not unreasonable.

This is precisely how the present "economic emergency" must be viewed: as a correction. Mexico is undergoing the natural convulsions that are necessary when fundamental structural changes inherent in the North America Free Trade Agreement (NAFTA) take place. Despite the frantic headlines screaming the end of Mexico as 1995 began, the current "crisis" will be beneficial for Mexico—and the United States—as the processes unleashed by NAFTA continue to transform the business landscape of Mexico in due course.

For the corporate officer, the striking differences in the perceptions of Mexico should reveal more about expectations than realities. It is unrealistic to expect an economy that had been rising to do so forever, without a contraction. At the same time, those inclined to despair are being unfairly pessimistic. Caution is in order, both going in, staying put, or getting out of any business venture. The unrealistic expectations, occasioned, in part, by Mexico's entry into the North American economy, have resulted in a considerable disappointment to those who expected a developing economy to be integrated into the world's largest economy without dislocation along the way.

This seeming reversal in Mexico's fortunes has profound implications. It is, in fact, fortuitous, for it makes the arguments and strategies discussed in this book all the more relevant. Mexico is still there, and NAFTA is still in place and intact. The opportunities, arguably, are more enticing now that a devalued peso has made the Mexican economy a more attractive investment. Indeed, the current challenges offer corporate America a greater array of options in establishing a Mexican presence.

The good news of the December 1994 devaluation and its aftermath is that the process of Mexico's integration is being accelerated. The Mexican government has been compromised by current circumstances. As a consequence, to ensure adequate financial liquidity, Mexico is changing its laws, permitting foreign banks to play a greater role than had been previously envisioned by NAFTA. Mexican banks, encumbered with an alarming proportion of nonperforming loans inherited from the period in the eighties when the banks were nationalized, are now threatened by dollar-denominated obligations. The solvency of several large banks is now uncertain, and the profits of all Mexican banks have been virtually wiped out, which will facilitate American banks' penetration of the Mexican market.

The welcome news of the accelerated opening of Mexico's financial and banking sector to American interests is only surpassed by the decision to increase foreign revenues through a massive privatization program. Mexico's "family jewel," the state-owned oil monopoly, Pemex, will now be greatly redefined to permit American companies a historic opportunity. Since its creation—as a consequence of Mexico nationalizing of foreign oil companies' holdings in the thirties—Pemex has grown to become one of the largest companies in the world and one of the most inefficient and corrupt as well. Valued at well over $100 billion, Pemex was excluded from NAFTA negotiations for political reasons. The financial crisis now confronting Mexico, however, opens vast new opportunities for corporate America. It is now anticipated that Pemex will be privatized during the current administration, which would be the crowning achievement of NAFTA. The economic consequences are therefore more promising, once the initial shock of the devaluation makes itself felt throughout the Mexican economy in 1995 and beyond.

The greatest concern, however, is political and not economic. The eighteen-year program to get Mexico up to speed has, in a sense, been derailed. In 1982 a long-term program was implemented that envisioned a three-part strategy for the development of the Mexican nation by the year 2000. The first part began in 1982 when Miguel de la Madrid took office and Mexico confronted enormous economic difficulties precipitated by the international debt crisis. For six years Mexico pursued a program of austerity and the beginnings of reforms, highlighted by Mexico's entry into the General Agreement on Tariffs and Trade (GATT). The second part began in 1988 when Carlos Salinas assumed the presidency, and Mexico embarked on a program to accelerate the dismantling of the statist development model: Mexico sold off state-owned firms, modernized its economy, and successfully negotiated the passage of NAFTA. The last part began in 1994 when Ernesto Zedillo became president. What was envisioned to be a "caretaker" presidency, which would see political reforms—actually recognizing the victories of opposition parties—and would oversee the preprogrammed implementation of NAFTA, has now been made more arduous.

A man of undistinguished intellect, chosen for his ability to manipulate the more recalcitrant elements within his own party, Ernesto Zedillo now confronts the expectation that he demonstrate leadership. The handling of the devaluation, the subsequent turmoil in his cabinet, his alarming inability to reassure either the Mexican public or foreign investors, and his lack of charisma continue to undermine Ernesto Zedillo's credibility. A man who has led a sheltered—and closeted—life, Zedillo is ill at ease when facing the public and has been unable to show leadership when required. His address to the nation following the abrupt devaluation—postponed five times after having been delayed several days—only highlighted his vulnerability. "It was apparent," a senior official at the International Monetary Fund lamented, "that this man is in over his head." That sentiment was evident within and outside Mexico. An official at the Bank of Tokyo, who was monitoring developments in Mexico for the Japanese government, stated that "If Mr. Zedillo's first month in office is any indication of what the next six years offer, then we can expect tremendous disorder in Mexico for the remainder of the century."

What is disturbing, then, is this absence of vision and honesty. A man who is not true to himself can hardly be expected to be true to others. As the first year of the Zedillo administration unfolds, it is imperative that Zedillo show the kind of leadership and capability required to lead Mexico at a time when the country is being economically integrated into the North American economy. The economic foundation—and prospects—for Mexico are enormous. Prudence, however, is always advisable. It was never that sunny in Mexico in 1994, but then again, it isn't that bleak in 1995 either. There are always risks, but therein lie the most enticing opportunities.

Introduction

On December 1, 1994, Ernesto Zedillo was sworn in as president of Mexico. If he manages to serve out his term, President Zedillo will govern Mexico to the year 2000. In the next six years, the North America Free Trade Agreement, known as NAFTA, which was implemented January 1, 1994, will transform the landscape of the Mexican nation in fundamental ways that no one ever envisioned. For corporate America, the opportunities are immense, for an enormous market has been opened up. Mexico, a nation of over 85 million consumers, is a nation of 85 million unfulfilled desires.

Indeed, that NAFTA was ever negotiated at the initiative of former Mexican president Carlos Salinas de Gortari is evidence of the enormous failure of the socialist aspirations of the Mexican Revolution. That revolution, which was the bloodiest military engagement ever waged in the Western Hemisphere and which ended in 1917, gave rise to an authoritarian political structure that failed to deliver on its most fundamental promises. That Mexico is a country where, by official estimates, half the people live in poverty, and which has witnessed 10 percent of the population fleeing for exile, mostly to the United States and Canada, serves to underscore this point. Another country with statistics as alarming as these is Cuba, another landmark on the Boulevard of Broken Revolutionary Dreams. The forced exodus of approximately 8 million Mexicans from their country—creating strains in the United States that are nowhere more evident than in Californians' widespread support for the anti-immigrant

Proposition 187 in November 1994's elections—and the mere fact that Mexicans live in despair and want have compelled Mexico to abandon all pretense of sovereignty and to secure her future to that of the United States and Canada. Mexico, in essence, has freely chosen to be integrated into the American economy—and, along with Canada, by implication the American dream—to form North America Inc. Make no mistake about it, Mexico is undergoing a series of changes that alarm with their speed and that delight in revealing the latent and pent-up demands that, prior to NAFTA, were but dormant desires.

For corporate America, large and small companies have seen a boom in exports to Mexico during the first year of NAFTA. As someone who has been living in Mexico during this time of revolutionary change, it has been astounding to witness the unabashed enthusiasm with which the Mexican public, as well as Mexican businessmen, have embraced all things American. The accusation that this book is a portrait of Mexico seen through gringo eyes is inevitable. But it has been delightful to witness the honesty with which Mexicans have rejected their socialist development model and the earnest manner in which they have conceded that the Mexican Revolution has been a failure. By so doing, Mexicans have made significant strides toward democracy.

In such an environment, the opportunities for corporate America are enormous. Mexico offers tremendous opportunities, both on a business level and in personal terms. The Mexicans are a warm and generous people who have suffered under the oppressive rule of a violent political party and who are only now beginning to break free and experience the beginnings of democracy. This book is an examination of Mexico as it continues a program of systematic integration into the North American economy. The book offers an analysis of the Mexican character, peculiar and perverse, and the historical forces that have shaped the fragile Mexican psyche.

"Mexico" is an idea whose time has gone. As decisively as the collapse of the Soviet Union signaled the most definite conclusion to that utopian undertaking gone mad, so has NAFTA concluded its Mexican counterpart. To be sure, the United States and Canada are embarking on a grand experiment, incorporating Mexico, a Third World country, into their very own. The statistics repeated by officials in Washington, Ottawa, and Mexico City are as familiar as they are dull: The implementation of NAFTA, which began on January 1, 1994, will create the largest trading bloc in the known universe, consisting of more than 360 million consumers in an economy that will surpass $7 trillion.

But the consequences of what we have done are more than economic. The emergence of Mexico as an intrinsic partner in America's and Canada's future offers a powerful narrative that will shape our destiny as the new millennium approaches, for NAFTA is the political recognition of the end of "modernity" and the limits of the nation-state. Economic reforms and openings have political consequences. Mexico is in the process of implementing reforms that will mirror the U.S. legal system, thus radically altering the framework in which Mexican society operates. And in the same manner that the United States and Canada established free trade, social issues such as dissimilar health systems were causes of debate. What is evident is that economic actions have political consequences. It is naïve to believe that the historic conceptualization of the nation-state as it exists can survive the needs of modern economies. The proliferation of economic trading blocs, whether it be NAFTA or the European Common Market, constitutes evidence of the limits of the nation-state. In this sense, then, Mexico's unilateral willingness to revise her laws—from banking to environmental—is evidence of the systematic surrender of economic and political sovereignty. The economic needs of Mexico require political changes of historic proportions, something with which Mexican rulers have no problem. NAFTA is the surrender of economic sovereignty, implying the surrender of political sovereignty as well.

Mexico as a nation-state itself is a mosaic of peoples and ethnicities held together by the bureaucracy of authoritarianism and the authoritarianism of bureaucracy. The violence that has erupted in Mexico since the implementation of NAFTA is ominous, especially since this parallels the process of nation-state disintegration that is going on in many parts of the world. In too many instances, the introduction of democratic reforms (meaning the synergies of horizontal social organizations) in authoritarian countries (meaning controlled vertical social organizations) has not brought about a positive new unity but has had the opposite effect of unleashing divisive forces.

The understanding of modernity in the twentieth century is closely linked with the rise of the Industrial Revolution and the organizational requirements of the economies of scale, first in economics and then in the political structure of the modern "nation-state." The emergence of the "synergies" of a "horizontal" organization and the "networking" possible only with a technology-based "Information Revolution" (ascendant in the second half of this century) is first felt in economics, then in politics.

Karl Marx criticized the alienation in the workplace of the industrial capitalist world, an alienation born of a vertical bureaucracy in which power and authority are dispensed from top to bottom and where human beings are reduced to the functions they perform within the industrial organization. The worker is "dehumanized" by the segmentation of tasks, the differentiation of rank and status, the rote nature of the labor in the modern factory. The individual within this system of labor is relegated to a narrow task whose constricted nature impoverishes aspirations and demoralizes the spirit.

Max Weber analyzed the organizational structure of the bureaucracy and found compelling evidence that the same forces that exacerbated the plight of workers in an industrial setting also applied to workers in a bureaucratic one. The workplace alienation created by the segmentation of activities in a modern factory, he argued, also occurs in a modern bureaucracy. The strict and rigid system within an organization and the differentiation of autonomy through a division of rank, privilege, and authority both functioned to distribute power—and freedom—in an unequal manner throughout a bureaucracy. Weber argued that these distinctions in power resulted in despair.

Mexico came into existence as a modern nation-state against this philosophical background and historical context. The power in the modern Mexican state resides in the authority that it dispenses through its bureaucracy, which suffuses the whole of Mexican society. Not unlike other authoritarian countries, the political economy of Mexico, since the conclusion of the Mexican Revolution in 1917, is characterized as a mixed economy in which the state dispenses patronage with impunity.

The philosophical rationale for such a system is based on both the world-view of the "Indian" and the intellectual conceptualization of the modern nation-state. That "Indian" societies throughout Mesoamerica were founded on communal notions of social organization proved fortuitous. Communalism in fact bolsters socialism in theory. Both methods of political arrangements imply bureaucracies capable of organizing human societies. The economic requirements of Mexico early in this century—transforming itself from a battlefield into a nation-state and initiating programs for economic industrialization—occurred at a time in the history of the world when bureaucracies were linked with modernity.

Mexico aspires to nothing if not modernity, as manifested through the implementation of the bureaucracy of the modern nation-state that parallels the bureaucracy of the modern factory. The promise of the Industrial Revolution—inventions that held a future of leisure and plenty— were false dreams, Marx and Weber argued. Instead of freedom, the individual would become enslaved to machines and the requirements of bureaucracies (economic and political) that were necessary to run industry and the state. The oppressive nature of these human relationships—many people on the bottom and middle levels of a hierarchical organizational pyramid where a few at the top enjoyed power—held no hope. Weber believed the designation of tasks, with its defined parameters of restricted autonomy, created "iron cages."

A compelling and lovely metaphor, Weber's "iron cage" poetically described the future then unfolding: Modernity would result in the enslavement of mankind. For most of the century, Mexico has been in step with the rest of the world. When the Bolsheviks seized power in Russia in 1917, the Mexican Revolution (which was really a civil war) also ended. When the Bolsheviks established the Soviet State and then embarked on a communist program that abolished private property, as well as human rights, Mexico created an authoritarian, bureaucratic nation-state with a mixed economy (more socialist than capitalist) and with mixed records on respecting human freedoms. When the United States implemented the New Deal, Mexico was busy with its own version. When the United States declared the War on Poverty, Mexico was also waging war as best it could, which meant bringing the "Indians" into the modern world.

The modern bureaucracy of the organization, both economic and political, becomes a prison, a constrictive armor that imprisons the individual. Weber mourned this and saw the future as a horrific nightmare in which men and women would be reduced to functions, not individuals. Others voiced the same fears. Aldous Huxley warned of a future without hope. In *Brave New World*, he predicted a totalitarian state in which the dignity of the individual no longer existed. The rise of fascism in Europe—Hitler and Stalin—was cited as evidence that this vision of the future would unfold. The twentieth century, many believed, would herald the beginning of the enslavement of mankind, not its liberation. Others dismissed all this as hysterics.

Mexico's nation-state paternalism, after all, delighted in its power of vindication: Mexico in the forties, fifties, and sixties was a model of nation-state building and of economic development. The vertical bureaucracy that enslaved men and women in Weber's iron cages was a triumph, from an organizational point of view.

Then something happened. History did not end, as Marx predicted, and his communism was assaulted by an unexpected antithesis: "postmodernism." Not unlike the nineteenth century when economics led the way, in the twentieth century economics also changes our understanding of the world first. Weber's vision of the surrender of the human being to the objective demands of rationality and value-as-function is undermined by the emergence of a new paradigm of human organization. In the same way in which the invention of the printing press revolutionized the role of learning or in which the invention of the lightbulb revolutionized nighttime activities in the life of mankind, the Information Revolution stands to turn on its head our understanding of bureaucracy and the systems of organizations throughout human societies, both in economic and political terms.

The recognition of such a thing as postmodernism is itself an act of repudiation. It is a recognition that, unbeknownst to us, there are forces at work that reverberate throughout human society. The heralded "de-differentiation" refers to the collapse of the parameters that constrict and define Weber's world. It is the beginning of the recognition that there are forces beyond that alter our understanding of power-as-authority, knowledge-as-rank, and bureaucracy itself. The very notion of "de-differentiation," which can be more readily understood as horizontal organization in which networking and access to information play pivotal roles, undermines the monolithic future foretold.

Indeed, the economies of scale of the industrial age now give way to dissemination of information—and power—through technological advances that no one could have predicted. The proliferation of autonomy undermines the hegemony of a hierarchical pyramid. A horizontal bureaucracy, linked by modems and computers, faxes and electronic bulletin boards, is characteristic of the postmodern world, which, in fact, is the world of the Information Revolution. Not unlike the Victorian Age, which is now considered the beginning of the modern era, perhaps the conclusion of World War II, the creation of the Bretton Woods System (economic), and the cold war (political) characterize the emergence of what is called the postmodern epoch. This transitional phase may very well constitute a bridge to what is more commonly referred to as the Information Revolution.

Free trade refutes the centralized economy of the Mexican nation-state in no uncertain terms. NAFTA anticipates the end of modernity and with it our understanding of the nation-state. In August 1982, after desperate attempts to stave off disaster, Mexico was forced to admit defeat, devaluing the Mexican peso, freezing dollar accounts, imposing foreign exchange controls, and, ever at the vanguard of such things, ushering in the international debt crisis.

La crisis, as this national hangover was called, marked the beginning of the end of the Mexican protectionist development fantasy. Improbable Mexican utopian dreams and inexplicable socialist schemes, catalysts of the elaborate paternalistic political economy that subsidized idiocy as much as it patronized the Mexican, fostering lingering resentment borne of frustrations, had come to nothing.

The harsh reality of bankruptcy made itself felt through *la austeridad* that accompanied *la crisis*, and *austeridad* that was engineered by American consultants and by officials from the International Monetary Fund and the

World Bank, sold to the Mexican masses by public relations firms from London, scrutinized by public and private officials in various European capitals and several American financial centers, and approved by representatives of Japanese interests, all ensuring that the Mexicans didn't take them down as well.

The top-down pyramid was crumbling, for the age of postmodernity was at hand; Mexico, not unlike many other nations around the globe, experienced the consequences of irrational economic policies taken to their logical conclusions. That Mexico was able to manage to hold on for as long as it did was due to the windfall revenues from oil exports, income upon which other nations with bankrupt ideologies, such as the former East Germany, were unable to depend.

The demise of Mexican modernity was confirmed when Mexico, reluctantly, became a member of GATT, a condition for being bailed out of her debt crisis. The death of the Mexican Revolution officially came quietly in the night as December 31, 1993, became January 1, 1994, which is when NAFTA took effect, thereby ending seventy years of spectacular surrealism and modernity. Mexico's ruling party and the state became one and the same, which is similar to such totalitarian regimes as the Soviet Union and the People's Republic of China.

The idea was to direct the development—political, economic, social, and cultural—of the nation in an effort to consolidate the aspirations of the Mexican Revolution and accelerate the development of the new state. These objectives, and the method by which they were to be achieved, happily coincided with the traditional communalism of the "Indians" and the indigenous peoples of what now had become Mexico. Communalism, which can be interpreted as the surrender of the individual to the interests of the group, now became modernity, which required the surrender of the individual to the needs of the nation-state. The creation of Ruling-Party-as-State and then the State-as-Big-Brother was the triumph of progress.

And who is against progress? NAFTA is progress and constitutes the surrender of the sovereignty of the nation-state to the network of the Information Age. The demise of centralization and of Aztec imperialism constitute the birth of democratic forces that are uncontrollable, that revitalize dormant regionalism, and that herald a postmodernism that is horizontal in nature, accessible to all individuals regardless of the position that they occupy in their society's hierarchy. Anyone can turn on the television and send a fax; thus, anyone can challenge the modern nation-state. The future as predicted by Weber is now changed in fundamental ways that render his "iron cage" a cage with an open door.

Where Mexico ends, America begins. The weightless nature of the postmodern border, like shifting desert sands that disorient by changing points of reference across an uncertain landscape, creates a new paradigm, an unfamiliar and ambiguous wasteland filled with apprehension.

The laws of nature—*for every action there is an equal and opposite reaction*—take precedence over the laws of nations—*May I please see your work papers?*

The border between the United States and Mexico dissolves, becomes weightless and is real only in a metaphysical sense. Rand McNally maps document what exists only on paper. Under NAFTA the terms of trade have changed, as has the border: The United States, Canada, and Mexico are reincarnated as states of mind, not states of sovereignty, something trade negotiators on each side of every border failed to consider. The tensions exacerbated by greater economic integration, and the implicit movement of peoples across borders, is nowhere more evident than in Californians' enthusiastic passage of Proposition 187.

Precipitated by the Information Revolution, a horizontal organization, linked by networks where information is currency, is replacing the vertical organization of traditional bureaucracies. The proliferation of information systems across all levels of an organization—and throughout society—is the natural evolution of the progress of technology.

The ability of horizontal organizations to foster autonomy and empowerment for the individuals within the organizational structure liberates in ways that Weber could not even begin to imagine. Far from being an iron cage, the postmodern period is contributing to a renaissance of individual creativity where a premium—a commercial, social, and political value—is placed on the ability to use technology to further the dismantling of the rigid power structure of the organization.

The irony of the end of the twentieth century is the recognition of the need to diminish the power of bureaucracy. This is evident not only in an economic setting where, to remain competitive in global markets, corporations are engaged in programs of restructuring designed to do away with traditional bureaucracies in an effort to tap the synergies of their employees. North America, Inc., is the political restructuring of the nation-state.

The primitive industrial organization of England in the nineteenth century—which was the inspiration for Marx—and the primitive bureaucratic organization of the state in the early part of this century—which was the inspiration for Weber—no longer apply. The ease of transmitting and managing information, the invention of new technologies, represents the opportunity to move into organizational structures unimagined by Weber or Marx. If the narrative of industrialization in the modern era was characterized by differentiation—a segmentation of roles and functions necessary for the operation of both the factory and the organization—then the narrative in the postmodern era is becoming a "de-differentiation," which is an arcane way of describing horizontal structures linked by networks of information.

The alienation of the workplace decried by Marx is becoming the empowerment of the worker through synergies. The market-driven evolution of a salariat economy based on an emphasis of market service functions and creativity is a major force in the marginalization of industrial production: Power resides not with those who make televisions, but with those who make the programs that people want to watch on television.

Is the demise of the Soviet Union as much a political revolution as it is the dismantling of the iron cages of a political bureaucracy that Weber feared? Is the emergence of a horizontally organized company, such as Apple Computer, evidence of the success of that kind of bureaucratic structure over the inherent limits of a vertical Chrysler Corporation?

Are the changes in Mexico—dismantling the hegemony of a centralized bureaucracy, the introduction of market reforms, the adherence to international accords, such as GATT and now NAFTA—evidence of the limits of vertical bureaucracies in the political structure of the nation-state?

Not all of Mexico's conquered peoples welcome liberation inherent in a horizontal network. In Chiapas, on the first day of NAFTA, there was a terrifying reminder that not all men and women want to be free, that there are those perfectly happy within the confines of an iron cage. There is comfort in the familiar, and the political challenge for Ernesto Zedillo is to contain the radical forces within Mexico that are willing to resort to violence to ensure that a leftist social structure survives into the next century.

The surrender of economic sovereignty and the synergies of a horizontal paradigm erode the political sovereignty of the Mexican nation-state. With NAFTA, the center of Mexico's universe has thus moved from the ruling party's offices in downtown Mexico City and is now linked by modems to Corporate America in Anywhere, U.S.A. A realignment now begins to take shape as Mexico's peoples and regions come to terms with the new gravitational force fields pulling at them. The states that comprise Mexico must now dance in disciplined orbits around these brighter, more promising celestial stars that shine brightly in the American universe.

As the authoritarianism inherent in Mexico's ruling-party patrimonial system is dismantled, ethnic and regional differences that have remained frozen in terror for almost seventy years are rekindled. Mexico has the potential of becoming Yugoslavia once the iron cage is removed from her equation. The Balkanization of the geographic expression that Rand

McNally identifies as Mexico stands to become real, as Mexico is torn asunder, drifts into civil turmoil, baptized anew in human blood, and transcends "nation-statehood."

But the future cannot be denied. The irony of the end of the twentieth century, therefore, is the emphasis on diminishing the power of bureaucracy. This is evident not only in an economic setting where, to remain competitive in global markets, corporations are engaged in programs of restructuring designed to do away with traditional bureaucracies in an effort to tap the synergies of their employees, for the way to increase productivity is by increasing worker satisfaction.

The Information Revolution has rendered the analysis of Marx and Weber obsolete, for the world they describe no longer exists. The conflict confronting Mexico becomes apparent. Mexicans now vacillate in ambivalence. Mexicans long for the promise of democracy but remain unsure if it is worth the burden of responsibility. The comforts of being taken care of melt away in the face of the postmodern paradigm now unleashed throughout the world. Our understanding of bureaucracy is changing and with it our notion of the company and the nation-state.

When the door is opened, after all, the iron cage no longer imprisons. Mexicans no longer want to be imprisoned. The question, however, remains if they can will themselves from their past.

Part I

The Corporate Integration of the Mexican Economy

1

The Integration of
the Mexican Economy

> Only if you encounter someone else are you able to reflect on
> yourselves.
> —Paul Tillich

American businessmen arriving in Mexico City for the first time experience similar sensations. The first thing that strikes them is the filth of the Valley of Mexico as their plane descends—Mexico City boasts the world's worst air pollution. Then there is the chaotic drive by taxis to the tony Zona Rosa district where hotels such as the Sheraton María Isabel are located. After settling in, they go for a stroll along the Paseo de la Reforma to stretch their legs after a long flight and gather their thoughts for their upcoming meetings. As they stroll along Mexico's finest boulevard, and as they look around them, walking along the landmark Angel de la Independencia monument and the surrounding colonial and contemporary buildings, some of which are askew, sinking into the lake-bed on which this capital was built, Americans are struck, and disappointed, by how shoddy everything looks.

It is then that fatigue sets in, part jet lag, part the apprehension of being in a foreign land, part the realization of how substandard Mexico is in fact. But American businessmen are descending into Mexico City in greater and greater numbers as the forces unleashed by NAFTA make themselves known. There are far too many opportunities to permit a market as compelling as Mexico to be ignored. Indeed, the United States and Canada are embarking on a grand experiment, incorporating Mexico, a Third World country, into their very own.

The consequences of what we have done are the invention of North America, Inc. Indeed, the United States, Canada, and Mexico have, in fact, embarked on a journey of self-discovery by forging closer links with one another. It is only appropriate, therefore, that now that the whole of North America is one big happy family, we each learn about our new relations and how habitual suspicions give way to harsh realities. This will reduce surprises that are bound to arise as our common North American future begins to unfold before us.

To be sure, Americans and Canadians have no idea what they have stumbled into. Mexico, so often judged harshly by Americans—an incomprehensible land of visceral nature—or dismissed as mere entertainment—tropical vacations filled with margaritas—must now be understood as a separate society that is being incorporated with daunting speed into the fabric of the American and Canadian political economy. The emergence of Mexico as an intrinsic partner in America and Canada's future offers a powerful narrative that will shape the destiny of Americans, Canadians, and Mexicans alike as the new millennium approaches with discomforting speed, amusing as much as it alarms. Whereas in the nineteenth century America moved West, fulfilling its Manifest Destiny, Mexico has embarked more insidiously toward the North, settling landscapes—California, the American Southwest, Texas, and points beyond Mexico's cherished "safety valve," a geography that it has so longed for but that proved ever so elusive, until now.

Americans and Canadians, too, believe that by making the most of Mexico's "cheap" labor and enormous natural resources, they can improve their competitive advantage on a global level, as well as ameliorate the social and political disruptions occasioned by all that annoying illegal immigration from Mexico, economic refugees from that festering economic basket case. It isn't that America is enthusiastic about Mexico. America is not enamored with the prospect of militarizing the border should things continue in the future as they have in the past and should Mexico decline to the level of those ridiculous banana republics.

Americans, in brutal honesty, are appalled by Mexico. The visceral nature of Mexico, its vulgarity and coarseness, its senselessness that offends exquisite American sensibilities, its mortifying indulgence of base passions, its amusing childlike innocence—not the desert wastelands of the American Southwest and the Mexican Northwest—are what really have separated Americans and Mexicans. The discussion presented here attempts to allay American and Canadian fears. It is an effort to ease the minds of our reasonable neighbors by explaining why Mexico is the way it is and how it came to be this way.

American enlightenment stands in stark contrast to Mexico's medieval enslavement to passions and emotions. The apprehension and fear that overwhelm Americans as they behold Mexico and her surreal landscape is as real as it is inescapable. What we have here is the Age of Reason looking into the face of the unreasonable, the Age of *Un*reason. If America (and Canada) represents the Age of Reason made manifest, then Mexico (and Spanish America) represents the Age of *Un*reason. An American of Mexican ancestry, Richard Rodriguez, recognizes this, albeit accidentally. Of San Diego he writes in *Harper's* magazine: "Late at night, on the radio call-in shows, hysterical, reasonable American voices say they have had enough. Of this or that."[1]

Still, somehow as surely as Mexico extends her influence into America—spilling over the border into California at San Diego, wading ashore the Rio Grande into Texas, extending farther and farther into America and reaching Canada—the economic, corporate, and institutional forces set in motion by NAFTA promise to accelerate processes already underway, so does America penetrate Mexico and points farther south.

There is a give and take. The question, then, remains who will do more giving and who will do more taking?

Our futures—which is to say, our ordeals—are linked as one. What public officials and economists and corporate leaders hail as "North America, Inc." represents a defining moment in the histories of the three nations of North America. Hysterical, reasonable American voices may fear, in fact, that Mexico's unruly unreasonableness will contaminate America, undermining centuries of work to spread civilization across the daunting wilderness of this vast continent.

California and Texas, especially, have been at the front lines, aghast in horror as Mexico has been spilling over the border. The hysterical, reasonable American voices that resonate throughout the darkness of night are apprehensive, reluctant to understand what to make of the ebbs and flows, the rising floodwaters of illegal immigration, of the burgeoning frustrations in America's failure to assimilate these incomprehensible people. American voices denounce the unreasonableness of the Mexicans, of the Latins, of the Southeast Asians, of all these Third World peasants. Americans fear that, under the guise of fashionable "multiculturalism" chic, great multitudes of people will tear asunder American civility with their backwardness, their stupidity, their baggage, their festering wounds. American voices lament the futility of rendering reasonable these unreasonable people. American voices decry the deterioration of American life that these alien peasants leave in their wakes, transforming the promise of the American Dream into a damning, unrelenting staccato of chaos.

American and Canadian misgivings are also Mexican misgivings. There is as much excitement as there is dread in Mexico as it faces the unknown consequences of what the future holds. Mexican ambivalence toward the promise of NAFTA—stated by its ruling party overlords to be desirable, but insecure in its own ability to judge for itself—Mexico remains unable to articulate the uneasiness that it feels, unable to phrase in words the inescapable thought, however fleeting it may be, that this is somehow a ploy, an insidious ploy at that, by powerful neighbors to *use* Mexico and the Mexicans, as has occurred so often in the past. Thus, a disquieting silence paralyzes Mexico, rendering the Mexican passive in the face of, what well may yet be, another so-called "bandit raid." This sentiment, bordering on resentment, is beginning to become more widespread in Mexico as the stark realities of NAFTA are felt; American businessmen are arriving in Mexico City by the planeload to make deals, whereas hardly a Mexican businessman travels to New York for the same purpose.

Mexico, it seems, has nothing to offer, except the cheap labor of her people and the prizes of her raw materials—oil, precious metals, land, fruit, sunshine. The United States and Canada, by contrast, have everything in the world that the Mexicans desire. Within the first year of NAFTA, this perception became more than evident as Mexico's trade deficit soared to staggering proportions, and were it not for revenues from oil exports, the Bank of Mexico's dollar reserves would have been depleted, triggering a sharp devaluation of the Mexican peso. The one-way nature of free trade, then, is only now being felt throughout Mexico.

Ambivalence, then, characterizes both Mexican and American business-men, which is exacerbated by historical misunderstandings and a cultural abyss that divides entrepreneurs from both sides of the border. The fundamentals of conducting business in Mexico, however, have been, and are continuing to be, greatly simplified. The economic development model that made imports difficult have all but vanished. In the new paradigm created by NAFTA, it turns out, America has everything to sell and Mexico has nothing to sell, save the same primary products that it has been selling to established markets for decades and that it then imports as finished products; Mexico sells oil to the United States only to buy it back in the form of unleaded gas, betraying the complete backwardness of Mexico's development schemes of the past seven decades.

The opportunities for corporate America, therefore, are tremendous, but sound strategies for the penetration of the Mexican market must be developed and implemented. The Mexican market offers its own set of challenges; but as more and more American companies are discovering, Mexico represents a ready market, eager for American goods and anxious to participate in the active integration of the Mexican economy into the whole of North America. The metamorphoses now taking shape in Mexico were inconceivable a decade ago, and the unbridled enthusiasm with which Mexicans are receiving the arrival of corporate America has few, if any, parallels in history anywhere in the world. The time is right. The market is right. The opportunities have been delivered within a political accord that affords protection, guarantees, and a level of certainty.

NOTE

1. Richard Rodriguez, "Across the Borders of History," *Harper's*, March 1987, p. 43.

2

Assessing the
Mexican Market

Since the implementation of NAFTA, the number of opportunities for American companies to increase their commercial dealings with Mexico has continued to grow at an accelerating pace. The pent-up demand from decades of protectionism, coupled with a natural predisposition to purchase American products, has resulted in greater and greater exports to Mexico. There are many ways in which Americans can take advantage of the boom in the Mexican market. Without becoming directly involved in establishing a presence in Mexico, the most accessible way to increase exports is to establish licensing agreements. For other firms, joint ventures and strategic alliances with Mexican firms offer an opportunity to establish a more visible presence in the Mexican economy. Larger companies, on the other hand, are likely to establish their own subsidiaries in Mexico.

Whichever strategy is chosen, however, depends ultimately on the goals of the firm, the market analysis, the long-term strategies, and the level of financial commitment deemed appropriate. A preliminary analysis of the Mexican market indicates that American companies have a natural advantage in assessing a product's potential in the Mexican marketplace. Decades of growing expertise in selling to the growing Hispanic and Latino markets throughout the United States have given corporate America an insight into the psychology of the Spanish-speaking consumer. Mexican firms, on the other hand, have virtually no expertise in selling to an English-speaking consumer. Thus, while American firms are poised to enter Mexico, few Mexican companies threaten to enter the United States.

NAFTA, critics have argued, has handed American companies an unfair advantage, so to speak.

MARKET AREA PLANNING

Under the terms of NAFTA, Mexico ceases to be a foreign market in many ways. The Mexican market, therefore, is rendered more akin to the Spanish-speaking markets in the United States, with which American companies are already accustomed. Indeed, the expressed and revealed preferences of the Mexican consumer are familiar to American marketers. Over the past two decades, Hispanic and Latino consumers in the United States have garnered greater affluence and visibility. In response to this growing market, corporate America has targeted marketing campaigns tailored to the specific characteristics of individual market segments. The Cuban consumer in Miami has different tastes than the Puerto Rican consumer in New York, which are different from the Mexican consumer in Los Angeles. For Mexico as a whole, the consumer profile is more affluent and sophisticated than the Latino consumer in Los Angeles, but not nearly as much as the Hispanic consumer in south Florida.

American firms exporting to Mexican consumers need to bear in mind that the purchasing power of the Mexican consumer approximates that of the Cuban resident of Miami more so than the Mexican-American consumer in Los Angeles. The reasons for this are several, but they have to do with race and the social status of the consumer. Whereas Miami Cubans are white and educated, California Mexicans are not. In Mexico, the growing middle class is both white and professional, and the tastes are similar to that of the vast majority of Hispanics in Miami. Mexicans in California and Texas, on the other hand, are not as educated and come from a more Native American background, rendering them disenfranchised minorities within minorities, in both Mexico and the United States.

The corresponding consumer patterns clearly reflect these differences. For corporate America, a sound strategy is to fine-tune consumer campaigns that are in place for the Hispanic markets of south Florida and that reflect the cultural nuances of the Mexican marketplace. It is counterproductive to rely on marketing programs targeted for the Latino markets in California and Texas, given that it is only a white, middle-class consumer in Mexico that is likely to afford American products.

Conversely, at the high end of the market—interior designing services, expensive jewelry—the Mexican profile approximates those of American consumers in such markets as Long Island, northern New Jersey, or Florida's Broward County. Consumer purchasing patterns are strikingly similar, as are disposable incomes. The patterns are familiar, as the preferences and the marketing strategies should also be. Apart from an ethnic twist, the consumer preferences are unremarkable; nor are Mexican consumers particularly demanding. Having been denied access to First World markets for so long, they are grateful for anything that approximates their needs.

As a general rule, if a product sells to the Spanish-speaking consumer in south Florida, it will do well among the Mexican middle class. The reasons, ironically, also lie in the class aspirations of the Mexican middle class. Affecting sophistication, the Mexican middle-class consumer attempts to emulate the standard of living achieved by the professional Cuban-American community in the United States, with a "Mexican" ethnic flavor. There is a discomforting resentment between Mexicans in the United States and Mexicans in Mexico that puzzle American observers. That the two groups seldom interact and have tenuous relations, often tinged with suspicion, supports the view that the Mexican Revolution has failed; Cubans in Miami and Cubans in Cuba are on opposite sides of the political spectrum, as the animosity between Cuba and the exile community demonstrates. The existence of similar tensions between Mexicans suggests that Mexicans in the United States are viewed as exiles, albeit economic ones, in the estimation of Mexicans who choose to be—or are stuck—in Mexico.

This distance, which is reinforced by class differences—Mexicans in America remain mostly in the working class, whereas Cubans in America are professionals—contributes to the market segmentation evident among Mexican middle-class consumers. Marketing programs, and expectations, should be geared toward understanding the subtle effects of class and status on expressed and revealed preferences of the Mexican consumer. To be sure, there is an enormous market of millions of Mexicans whose consumer profiles approximate that of Mexicans in the United States. But the challenge there is the stark reality that these consumers have limited disposable income, and Mexico continues to subsidize basic consumer goods as part of its political agenda. There are restrictions, for example, on the sale of powdered milk, and price controls are in force for items such as bread. An economy where these things are necessary reveals a great deal about the affluence of its consumers.

Business Opportunities

For about forty years, Mexico restricted imports as part of an import-substitution program designed to allow domestic production to satisfy the nation's demand. This resulted in the development of inefficient industry;

comparative advantages were disregarded, and a captive market paid a premium for goods and services that were not on par with international standards. The proliferation of such inefficient industry, fostered through state intervention and nationalist policies, resulted in self-sufficiency of sorts, however inefficient it may have been.

This economic development model had its limits, and the growing Mexican population required greater economic choices. With significant proceeds from oil exports and an increasing amount of foreign loans, the Mexican government embarked on a program to accelerate economic development, which included the development of an in-bond industry, known as *maquiladoras*, and the development of resort communities to host greater numbers of foreign tourists. That the Mexican State relied on significant dollar earnings through the state-owned oil monopoly afforded the government ample funds to finance a vast array of spending programs to keep its development model afloat. In the seventies, as the Arab oil embargo pushed the price of oil up, and as new reserves were discovered in Mexico, the Mexican government's revenues soared, as did the number of loans extended by foreign banks and lending organizations. Unlike the Saudis, who have been successful in managing their wealth, Mexico, for a variety of reasons, proved less successful in handling incomes. When the price of oil began to decline, spending levels could not be sustained and a series of problems developed that came to a head in August 1982 when Mexico devalued its currency and formally announced that it could not meet its international obligations, ushering in the international debt crisis.

The 1980s in Mexico are remembered as the "lost decade" in which austerity measures resulted in a sharp decline in incomes and standards of living. The ensuing economic crisis forced Mexico to abandon its nationalistic development model and, by joining GATT, it joined the community of nations, embarking on a program to open its borders and adopt free trade. These policy changes were encouraged by young Mexican ministers and officials who, for the most part, were educated in the United States and sought to abandon the rhetoric of the Mexican Revolution in favor of a modern economy. The negotiations that led to NAFTA were the result of a concerted campaign to "render reasonable" the Mexican political economy, which is nothing short of a revolution.

For corporate America, which had long been relegated to a restricted role in the Mexican economy, U.S. subsidiaries that produce for the small Mexican market and that are restricted to the production of goods for export now have ample opportunity to expand in Mexico with an enormous amount of freedom at their disposal. Under the new terms of trade, corporate America now faces almost no barriers in developing opportunities in the Mexican market. Indeed, NAFTA is resulting in a phenomenon that few expected: Whereas Americans, such as Ross Perot, feared a Mexican "invasion," what is actually occurring is an American takeover of the Mexican economy. The speed with which corporate America is extending into all areas of the Mexican market astounds in its completeness—and in the enthusiasm with which Mexicans are embracing all things American.

For industry, the opportunities are remarkable. Mexicans, for historic reasons that will be addressed later on, have a natural predisposition to favor American goods. This bias in favor of American products is, in part, a political statement in protest against the statist development model of the previous half century. For Mexicans who have long awaited the opportunities afforded their counterparts in the United States and Canada, the ability to have a choice—whether it be choosing a pizza as opposed to an enchilada or choosing which political party to vote for in an election—is a novelty that delights. As a result, America is in; witness the Mexican teenagers standing in line to enter the Hard Rock Cafe, the Mexican Yuppies buying everything off the shelves of the Sharper Image store in Mexico City, or the trucks filled with merchandise and waiting to cross from the United States into Mexico. There are few times in history when a market of 90 million consumers, who happen to be next door, are presented on a silver platter. Mexican President Carlos Salinas, a Harvard-educated Yuppie who loathes the statist development model that brought Mexico to economic ruin in 1982, has delivered Mexico to corporate America with no apologies.

Alliance Partner Analysis

The identification of suitable partners is made difficult because of language barriers and the different methods of determining the credit-worthiness of Mexican companies. The implementation of strategic plans, however, requires a comprehensive analysis of potential Mexican partners. The strengths and weakness of potential partners is a task made more arduous by the relative strength of American firms vis-à-vis Mexican counterparts. As such, familiar tools of analyzing financial statements of potential candidates and scrutinizing marketing programs are only one component that should be considered. In Mexico, where business dealings are personal friendships, it is the nature of one's friendship with the Mexican managers that is the basis of trust and that inspires confidence. As important, too, is an assessment of the relative development, or lack thereof, of the targeted market. A firm that is small but knowledgeable and whose managers are eager to work may better serve the strategic objectives of opening a market. The longevity of the firm, too, speaks volumes about that firm's ability to negotiate in uncertainty and volatility, which characterizes many emerging markets.

Entry/Exit Barriers

The proximity of Mexico reduces barriers to entry and exit. New foreign investment laws facilitate the transfer of funds from one country to another, expediting the repatriation of profits as well as the infusion of capital for expanding investment levels of the operations of a Mexican strategic business unit (SBU). For many American companies, fortuitously, it becomes far easier to reduce the costs and risks of entering the Mexican market through the use of agents and representatives. As a consequence of the modifications to Mexican laws, it is now easier to enter the Mexican market via licensing and franchising. There has been a boom in American companies franchising their operations in Mexico. Legal guarantees that were once lacking now offer protection to American firms, since intellectual property was not well defined under Mexican laws. The ability of easing into the Mexican market through the use of agents and licensing agreements is a viable way of reducing initial entry and exit costs while the long-term potential of the market is assessed.

Competitive Advantage

Corporate America enjoys an envious position in entering the Mexican market. As a result of the import-substitution development model pursued for half a century, few Mexican companies can hope to compete on American turf. Apart from notable exceptions, like Cemex, which manufactures cement and which controls a sizable portion of the U.S. domestic production, few Mexican companies are in a position to compete against American companies in the United States. No Mexican retailer is prepared to battle Saks Fifth Avenue or Nordstrom, no Mexican firm represents competition for Intel or IBM. Thus, corporate America can rest assured that its domestic operations will be unaffected by Mexican competitors, whereas the opposite cannot be said.

Corporate America, under NAFTA, now enjoys carte blanche in the systematic penetration of the Mexican marketplace. Ironically, the process of seizing large portions of market share in different Mexican niches is facilitated by the wave of privatizations that occurred in the eighties. Under the Salinas administration, significant segments of the Mexican economy were privatized, from banks to airlines; the wholesale dumping of public sector entities contributed to the proliferation of newly privatized companies whose managers face a learning curve. The Mexican banking system, for instance, remains among the most inefficient and backward in the developed world, so much so that NAFTA offers provisions for a one-time, three-year moratorium should American and Canadian banks take over the Mexican banking system too quickly. Already, dozens of foreign banks have filed applications to enter the Mexican banking system, while no Mexican bank has expressed an interest in competing with banks in, say, New York or Toronto.

For corporate America, the natural competitive advantages astound in their extensive nature; an entire market characterized by managers who are struggling with a learning curve at a time when deregulation is changing the rules of the game is there for the taking. In terms of success, the expansion into Mexico is one in which a competitive advantage and a customer profile inherently prefers American products and facilitates the establishment of a sustainable strategic presence throughout all economic sectors. The fear, often voiced by Mexican liberals and categorically ignored by Mexican technocrats, is that in a matter of a few years Mexicans will be reduced to being employees of American companies.

Relative Market Strength

The relative weakness of Mexican companies in the age of free trade constitutes a significant advantage for American firms. The Mexican economy is a small fraction of that of the United States. The Mexican economy is an emerging market, while in many key sectors the United States is a mature market. For these reasons the performance of a Mexican SBU stands to show higher rates of growth than operations in the United States. Thus, assessing relative performance requires the establishment of reference points and benchmarks that reflect the strategic differences of these markets. A contextual analysis offers insights into the identification and assessment of opportunity costs, as well as the establishment of milestones in cost positions, differentiations, and the successful development of focused markets. For the American manager, then, the challenge becomes one of competing, not against other Mexican competitors, but with American competitors that also are pursuing market shares in Mexico. It is GM battling Ford and IBM battling Apple and McDonald's battling Burger King—all speaking Spanish. The relative strength, then, lies in establishing a Mexican SBU first, and then expanding before competitors establish a presence of their own.

Strategic Thinking

With a sense of the urgency in opening up a Mexican presence—K-Mart and Wal-Mart are poised to compete head-to-head throughout Mexico beginning in 1995—the information compiled from contextual analyses of competitor and industry positions indicates how long-term strategic goals are modified to reflect the changing regulatory, legal, and business environment. The emergence of competitors—or the absence of familiar competition—will determine whether strategic alliances, joint ventures, partnerships, or acquisitions are the optimal way of establishing a sustainable presence in the Mexican marketplace. The importance of conceptualizing the Mexican market as a mosaic of distinct regional markets, but with similar themes, allows for the development of segmented market strategies.

Strategic Objective

The short- and medium-term objectives are defined. For consumer products and service companies, the opportunities for immediate sales are enormous. Mexico, because of historic trade barriers, has offered significant returns on investment. While competition is beginning to be felt in key consumer markets—consumer products, fast-food franchises, electronics—in many other areas profit margins remain higher than in the United States or Canada. The lack of a sophisticated infrastructure, the absence of fierce competition, the premium paid for catering to niche markets—all contribute to the feasibility of higher profit benchmarks. Management objectives should reflect the feasibility of exporting or servicing a market for whom the novelty of the product represents a measure of status that is often difficult to achieve in mature markets in which consumers are jaded and face greater choices as a matter of course.

Leadership with Vision

Success in establishing a significant presence in Mexico requires an aggressive approach best handled in conjunction with a Mexican partner who is familiar with the national and regional marketplaces. The timetable that NAFTA establishes for bringing down trade barriers has contributed to an emphasis among Mexican managers on identifying American associates. The philosophy—or fear—is that it is better to be in an alliance with an American company today than in direct competition tomorrow. The heightened sense of competition—if not dread—throughout corporate

Mexico is contributing to an explosion of alliances and joint ventures. In the next twenty-four months, for instance, major retailers throughout corporate America will begin entering the Mexican marketplace in association with existing retailers. Whether it is Wal-Mart or Office Depot, these firms, in joint ventures and alliances with Mexican partners, will begin to dot the Mexican landscape in a significant way. The priority for firms in corporate America, then, if unable to establish a presence of their own, is to identify key players for securing strategic market positions.

Identify Future Goals

Within an overall market plan, a growing Mexican presence needs to be established. Rather than conceptualize a Mexican subsidiary or sales revenue as a "foreign" operation, the emerging interconnected nature of North America, Inc., suggests that Mexico be considered as an SBU that generates a cash flow, either from direct exports, licensing fees, or joint venture sales. Within this framework, the success of an SBU can be analyzed in a more traditional manner. In view of the fact that Mexican labor, commercial, tax, and business laws are being reformed to reflect more closely the legal systems of the United States and Canada, Mexico will make more "sense" to American managers as the next century approaches. Indeed, tremendous progress has already been made in rendering more sensible Mexican laws concerning copyrights and intellectual property, which is of significant importance for computer software firms.

Establish Objectives

Management needs to understand how to establish priorities for assessing what constitutes progress in the Mexican market. A mistake often made is to rely exclusively on an initial cash flow figure while neglecting the sustainability of that growth. Competitive strategies must be tailored to reflect the need to enhance market position in a fundamental manner. Consider the setbacks suffered by fast-food companies that entered Mexico. At first, the novelty of American companies, such as McDonald's and Kentucky Fried Chicken, resulted in spectacular sales, in much the same way in which Planet Hollywood would cause a sensation whenever a franchise opened somewhere in the United States. The initial sensation, however, peaks after a few months and the failure to have tailored a marketing program to sustain sales results in a deteriorating cash flow. While there are companies, such as McDonald's, that can sustain remarkable sales in Mexico City, franchises in other locations have not been able to duplicate the success. For American firms, the challenge remains to establish benchmark objectives that reflect the creation of a sustainable presence in the Mexican marketplace, long after the initial fanfare subsides.

Assign SBU Missions

Consistent with this, the Mexican SBU must have a working plan that recognizes the distinct needs and responds to the preferences of the Mexican market. The Mexican SBU must have the resources, in both human and financial terms, to carry out its mission adequately. This requires the presence of bilingual, if not bicultural, officers who can understand the nuances of the Mexican psyche and culture. As Mexico becomes more of a domestic market, it may be appropriate to consider Mexican operations as an SBU, no different from the differentiated market segments in the United States as a whole.

Determine Risk Adversity Levels

The risks of conducting business in Mexico are diminished in the age of free trade. The rationalization of the Mexican legal system and norms of doing business contributes to a sense of greater stability. This is not to say that Mexico approximates a mature or stable market in a traditional sense. In the nineties, the threat of a devaluation exists, if for no other reason than that the mounting trade deficit is depleting the central bank's reserves at an astonishing rate. Of greater importance is the continuing— if not spreading—level of political violence. The dismantling of the structure of a ubiquitous hegemony faces stiff resistance from those sectors of Mexican society that benefit from the status quo. Armed rebellion and political assassination among the ruling elite has cast a shadow over the continuing stability. For American managers, a prudent and cautious response to disturbances is recommended. Things have a way of working themselves out in Mexico, and a society that remained stable during the 1982 international debt crisis suggests that the process of democratization, however painful at times, will be peacefully resolved. Nevertheless, Mexico as an SBU occupies the higher ranges of risk.

Establish Portfolio Balance

The diversity of opportunities in the Mexican market is great. The designation of an SBU for the Mexican market should incorporate a strategy to develop opportunities in different market niches that conform to the overall long-term goals of the firm. The traditional practice of dumping outdated and obsolete products on the Mexican market is becoming increasingly difficult; where trade is freer, consumers are less desperate for whatever they can secure. Market niches in related fields must be developed in a way that allows for an overall balance that provides an entire range of goods and services to the more demanding Mexican client.

Determine Resource Commitment

It is expected that as competition continues to accelerate, profit margins will decline. Whereas in earlier decades the captive nature of the Mexican market assured handsome profit margins, in the nineties the level of commitment, or investment, of a firm will be determined not only by revenue figures but also by a continuing analysis of the market. Management's commitment to providing resources for an expanding Mexican SBU development requires access to timely input. The potential for growth and for further development of existing markets requires an enhanced level of commitment; Mexico is neither foreign nor distant any longer.

Identify Threats/Opportunities

Apart from the threat of a currency devaluation or political violence, the greatest threat for corporate America resides in competition from other American firms that enter the Mexican marketplace. The desperate search by Mexican firms to secure alliances and joint ventures with their U.S. and Canadian counterparts since the conclusion of trade talks is now being felt as company after company announces plans for this or that venture. For corporate America, the real threat is of being left behind as competitors move in and establish a presence in the Mexican market. For firms already established, the mere existence of a track record stands to offer a false sense of security. Complacency is a threat; after withdrawing from the market for twenty years, for instance, Pepsi-Cola reentered several key markets, the resort of Cancun among them, and the competing cola wars with Coca-Cola produced an all-out war that has shaken the Coca-Cola distributor in the region in a dramatic way.

Anticipatory Strategies

The development of competitive strategies is continuously changing as markets in flux settle. What became a threat for Coca-Cola was, in turn, an opportunity for Pepsi-Cola. What sets superior management apart is the ability to discern how opportunities will emerge and what strategies are most able to develop these opportunities. For corporate America, the whole range of Mexico is now open, particularly as the Mexicans themselves aspire to become more and more like Americans, in standard of living, in aspirations, in consumer tastes. The process of regional differentiation is already clearly defined; the north of Mexico resembles the American Southwest while the south of Mexico still resembles the banana republics of Central America. The natural drifting, coupled with the simple matter of geography, argues for a strategy to penetrate Mexico City, where a quarter of the Mexican people live, then move to the cities of Guadalajara and Monterey. Reaching these three cities assures reaching 70 percent of potential markets.

Implementation

The whole of Mexican geography offers the opportunity of convenience. For most businesses, it is possible to reach up to 85 percent of the Mexican market by targeting Mexico City, Guadalajara, and Monterey. These cities, connected by easy flights to each other, give corporate officers a handle on the more significant markets in the country, as well as better control in implementing a corporate strategy and consulting with Mexican partners and managers. The most insightful analysis and the most meticulous plans are less useful if something is lost in the translation. In an era of fierce competition, the mark of leadership is in implementing strategic thinking for securing a firm share of the Mexican marketplace.

Aggressive Marketing

Consistent with these aims, an aggressive marketing program is problematic. While the objective of convincing the customer that one's firm can meet the needs of the client's value chain, American style marketing offends the more Old World and gentlemanly manners. Indeed, Mexicans, more so than other Latin Americans, affect a style of manners and civil conduct that are formal, to such a degree, in fact, that Mexicans are ridiculed by other Latin Americans—Argentinians, Colombians, and Venezuelans, in particular—for such affected manners. In the Mexican context, however, American managers must be aware of the conflict within the Mexican business community. The generational gap between the older generation of Mexican managers, who have lived their entire lives in a protectionist economy, and younger Mexican managers, who look to their

American contemporaries as a role model, is enormous. Mexicans are in the midst of changing how they do business; how they sell to the public and how the standards divide direct from aggressive and acceptable from rude are redefined in the new paradigm of free trade. What may be acceptable in the United States may be seen as overbearing in Mexico. And what holds true for marketing practices also holds true for management styles. Corporate America, for instance, must come to terms with the undeniable fact that the most capable managers in the United States for helping to develop the Mexican market are Cuban Americans, who are seen as arrogant by Mexicans. This dilemma is addressed at length in the next section. For the implementation of strategic thinking, however, it is important to recognize not only the Mexican aversion to what is seen as straightforward marketing campaigns but also the conflict emerging from the Americanization of marketing values and styles.

PECULIARITIES OF THE MEXICAN MARKETPLACE

The traditional approach to strategic thinking has to be modified to reflect three distinct characteristics that render Mexico peculiar to American managers. Apart from the obvious differences—Mexico is a society where Spanish is spoken and where there is a great deal of Native American influence, and it has evolved from the historical forces brought over from Spain, not England (as was the case in the United States and most of Canada)—there are other, more relevant, factors at work. If corporate America is to treat Mexican operations as an SBU, then it must understand that this SBU will be different because of possible currency devaluation, the threat of political abductions, and the jealousies stemming from competition between Mexicans and American managers of Cuban descent. Each of these categories offers insights into how to best develop and implement strategic thinking for establishing a profitable Mexican presence.

Exchange Rates

An important consideration in conducting business in Mexico is the stability of the peso. Under the Salinas administration, the Mexican currency traded within a narrow band, part of a controlled devaluation. The Salinas administration "politicized" exchange rates, however, preferring to let the peso become overvalued for the sake of the confidence a "stable" exchange rate would inspire. This policy became unsustainable in the second half of 1994 for three reasons. First, Salinas underestimated the lack of competitiveness of the Mexican economy in a context of freer trade.

While Mexicans exported more, they imported far more. The result was a rapidly deteriorating trade balance, draining the reserves of the Bank of Mexico. Second, Salinas politicized the economy, increasing money supply to finance overtures to the Zapatista rebels in Chiapas and to subsidize the ruling party's campaign in the presidential elections; bribing peasants and flooding the airwaves with political advertisements does cost money. Third, the anticipated capital inflows, mostly from Japan, did not materialize in 1993 or 1994. I remember seeing a frustrated Salinas pacing, angered at the recalcitrant Japanese officials, lamenting that the Japanese "were going to miss the boat." Then again, the *Titanic* is a ship well worth missing.

As a consequence, the prevailing exchange rates became unrealistic. This policy of a controlled devaluation while providing a firm foundation for conducting business in Mexico, created liquidity problems in the short term. When Ernesto Zedillo took over in December 1994, he inherited an overvalued currency, a deteriorating trade deficit, and weakened investor confidence occasioned by both the caliber of the members of his Cabinet and by the continuing unrest in the states of Chiapas and Tabasco. These problems proved insurmountable within the first month of his administration, and once it became apparent that pressure on the Mexican peso continued to intensify, the Bank of Mexico, in order to protect its dwindling reserves, withdrew from market intervention. In the aftermath, the Mexican peso was sharply devalued, from approximately 3.50 to the U.S. dollar to, at one point, over eight to one. The extraordinary reaction was further aggravated by the inexperience of the Zedillo administration, but once the peso recovered to the 6–6.50 trading range, there was relief that the long overdue "correction" had at last taken place.

The challenge for the Zedillo administration is to curb inflationary pressures that stand to erase the benefits of a correction as massive as this one. It is anticipated that, while the Mexican economy being inherently so "dollarized," a conservative fiscal and monetary policy, similar to that implemented by Miguel de la Madrid in 1982 and continued by Carlos Salinas in 1988 will reign in the fears that a cycle of inflation and devaluation will exacerbate an already delicate situation. The enthusiasm with which Mexican companies and consumers have been purchasing American goods, made more feasible under the liberalized terms of trade, continues unabated. This "imported" inflation limits the choices afforded the Mexican government; Mexico is now so dependent on the U.S. dollar that it must consider the interests of American investors first and the Mexican public second.

Corporate officers should be aware, moreover, that unlike other countries where there is a backlash against a "flood" of American products, in Mexico it is the contrary: The resentment is against any government that hinders access to U.S. goods. Therefore, the political pressures on President Zedillo confronts a credibility and legitimacy problem of enormous proportions. It is unfortunate that the Mexican peso is not stable enough to be traded on future markets, which would allow for greater stability in business transactions. Experiences with the 1982 debt crisis, which saw a series of devaluations and exchange rate controls, suggest that several strategies familiar to currency managers offer reassurance, given that the Mexican economy remains sound, and the timetables contained in NAFTA remain in place.

It is true, however, that the first year of NAFTA has been volatile: an armed insurrection in the southern state of Chiapas, political assassinations, a sharp devaluation of the Mexican peso, and an extensive market correction in Mexican issues traded on the New York Stock Exchange. The economic dislocations occasioned by all this, moreover, are the necessary convulsions and turmoil that is expected when Mexico's small economy is integrated into those of the United States and Canada. The market correction and currency fluctuations are a normal process of change and integration, particularly when the disparate inflation rates and politically motivated central bank intervention had distorted the exchange rates. Sudden shocks, however unpleasant, are not catastrophic, particularly when the underlying fundamentals are solid, and they remain so.

This is not to say that such violent movements are welcome. Fortunately, there may be other strategies to address the issues concerning currency exchange rates. The Minister of Finance under the Salinas administration, Pedro Aspe, presented several position papers at international conferences that addressed the idea of establishing a single monetary unit for North America—specifically, the U.S. dollar. While such an eventuality may be years away, it is significant that one of the most important Mexican officials is even contemplating such an option, at a time when nationalism issues dominate Mexican public life.

Should Mexico, at some point, adopt the U.S. dollar as legal tender, however, it is important to recognize what such a policy change would entail. Mexico, by virtue of its inability to print U.S. currency, would, in effect, surrender control of the money supply, and, therefore, of interest rates. In turn, however, it would enjoy a stable currency, ending the possibility of a devaluation in the monetary unit with which it conducts business in North America. Surrendering control of the money supply is not too much to ask of a government that has never been able to handle such a responsibility. As NAFTA unfolds, certain Mexican markets already are seeing U.S. dollars circulating interchangeably with Mexican pesos. While it is nothing new to have cash registers that accept—and give change—in either currency, this practice is spreading to other areas, most notably the beach resorts, like Cancun. In a matter of years, as Mexicans become more familiar and comfortable with the circulation of American dollars, policy changes consistent with the hypothetical arguments expressed by Pedro Aspe would be easier to implement.

Political Abductions

Throughout most of the seventies, the possibility of political abduction was a common concern in Europe where quite a number of terrorist organizations operated freely, most notably in Italy. During the 1980s, Mexico began to be, increasingly, characterized by abductions as well. The kidnapping of businessmen, known as *rapturas* in Mexican colloquial Spanish, constituted little more than an inconvenience. For the most part, it was one branch of the police or state security apparatus that was responsible for the abduction; thus, the life of the victim was seldom in danger, and once payment had been made, release was almost guaranteed. Indeed, toward the end of the eighties the kidnapping of Mexican business-men had become so commonplace that it hardly raised an eyebrow. (In a perverse twist of events, several newspapers speculated on businessmen likely to be kidnapped, thereby giving a certain social status to being important enough to be abducted.)

During the nineties, however, the nature of these kidnappings began to change. Whereas before the pattern was familiar, would-be clandestine rebel groups saw these *rapturas* as a way of securing funding for terrorist activities. From the point of view of the business community, the stakes had changed; it's one thing to be kidnapped by an unscrupulous police chief who wants to add a pool to his home and quite another to be kidnapped by terrorists who want to secure weapons to overthrow the state.

The Zapatist rebellion—which declared war on the Mexican government on January 1, 1994, the first day NAFTA went into force—is believed to have secured a great deal of funding from the ransoms collected from prominent businessmen in the state of Chiapas over the last few years. And there has been much speculation about the use of the ransom paid for the most celebrated kidnapping in Mexico since the implementation of NAFTA—

specifically, the $30 million paid for the release of Alfredo Harpú, one of the owners of Banamex, Mexico's largest bank.

For the American businessman, the chance of being kidnapped in Mexico is small. The threat to one's Mexican partner or associate, however, is not. The Mexican associate to whom this book is dedicated, for instance, was kidnapped a few years ago. It was an ordinary and unexceptional thing. As Mr. Canto approached his automobile one day after leaving his office and was about to unlock the door, a pick-up truck pulled up next to him. Before he realized what was happening, another man appeared from the side, grabbed him by the elbow, pointed a gun to his side and told him to get in. In less than a minute, he was whisked away, and the tedious logistics of securing his release were underway a few hours after he called the office to inform us that he had been abducted. This is Mexico, so there is no point in calling the police. In Mr. Canto's case, it was just as well, because he had been kidnapped by the police; so in a perverse sense, his whereabouts and personal safety were secured.

Mr. Canto's *raptura*, it should be pointed out, took place in the eighties. In the nineties, things are riskier. In all likelihood, the kidnappers are trying to secure funding for armed rebellion, which makes matters more difficult: Since the police are not responsible for the abduction, then no one really knows who or where the victim is being held. In the case of Alfredo Harpú, one of the world's wealthiest men, it took months of belabored negotiations to ensure his safety and secure his release.

As a variation on this theme a few years back, roadblocks were set up along back roads for the collection of "tolls" or "taxes." More amusing than kidnappings was one such incident that happened to this writer. While driving along a remote highway in the state of Chiapas, I came upon some logs thrown across the road. A few armed peasants brandishing machetes approached my vehicle to inform me that they were collecting a "revolutionary tax" of some sort. For the sake of argument, I negotiated a price for which the road would be cleared, which was the equivalent of about $30, and then I was allowed to go on my way. Encountering individuals who collect such "taxes" to finance popular uprisings is not that common an occurrence these days, but kidnappings remain a real threat.

In the case of Mr. Canto, it was a simple matter of securing the ransom for his safe release and of a few missed meetings. To make this surreal scenario the more ludicrous, Mr. Canto's chief concern was whether the ransom paid was a tax-deductible business expense; Mexican tax law is unclear on this matter. A Mexican friend, playing the provocateur, argued that this was the Mexican equivalent of making a donation to the policeman's association. The entire subject takes on a surreal aspect that defies the most fundamental ideas about decency and civility. To argue that these are "extra-official" sources of funding for law enforcement agencies astounds in its sardonic duplicity. That may very well be the case, but this is a fact of life for corporate Mexico, which means that the risk to Mexican partners and associates of corporate America is considerable, especially as the level of violence in Mexico continues to increase and the authoritarian development model continues to crumble. Adequate personal safety insurance is recommended, as is appropriate personal safety for corporate officers.

American Managers of Cuban Descent

For English-speaking Americans, there is a danger in making the assumption that the Mexican middle class is identical to professional Cubans in Miami. There is an even greater danger in making the assumption that Cuban-American employees are the logical choice for spearheading efforts in penetrating the Mexican market. While Anglo Americans remain oblivious to the subtle differences among competing Hispanic groups within the United States, there are significant cultural, political, and racial nuances that create friction. Mexico, for instance, has always maintained friendly relations with Cuba—something that has long angered the Cuban exile community in the United States. Mexican foreign policy in the second half of the twentieth century has been that of containing American imperialism in Mexico's sphere of influence.

This political distinction has resulted in Mexico's offering aid and assistance to Fidel Castro in Cuba, to Salvadoran rebels (who long maintained public relations offices in Mexico City, underwritten by the Mexican government), and more recently, extensive subsidies to the Sandinistas in Nicaragua. Thus, Mexicans have seen themselves as the benefactors of the Cubans. In the United States, however, Cubans have had no need for Mexican benevolence, and, quite the contrary, Cuban Americans have snubbed Mexicans. The more obvious reason is self-evident: Mexicans support the communist regime in Cuba, which is the reason why there is such a large exile community of Cubans in the United States.

There are other reasons as well. Cuban Americans, for instance, cannot understand why Mexico, blessed with so many resources and occupying such a strategic geopolitical place, remains such a backward country. Cubans in the United States, who have been Americanized in the ways of the First World, show little sympathy for the lethargic nature of Mexican society, which accepts a political hegemony that denies Mexicans democracy and freedom. Moreover, Cubans in the United States cannot understand the "Indian" mentality of the Mexicans, and, quite frankly, feel racially superior to the darker skinned, "mestizo" mass of Mexicans. Cuban Americans are white. Mexicans are not.

In the eyes of Mexicans, Cuban Americans are arrogant and overbearing. Their success in America, which stands in sharp contrast to the failure of the Mexicans to achieve equal footing in American society, disturbs the Mexicans, who are again reminded of their inadequacy, of their perceived inferiority. American Cubans look down on the Mexicans for being backward. Mexicans see American Cubans as cocky and as feeling superior to Cubans in Cuba, which is a point made more complex by the fact that Cubans in Cuba are not white, but black and mulatto. Corporate officers must be sensitive to these racial points of contention, which is frustrating, for Cuban Americans as a group are the most qualified professionals throughout corporate America for helping transform Mexico into a developed nation.

The differences in the level of achievements between Cubans and Mexicans in America is remarkable. Americans fear an invasion of Mexican immigrants as a consequence of NAFTA. But the fear has to do with the ability of Mexicans to make it in American society. If the Cubans, immigrants of the Spanish-speaking world, can arrive in the United States and make it to the top—whether it is Desi Arnaz, who built one of the most important production studios in Hollywood in the fifties and sixties, or Roberto Goizueta, whose total compensation package has approached $100 million a year as head of Coca-Cola Company in Atlanta in the eighties and nineties—then the fear of "chaos," as Latino writer Richard Rodriguez characterizes Mexican immigration to the United States, is not endemic to the peoples of Latin America. Cubans have been praised as "exemplary" Americans, by conservative commentators such as George F. Will, which is a characterization that has never been made of the Mexicans.

If by fear of chaos Americans mean that Mexicans represent disorder run riot, then what we are dealing with is the absence of reason. If Mexicans bring chaos on their backs, they bring unreasonableness. When Americans stand in San Diego and look at Tijuana and a dread bordering on despair takes hold, it isn't a standoff between Protestantism and Catholicism, and it isn't England alarmed by Spain. On the border between San Diego and Tijuana, then, reasonable people grow exasperated at the presence of unreasonable people.

Cubans, as their success in America attests, on the other hand, are reasonable folk, something the Mexicans obviously are not. To nineteenth-century Europe, Mexico was a horrific vision of chaos reigning supreme.

To twentieth-century America, Mexico is chaos on the border. To reasonable Mexicans, Mexico remains what it has always been: an uneasy coexistence between the possible and the impossible, a struggle to make sense of the nonsensical, of accommodation and patronage.

The difference between the Mexicans and the Cubans, then, is the distinction between Passion and Reason. It is a difference that rests on the undeniable fact that in a market economy, Reason is rewarded, whereas Passion is not. The laws of supply and demand, of scarcity and desirability, govern human life in unexpected ways. Therefore, Mexico enters America through the kitchen door—as a dishwasher, as a busboy, as a cook—and then in a grocery bag—as a jar of salsa, as a bag of nacho chips, as a cardboard box containing low-calorie frozen burritos. Cuba, on the other hand, enters America through the front door—table reservations for six at nine o'clock here, a private catered dinner party overflowing with champagne there, and then as guests—as potential buyers of one's home, as interior decorators, as guests of honor at a cocktail reception on one's poolside terrace.

In *The Exile*, David Rieff reports Gloria Sanchez, an outspoken Cuban Miamian, as making the following point: "Anglos [non-Cuban white Americans] hate us . . . because we are not like Mexicans or Puerto Ricans. We won't get down on our knees. We accept some of America but not everything. We weren't just peasants."[1] Whereas the Mexicans in America are merely *peasants*?

Cubans can participate in American life and rise to the top by virtue of their Reason—the evidence of which lies in their education, their philosophies, their ability to use automated teller machines, to run their own businesses, to stand up for their rights, to become involved in civic affairs, to succeed, as America has defined success. Cubans have masterfully succeeded on American terms.

Mexicans, on the other hand, are noticed by their failure—a failure seen in their *absence*.

Where are the Mexican mayors of Los Angeles? the Mexican doctors honored by the American Medical Association? the words of praise from George F. Will? the Mexican CEOs of *Fortune* 500 companies? the Mexican pop idols whom America's youth worships on MTV? the Mexicans whose lives offer evidence of unbridled financial success? the Mexican architects who build for future generations and are honored with awards from the American Institute of Architects? the Mexicans who have achieved the American Dream? What would be in a book about the achievements of Americans of Mexican ancestry?

Why are Cubans in America winners and Mexicans in America losers?

Comparing the contrast between Spanish in Los Angeles and Miami, Joan Didion reports the following:

This question of language was curious. The sound of spoken Spanish was common in Miami, but it was also common in Los Angeles, and Houston, and even in the cities of the northeast. What was unusual about Spanish in Miami was not that it was so often spoken, but that it was so often heard: in, say, Los Angeles, Spanish remained a language only barely registered by the Anglo population, part of the ambient noise, the language spoken by the people who worked in the car wash and came to trim the trees and cleared the tables in restaurants. In Miami Spanish was spoken by the people who ate in the restaurants, the people who owned the cars and the trees, which made, on the socioauditory scale, a considerable difference.[2]

A considerable difference to whom? To individuals who associate spoken Spanish with menial labor—people working at car washes and gas stations, as gardeners and as busboys? Perhaps. To individuals who are comfortable with spoken Spanish as a working-class language, one that would never be spoken by doctors, architects, lawyers, business executives, the wealthy? Perhaps. To the educated Spanish-speakers dining in the fancy restaurants, driving the nice cars, and shopping for pretty trees (with elegant homes thrown in with the purchase of those pretty trees)? Perhaps not.

To the Spanish-speaking Cuban executives in Miami, their success and their lives are natural; people eat in fancy restaurants and drive nice cars and own splendid homes in Buenos Aires and Madrid and Santiago and all through the Spanish-speaking world. That Miami now joins this community of Spanish-speaking cities is, alas, Manifest Destiny.

These are the philosophical arguments whispered among Latin Americans in the privacy of their homes. These are the ideas that linger in their minds and hearts—which affect how they go about doing business. The challenge for corporate America is to be sensitive to the feelings of the Mexicans, to be conscious of the perceived arrogance of the Cuban Americans, and to try to strike a balance, the need for culturally fluent employees to open up markets in Mexico, without offending Mexican sensibilities—the client, if not always right, should not be insulted.

A QUESTION OF TIME

A brief note on the concept of time is in order. American managers, who occupy a reality where time is money, have problems understanding the disregard for punctuality in Mexico. The stereotype of Mexico being the land of *mañana* is a correct assessment of the situation. What is neglected, however, are the reasons for the lax view of time and the subsequent disregard for someone else's time.

In Mexico, where questions of self-doubt linger pervasively and where, for a variety of reasons, people face challenges, a premium is placed on what one can have. In a country where people lack education, achievements, or opportunities, what one can have is manners. Courtesy becomes almost sublime, a contest as to who can be more courteous. It is not uncommon to spend awkward moments while one is holding the door open for another, who is waiting for the first person to walk through. "No, after you," one Mexican says to another, who responds, "Oh, no, but after you."

Another thing one can have is power: the power to make another wait, to dispose of someone else's time. The delays in starting meetings, in getting on with business, in making appointments, are all ways of exercising power. There is no intention to humiliate the person who is made to wait, but the point is to establish a pecking order. It is roughly analogous to the cliché in the United States that "the customer is always right." In Mexico, the customer has the power to make the seller wait. As such, there is a saying in Mexico that American managers cannot afford to forget: "El que se enoja, pierde," which means, "He who loses his temper, loses"—a warning that, in many cases, making someone wait is a test of sorts. Mexicans determine someone's patience, temperament, and manners by how that person responds to having been made to wait. The ability to make another wait, therefore, is not only used to demonstrate who has power over whom, but is also used to test character. Despite what is often written by Americans, being late or making someone wait is most often a calculated move, not a lax understanding of punctuality explained away by cultural factors.

Meetings that take forever to get started, lunches that drift into late afternoon, and constant delays are all means of assessing the other party. For hurried American managers, it will be of great relief to know that the new generation of Mexican businessmen are as rushed as the Americans are and that the point of being punctual is becoming the standard. Everything else about Mexican business life is becoming more and more American, and, happily, the notion of time is not immune to the effects of NAFTA.

NOTES

1. David Rieff, *The Exile: Cuba in the Heart of Miami* (New York: Simon & Schuster, 1993), p. 139.

2. Joan Didion, *Miami* (New York: Simon & Schuster, 1987), p. 63.

3

Management Strategies
for Mexican Alliances

There are many ways to take advantage of the unfolding opportunities in
the Mexican marketplace. For larger firms that desire to establish a
presence on a national level within the short term, the use of alliances offers
ideals opportunities to achieve these goals. The purchase of Mexican
companies, whether partial or complete, is a more complicated matter that
requires a considerable commitment, but in capital and strategic planning.
Businesses, on the other hand, that have an advantage in name recognition—
as many retailers and consumer producers do—can use alliances to gain
access to an immediate distribution network within Mexico with a company
that is knowledgeable about the marketplace and has a proven track record.

Regardless of the size of the targeted market, or of a firm, what remains
a paramount consideration is conceptualizing Mexico, not as a foreign
market, but as a promising SBU, not entirely within the domestic realm.
Mexican operations, therefore, must be considered as SBUs that operate
in a changing regulatory environment. Under the terms of NAFTA, after
all, Mexico is required to rewrite its laws, whereas the United States and
Canada have no regulatory changes to make. The purpose is to upgrade
Mexico's legal and commercial laws to world standards. As such, American
managers must consider Mexican operations as SBUs that function in an
uncertain and emerging business environment.

As such, the inherent dangers of corporate alliances are magnified in
international business transactions, which become more acute given the
ambivalent nature of the "international" status of Mexican operations as
North America, Inc., emerges. Americans, who have a distinct inclination

to favor individualism and independence, are often at a loss to understand the marked difference of the Mexican—and Latin American—suspicion of individualism. As safety is found in numbers, so too (for cultural reasons explored later on), Mexico's cultural history favors communalism and group efforts. Corporate Mexico is seldom self-reliant. In contrast, the culture of corporate America is founded on the notion of entrepreneurship. In a country where Horatio Alger is alive in Microsoft's Bill Gates, the cultural predispositions favor individual achievement. It has been noted that America has a Founding Father, not Founding Committees, which is presumably why Americans hold in contempt bureaucracies of any kind. Mexico, on the other hand, is a national entity invented on a hierarchical pyramid. Corporate America's natural predisposition for self-reliance tends to undermine successful alliances. Mexico's dependence on communal efforts, however, bolsters the chances of forming workable alliances. Indeed, the undeniable need of Mexican managers to come on-line also improves the likelihood that the cooperation mandated by the structure of a corporate alliance will be provided.

Companies form alliances with another firm for mutual benefit. Corporate Mexico has much to gain in technology and know-how from its American counterpart. In turn, Mexican firms have expertise in understanding the Mexican marketplace. Alliances, such as the one formed by Gigante and Office Depot—a Mexican retailer in an alliance with the office products wholesaler—offer the opportunities to bring together specific skills and resources in ways that may complement each other. The immediate benefits of these kinds of alliances is readily seen: Office Depot is expected to open thirty stores throughout Mexico within the first twenty-four months of NAFTA's implementation.

Corporate America is thus able to penetrate Mexican markets and to gain market share at a time when Mexico is undergoing significant change. Strategies designed to allow American companies to establish significant market shares in the nineties is an imperative, for consolidation is expected at the end of the ten-year period. The creation of adequate alliances, however, is a difficult matter. Apart from language and cultural issues, the success or failure of the alliance is dependent on how the venture is structured, the qualifications of managers placed in charge, and how the responsibilities and strategic missions are divided among the partners. Corporate America must be confident that it has chosen a Mexican partner who is able to facilitate the establishment of a comprehensive distribution network or who is familiar with the rapidly changing market realities.

In this chapter, I will discuss the strategic characteristics of a successful corporate alliance with Mexico.

DYNAMIC MANAGEMENT STRUCTURE

An alliance, in effect, brings together distinct and separate corporate entities. Each company enters into the alliance with its own corporate culture, implicit or explicit behavioral systems, and management strategies. Each corporation lacks an intimate knowledge of the operations of its partners. For the most part, it is upper management that initiates, negotiates, and approves of the nature of the alliance; and once the arrangement is underway, the day-to-day management is left to other managers. The personnel from each company involved in the alliance, therefore, may have far less working knowledge about the other members of the alliance. The ultimate success or failure of the alliance all too often rests in the hands of middle management. Thus, a dynamic management structure that can incorporate the talents of these managers must be in place. Their expertise must be used, confidence built, and voice heard if a responsive and flexible management structure capable of accomplishing the strategic mission of the alliance is to be met. This holds true for each member of the alliance; the best attributes of each firm must be harnessed for the benefit of the whole. This kind of management structure—one that creates a sense of unity between the participating parties and transcends both corporate cultures—however, runs counter to the romantic view of individualism that shapes the American business character.

ENCOURAGEMENT OF CALCULATED INITIATIVES

The dynamic management structure required by alliances includes the flexibility to take calculated risks. This translates into encouraging managers to develop their own initiatives and to implement decisions that are superior in their judgment. The areas of expertise of the managers working in an alliance must be tapped. In an increasingly competitive global marketplace, a firm must take advantage of all the skills and talents available to it. Consider a native Chinese manager who is skilled in the subtle nuances of Chinese culture, customs, and business climate. The opinions of such managers must be respected when developing alliances with Chinese entities or when penetrating the Chinese marketplace. An alliance that hopes to establish a profitable presence in China cannot hope to succeed if it dismisses the advice of its own personnel.

SYSTEMATIC TASK SETTING

The roles and responsibilities of each firm in the alliance must be clearly defined. The nature of the Mexican business environment is such that, for the most part, American firms provide technology, know-how, goods and services, as well as a significant portion of the financing, while Mexican companies provide knowledge of the marketplace, a distribution network, financial relationships, and a corps of employees knowledgeable and familiar with the client profile. Once a delineation of responsibilities is established, realistic benchmarks can be set and an equitable division of tasks established. Misunderstandings in marketing approaches must be avoided. Although tariffs and taxes are higher in Mexico, there is a predisposition to raise prices higher than Americans are used to setting. A cautious supervision of prices must be exacted, for the notion of market share remains an elusive idea among many Mexican managers. Therefore, detailed milestones need to be agreed upon, as well as timetables for meeting specific goals. A program of systematic task setting is paramount to success in the Mexican market.

EQUAL DISTRIBUTION OF AUTHORITY

Many alliances fail when internal power struggles detract from the mission at hand. Mexican companies, which tend to be sensitive about their relationship vis-à-vis American companies, are particularly sensitive and Mexican managers have a predisposition to believe their ideas or contributions are dismissed or are not as appreciated as they should be. Many Americans who have initiated, or expanded, operations in Mexico report a baffling breakdown in communication among managers. The cultural nuances of the insecure Mexican psyche, so easily bruised, is often at odds with the more straightforward American style. What many Mexicans interpret as evidence of arrogance, American officers see as "speaking directly," something seldom done in Mexico. Under these circumstances, it is imperative that the goals of the alliance, that a command of authority, and that attention, which many Americans believe borders on patronizing behavior, be lavished on Mexican managers. Even among the most savvy Mexicans, for instance, when a store or an office is opened, it is common to have a Catholic priest bless the premises, which includes the sprinkling of holy water. To Americans, who believe matters of faith belong in the realm of personal conscience, such public ceremonies are discomforting; attending the opening of a McDonald's where the first Big Macs are sprinkled with holy water does raise eyebrows, but more harm will come if such divergent cultural practices by Mexican partners are not politely indulged. Indeed, if an alliance becomes a collection of bruised egos, and if office politics dominates the nature of the alliance, strategies will fall prey to self-destructive behavior. Instead of imposing one partner's will on another, management must endeavor to work together to create a sustainable competitive advantage. Authority must therefore be distributed among the respective players in an equal and equitable manner that is mindful of the particular cultural differences between management styles and interpersonal behavior.

ENCOURAGE CALCULATED RISK TAKING

The emerging turbulence in the Mexican marketplace offers corporate America unique challenges. NAFTA is producing substantial dislocation within all sectors of the Mexican economy; the opening of Mexico has thrown everything into a flux in which every market is up for grabs. The more sustainable opportunities, therefore, lie with firms that are willing to accept the need for calculated risk taking in Mexico. The need to establish market positions and penetrate new markets requires that higher levels of risk be set within parameters of strategic planning than would otherwise be acceptable. Alliances and partnerships, after all, are themselves examples of calculated risk taking that expose the partners to the possible failures of others. The very nature of this act of rendering one's firm vulnerable is reason for caution in and of itself; for in an increasingly competitive business environment, it only serves to increase the number of unknowns. No one can be certain as to the success or failure of a given venture, or alliance. There are, however, certain steps that can—and must—be taken to give the venture the best chance of success. An adequate analysis of market conditions, forecasting, and strategic planning are all requisite before entering into an alliance. Furthermore, during the lifetime of the alliance, it will be necessary to modify strategies to keep current with changing economies or market conditions. The alliance that has the best chance of success is one that is flexible and encourages modifications or taking calculated risks, such as investing in new technologies, creating new markets, or even entering untested markets.

STREAMLINE COMMUNICATION CHANNELS

The amount of information generated each day as a direct result of an alliance is staggering and is only magnified by linguistics and delays in transmitting information across borders. These problems are magnified by the double conversion, financial in terms of peso sales to dollar equivalents and perhaps in terms of systems of measurements—Mexico uses the metric system while the United States does not. As a result, it is imperative to have key contact personnel among all partners who are primarily responsible for the efficient—and accurate—relay of information between the companies. It has been the experience of successful firms that enter Mexico to make sure that the Mexican partner has a technical person fluent in English in addition to the principal management contact. The task of streamlining all channels of communication between each firm and within each firm is imperative for the efficient transfer of information necessary for a successful alliance.

DEVELOP MULTIMANAGER ROLES

The most important factor in the success or failure of the alliance is the human factor. The team of men and women from each firm who work together are the managers who will determine the fate of the alliance. The individuals responsible for the day-to-day functions of the alliance must be qualified and able and must possess the skills demanded by the nature of the venture. This requires the creation of teams that consist of multi-faceted managers who possess the skills, knowledge, and drive required for success, which takes on a heightened sense of importance given the need for multicultural and bilingual managers who are salient in both cultural environments. Corporate America needs managers who are able to converse on several levels with their counterparts at Mexican companies, or within the firm's own Mexican SBU. The manager must be capable of filling such distinctive and diverse management roles as leader, administrator, planner, and entrepreneur. A leader ensures that the agreed-upon strategies are implemented and that adequate information is being communicated to those individuals responsible. Control of the project calls for the role of *administrator*, with a thorough understanding of the variables that are crucial to the venture's success, pinpointing the sources of trouble and developing corrective courses of action. The *planner* is devoted to monitoring the overall progress of the joint venture and determining whether its goals are consistent with the firm's goals. The *entrepreneur* seeks new opportunities within the scope of the venture and seeks ways to improve the implementation of its strategies.

CONCLUSION

When the strategic structure of the alliance encompasses these charac-teristics, the likelihood of success is increased and the risks involved diminished. The fact of business life in the age of free trade, however, is that far too many American managers fail to grasp the urgency of forging an alliance with Mexican companies within the parameters of a strategic structure. The competitive nature of the emerging North American economy and the fast pace of innovation demands that measured attention be given to the formation of an alliance that can deliver a sustainable, and profitable, presence in the Mexican marketplace. The rapid expansion of American companies into Mexico subsequent to the implementation of NAFTA has been astounding. The Mexican market represents an opportunity that offers strategic opportunities that must be taken advantage of before a period of consolidation begins to unfold as the 1990s end.

4

The Case of Infrastructure Assessment

Corporate America is in Mexico to stay. The market is too great, and so is the opportunity of contributing much good. The discomforting nature of employee relations notwithstanding, American managers need to be sensitive to the peculiar expectations within the Mexican context—and rely on a Mexican foreman to deal with these issues. Consider the current state of Mexican infrastructure in light of the demands precipitated by the implementation of NAFTA. Indeed, the opportunities for corporate America in upgrading Mexico's infrastructure is enormous. A brief over-view of two are highway construction and pollution abatement, which demonstrate the kinds of opportunities available in all areas of Mexico's economic development. Indeed, in many instances it is the lack of expertise and capable personnel that inhibit Mexico's ability to carry out the most basic of projects, such as building a bridge or controlling air pollution. The crisis of an insufficient number of capable professionals that Mexico confronts is the result, apart from Mexico's inadequate educational system, of a significant brain drain that occurred in the eighties, during the international debt crisis. At that time, significant numbers of Mexican professionals emigrated to the United States, where they have now established themselves over the past decade. In recent years, despite an improving economy, efforts by the Salinas administration to lure these people back to Mexico was not as successful as hoped.

HIGHWAY PRIVATIZATION

Mexico had a plan to build 4,000 miles of concession roads by 1994, at a total cost of $9.8 billion. To date, an investment of $4.6 billion has been made. Of this amount, two-thirds is private investment, and the balance is public, either from the government or from the state oil monopoly, Pemex. The highway privatization program has been plagued by continuing problems arising not only from poor engineering, but also from exorbitant tolls, which has reduced demand. Mexican companies, accustomed to enjoying the impunity afforded by tariffs and trade barriers, are struggling to adjust to the concept of price elasticity in pricing goods and services.

Additionally, the nature of the problems include the following:

• Construction delays. Of the thirty-two build-operate-transfer concessions granted since 1989—involving twenty-eight highways totaling 1,864 miles and four internal bridges—only nine projects are finished, and sections of seven are operating.

• Inadequate engineering services. Cost overruns and delays are compounded by inadequate government-supplied engineering services. Problems are further aggravated by lack of uniform truck weight restrictions on Mexican roads.

• Political process. The process by which concessions are granted is more political than it should be. Firms are expected to assume tort liability (and under Mexican law international arbitration for disputes is not allowed, further heightening risk), and traffic projections/high tolls undermine the profitability of the concessions.

For corporate America, there are tremendous opportunities in the following:

• Supplying engineering services to the Secretariat of Communications and Transportation (SCT)

• Project management services to firms that have won concessions, such as Dillingham Construction of Pleasanton, California

• Indefinite overall program management services to the Mexican government

At a meeting held in Manzanillo while NAFTA negotiations were underway, U.S. Federal Highway Administrator Thomas Larson characterized Mexico's privatization program as "a search for new ideas in design, construction and operation of roads." The minister of the SCT in the Zedillo administration has pledged to move to resolve the problems that the floundering highway privatization programs presently encounter.

Officials within the Zedillo administration argue that Mexico now faces no other choice but to facilitate the entry of American and Canadian firms to help in the construction of strategic highways and to improve the port facilities throughout the country.

POLLUTION CONTROL

Pollution in Mexico is of serious concern. The ozone levels in the Valley of Mexico continue to set new records, despite efforts to reduce the emission of pollutants. In the early 1990s, Mexico City residents saw the closure of public schools, industries were ordered to cut back their production by 75 percent, half of all vehicles were ordered off the streets, and people were told to stay indoors. The pollution problem in Mexico City is overwhelming, a high priority, and offers a significant, long-term opportunity for American companies specializing in the pollution control and abatement industries.

The air pollution control market can be broken down by the transportation, power, and industrial sectors. Transportation sector emissions are primarily being addressed through the production of cleaner fuels, fuel substitution, and the use of more efficient vehicles with catalytic converters. The power sector is shifting to cleaner fuels and efficiency improvements and is cleaning emissions with such technologies as electrostatic precipitators. The industrial sector produces a wide array of emissions (depending on the inputs), which are being addressed through process changes, fuel substitution, bag houses, precipitators, scrubbers, and so forth.

Clean Fuels Production

Petroleos Mexicanos, the state oil monopoly, known as Pemex, is implementing three projects to reduce sulfur levels to under 1 percent in fuel oil and diesel fuel for a total investment of $450 million. In addition, Pemex plans to invest $549 million in building eight new plants and modifying seven existing ones in order to produce higher octane gasoline.

Power Plant Air Pollution Control

While the Comision Federal de Electricidad (CFE) contends that most of its power plants are adequately equipped with air pollution control technology, an independent assessment is underway. CFE and the Instituto de Investigaciones Electricas have commissioned a detailed environmental impact assessment of seven thermal power plants in Mexico: Tula, Valle de Mexico, Salamanca, Rio Escondido, Monterrey, Manzanillo, and Mazatlan. This study is being performed by the Spanish firm Hidro-electrica Española, with Battelle and Radian as subcontractors.

Coal Power Plant Electrostatic Precipitators

Six 350 MW coal-fired power plant units are expected to be installed over the coming eight years. Units 1 and 2 of the Carbon 11 power plant at Piedras Negras, Coahuila, are expected to be operational in 1992. These units are conventionally financed and developed by CFE. Units 3 and 4 of Carbon 11 are to be installed by 1995. These units are being developed by Foster Wheeler, Mecanica de la Pena, and Bufete Industrial under a build-lease-transfer (BLT) arrangement. In 1998, two 350 MW units are expected to be installed at Sabinas. All of these power plants will require electrostatic precipitators.

Steel Industry Dust Collection

Air pollution control, through the installation of equipment to collect dust and iron particles, is being considered by Mexico's largest private iron and steel company and the country's eighth largest corporation (HYSLA S.A. de C.V.) according to a recent International Finance Corporation (IFC) study. Depending on the results of the engineering study, projects at various steel mills could be implemented, at a total investment of about $15 million.

Chemical Industry Air Pollution Reduction

The reduction of SO_2 and other emissions from a sulfuric acid and polystyrene plant is being considered by Industrias Resistol, S.A., Mexico's third largest petrochemical company, with twenty-five plants nationwide, according to the recent IFC study. The company's strategy is to achieve zero emissions to air, water, and land by the year 2000. The air pollution investment currently being contemplated is about $1.5 million.

Industrial Solvents Emissions Control

An important air pollution source is the emission of various gases from the use of solvents in auto painting, the production of paints, glues, and so forth; as well as printing and industrial cleaning. The implementation of these air pollution control measures awaits a definitive regulation from

Secretaría de Desarollo Urbano y Ecología (SEDUE), Mexico's equivalent of the Environmental Protection Agency (EPA). Indications are that this new regulation will take anywhere from one to three years to be issued, at which point stringent application is expected. Some companies are already considering adopting control measures.

Industrial Air Pollution Monitors

SEDUE is increasingly requiring industries to install their own pollution control monitoring equipment. For instance, one steel mill was required to install not only six particulate monitoring stations throughout the local town but also a meteorological tower within the plant.

5

The Paternalism of Employer-Employee Relations in Mexican Society

For American managers, the most daunting task of establishing a presence in the Mexican market resides in dealing with the Mexican labor force. Perhaps the tragedy of Mexico on a human level is that the Mexican people are the warmest, most generous and splendid human beings imaginable, yet they are completely lacking in the skills required for a modern economy. Their lack of training transcends race or social level, for as readily as one finds unskilled labor barely capable of sweeping a factory floor, one also finds engineers who cannot engineer and doctors who should not be practicing medicine. The impression that most first-time American businessmen have of Mexico City as they take strolls near their hotels in the Zona Rosa, namely, that everything looks shoddy, is correct, precisely because it reflects the levels of skills of Mexican architects, engineers, construction managers, and designers.

The long-term employee problems confronting American managers working in Mexico reside in the need to change the employer-employee relationship. In much the same way that Hispanic immigrants to the United States have had to abandon the customs of their native land, if Mexico is to become a vibrant participant in the world economy, it must discard its historic paternalism that causes men and women to become adult children incapable of taking care of themselves and that causes employers to be substitute parents for these adult children. Consider, for a moment, the structural and continuing problems associated with the heralded "maquiladora" program. It is expected that corporate America will employ one million Mexicans by the year 2000 in the thousands of in-bond plants operating and under construction in Mexico. The employee problems encountered in the in-bond industries suggest the kinds of problems that American employers of Mexican workers face.

INFRASTRUCTURE, TELECOMMUNICATIONS, AND FINANCIAL SERVICES

The inadequacy of Mexican infrastructure and education levels was the focus of NAFTA discussions. A fast-track series of measures were agreed upon that were designed to, over the course of a decade, accomplish the development of Mexico's physical resources. The one-way, United States-to-Mexico nature of this massive rebuilding effort requires that, in the short- or medium-term, it is American companies that will be the beneficiary of this economic activity. Analyzing the effect of NAFTA, Gary Clyde Hufbauer and Jeffrey Schott of the Institute for International Economics write: "In our scenario for the foreseeable future, the impact of NAFTA and associated Mexican reforms is to increase US exports to Mexico by $16.7 billion and to increase US imports from Mexico by $7.7 billion."[1] This dramatic rise in American exports to Mexico—and in Mexico's deteriorating balance of trade with the United States—will occur while the massive infrastructure projects needed to capacitate the Mexican economy to acceptable levels of efficiency and development are implemented.

Specifically, in the areas of infrastructure, telecommunications, and financial services, significant opportunities are found

Infrastructure

Within the next decade, the United States and Mexico will be connected by a network of trucking and railroad services that will extend north to south. Major privatization programs for highways and bridges are under-way. While these projects are financed by the private sector, the changing role of Mexican transportation regulation offers significant opportunities to American construction management firms. The Mexico City–Acapulco new privatized highway suggests the appeal of these kinds of infrastructure projects. Not all such ventures, however, have been successful. The Cancun-Merida highway is a troubled business venture, one in which poor construction and high tolls has significantly reduced the number of users.

There are, however, ample opportunities for highway expansion, bridge and tunnel projects, and the modernization of existing byways. For American companies in the transportation sector, too, there are opportunities of extending trucking and rail service into Mexico. Throughout the nineties, issues such as difference in truck weights and cabotage laws will be addressed, causing Mexican standards to conform with U.S. and Canadian norms. The antiquated nature of the Mexican trucking sector, characterized by an older fleet of inefficient vehicles, the relative inexperience of Mexican drivers in operating on modern highways, and the restrictive nature of entry into the United States suggest that while American truck and rail companies will benefit from greater access to Mexican markets, few, if any, Mexican firms are prepared to service American clients, apart from immediate border clients.

The binational commission established by the states that constitute both sides of the U.S.–Mexico border, too, has established committees to coordinate and determine how to best integrate the border infrastructure region. Federal funding sources, from both the U.S. and Mexican governments, as well as private funds, are being considered. Former U.S. Treasury Secretary Lloyd Bentsen, who is from Texas, has articulated the possibility of creating a special fund, financed through the sale of bonds backed by the U.S. government, for financing major infrastructure projects long the U.S.–Mexico border.

Telecommunications

Mexico's state-owned telephone monopoly, Teléfonos de México, known as Telmex, was privatized under the Salinas administration. Since this development, Telmex has engaged in a strategic program to modernize Mexico's telecommunication services. The capital-intensive investment has been financed, to a large degree, through the listing of Telmex American Depository Receipts (ADRs) on the New York Stock Exchange. Telmex in recent years, in fact, has become one of the most active issues on the New York Stock Exchange. It remains a monopoly, but under the terms of NAFTA, foreign competitors will be allowed to compete in the Mexican long-distance telecommunications industry. It had been expected that AT&T would join forces with Telmex. Because Southwestern Bell Communications is part of a foreign consortium that owns 10 percent of Telmex, however, AT&T feared that regulatory issues in the United States would restrict AT&T's ability to enter the Mexican market and provide long-distance telephone service into the United States.

Therefore, AT&T announced at the end of 1994 an alliance with Grupo Alfa, a Mexican conglomerate with far-flung interests, sending Telmex shares plunging and signaling a substantial opening of the Mexican telecommunications market. As early as 1997 there will be true competition, which suggests that the medium-term telecommunications sector will be characterized by market segmentation similar to that in the United States when MCI and Sprint emerged as AT&T's competitors for long-distance service. For Telmex, which is seeking an alliance with another long-distance carrier, the challenge remains of establishing a fiber-optics network throughout the country before the 1997 monopoly expires. For various reasons, it is the firm with an extensive fiber-optics network that will be able to rent these lines to other carriers. Telmex stands to generate revenue for the use of its fiber-optics network, regardless of who is the carrier.

These developments in value-added services, as well as the provisions in NAFTA that end almost all tariff and nontrade barriers to the imports of telecommunications hardware, offer significant opportunities for American firms to participate in the systematic upgrading of Mexican telecommunications. When Telmex was a state monopoly, telecommunications served a "social" and not "private sector" function. Public telephones, for instance, were free. Only after Telmex was privatized did public pay telephones began to appear. The rapid conversion of the social purposes of telecommunications has created an explosion in the telecommunications market. After decades of pent-up demand—Mexico remains a country where activating telephone service for a new customer can take several months—the transformation is astounding. Cellular phones, computer modems, fax machines, telephone equipment of all kinds are being imported by the truck- and containerloads. This virtual telecommunications revolution is not only contributing to the development of the economy but exacerbating the political crisis that Mexico confronts, as information— and power—is now transmitted in a horizontal framework, diffusing knowledge and influence through Mexican society.

Financial Services

Mexico has long been burdened by a primitive banking system that is inefficient. In fact, more than half of Mexico's population does not have access to banking services, and those that do are confronted with expensive fees for inadequate services. The sorry state of Mexico's financial and insurance industries is such that, under the terms of NAFTA, deregulation is phased in gradually until the year 2000. At that time, American and Canadian banks and insurance companies will have virtually unlimited access to the Mexican market. Mexican officials are cognizant of the threat to Mexican financial institutions in the face of direct competition from American and Canadian businesses, and there is a provision for a one-time imposition of restrictions should Mexican financial institutions lose more than 25 percent of the market by the year 2004.

The three-year moratorium is designed to protect Mexican financial institutions from the expected shake-up as the Mexican banking and insurance industries contract. In anticipation of the coming turmoil in these sectors, American banks have begun to establish representative offices and to comply with legal requirements for opening up business in Mexico. With the exception of Citibank, which operates under a grandfather clause, there are no American banks in Mexico at present, although it is expected that banks with significant Latin American experience, such as Bank of America, Chase Manhattan, Chemical Bank, and the Bank of Boston, are likely to dominate the Mexican market within a decade. The experience in other Latin American countries, such as Argentina where Citibank and the Bank of Boston hold considerable market share in the retail banking market, offers historical precedents for the long-term corporate strategies of U.S. financial institutions.

What holds true for banking, is also the case for the insurance sector. Mexico is presently characterized by expensive and inefficient insurance services, a problem made more pressing by the size of the market. The potential for tremendous growth is very real. Mexican firms and individuals lack adequate insurance coverage across an entire spectrum of services, and the strategic development of a sizable market represents a significant opportunity for corporate America. Strategic alliances like the one established by Aetna in 1994 lay the groundwork for the systematic takeover of the Mexican insurance market; Aetna enjoys a considerable competitive advantage given the economies of scale at its disposal: Computerization, actuarial analyses, competent personnel knowledgeable in financial investments, and familiarity with the U.S. domestic Hispanic and Latino markets represent formidable advantages. It is expected that within the next fifteen years, Mexican insurers will be acquired or allied to American firms, or they will no longer be in business.

Summary

The net effect of this is the wholesale transformation of the Mexican landscape in terms of the infrastructure available. The economic growth of Mexico can only be enhanced when these changes are implemented. The protectionism that fostered inefficiency and retarded the strategic development of key sectors will be, for all practical purposes, dismantled by the year 2005. Working with the natural advantages of each nation—the United States providing technology and capital, Mexico offering labor—

synergies can harness the tremendous potential of North America as an economic bloc. Of the automotive industry, Gary Clyde Hufbauer and Jeffrey Schott made the following observation: "As a consequence of NAFTA, within 10 years an integrated auto market will exist in North America. By world standards, the regional industry should be highly competitive. In fact, drawing on economies of scale and a variety of labor skills, North America could become the world's low-cost producer of autos and trucks, and a major net exporter of these products."[2]

What is true of the automotive industry, is also true of the insurance, banking, telecommunications, and industrial sectors. Of greater significance for corporate America, moreover, is the essential character of these emerging markets. There are American firms operating in Mexico, poised to serve not only the Mexican market. Through complementary trade agreements now being negotiated between Mexico and other Latin American countries, these American SBUs can then proceed to service other markets in the region.

In the immediate term, moreover, the wholesale upgrading of the Mexican infrastructure, telecommunications, and financial services sector is strengthening the ability of American firms to compete on a level playing field. American managers are comfortable with high technology, financial services, and an adequate infrastructure; Mexican managers are not. The implicit competitive advantage is not surprising. Mexico is becoming more American in the way it conducts business, whereas America is not becoming like Mexico. Indeed, American managers who have been doing business in Mexico for years have expressed surprise at the speed with which technological changes are taking place in Mexico. In the first year of NAFTA, for instance, Mexican telephones began to provide touch-tone service; now one can get lost in those annoying voice mail systems as easily in Mexico as in the United States.

"MAQUILADORA" REVOLVING DOOR

For all its noted success, Mexico's in-bond program, not unlike those of other developing countries, offers challenges to American employers. While the Mexican workforce remains among the most efficient and cost effective in the international marketplace, there are other hidden costs that are often overlooked, unanticipated, and discounted by promoters of this kind of economic development. These shortcomings, which liberal critics in the United States have pointed out in the past, are ever more evident as Mexican wage standards decline during the economic dislocation associated with the transitions envisioned by the implementation of

NAFTA. For American managers, the possibility of continuing labor disruptions in terms of employee turnover and dissatisfaction offer challenges for the efficient operation of facilities located in Mexico. Some specific issues follow.

Insufficient Incomes

The minimum wage jobs offered by the maquiladora program, while beneficial to the employer, are not sufficient to maintain a standard of living that is adequate. In the past, through a complicated system of price controls, subsidies, and transfer payments, the Mexican government was able to subsidize indirectly employee wages by controlling the price of basic foodstuffs, housing, and health care. The integration of Mexico into the world economy, however, and the need to balance the Mexican federal government budget, has resulted in a program of continuing cutbacks that represent the dismantling of the support network once in place. This bureaucratic system of social management, while intrinsic to Mexico's paternalistic political arrangement, has been discredited, while wages have not risen to reflect the cutback in social outlays. The celebrated "Solidaridad" program, begun in the De la Madrid administration and greatly expanded under the Salinas administration, represents nothing more than the glorification of the traditional "pork barrel" programs created to garner support for the ruling party. The programs initiated and completed under the Solidaridad banner have done little more than to serve as bribes to poor rural communities and to allow ruling party members a largesse from which to dispense patronage at their discretion. It has done very little to improve the lives of the millions of working Mexicans who continue to see their meager standard of living decline.

Employee Turnover

As a consequence, there is an enormous turnover in the personnel of the maquiladoras that line the border between the United States and Mexico. A frustrated American manager of a *Fortune* 500 company with assembly plants in Mexico suggested that a revolving door be installed because the employees come and go that quickly. Mexican officials discount this phenomenon, which is only to be expected. The minimum wages, the rote nature of the jobs, and the long hours have resulted in a labor force consisting of single women in their early twenties. These employees, many of whom move from other parts of the country in search of jobs, are also in search of husbands and in search of the chance to return home. The typical maquiladora employee is only working out of necessity; minimum wage, dead-end jobs are not a career path. Hourly compensation for a Mexican factory worker is $1.95, versus $15.60 in the United States, which is a considerable difference. These employees leave once they marry, or shortly after their first pregnancy, often returning to their hometowns or to the hometowns of their husbands.

Domestic Life of Employees

Consistent with the profile of the maquiladora employee, there is a social repercussion seldom addressed. While minimum wage jobs pay little, they pay more than outright unemployment. The character of the present maquiladora program in Mexico is one that favors the employment of women: They have greater discipline than men, are more submissive in following orders, have greater concentration required for rote work, and have smaller hands, which are useful in assembling components. In many households where maquiladora assembly plants are located, it is the woman who earns the larger paycheck. In a misogynist society such as Mexico's, an element of rivalry is introduced; Mexican men who, for cultural and historical reasons, feel inferior, are further threatened by recognizing that the wife is the main wage earner. The incidents of spousal abuse and alcoholism plague neighborhoods where maquiladora workers live, which only creates unexpected problems for American firms.

Relocation of Maquiladoras

Under the terms of NAFTA, incentives have been put into place to encourage the establishment of in-bond industries in areas away from the U.S.–Mexican border. The opening of a plant within the interior of the country creates management problems. In the past, American managers, many of whom live in the United States and drive into Mexico to work (returning home at night), have relied on Mexican foremen to handle "employee" problems. This delegation of responsibility for taking care of these issues and ensuring that operations remain uninterrupted is made more difficult if American managers are denied the comfort of returning to the United States after a day's work. In much the same way in which employee problems are now company problems in the United States— within the past ten years corporate America has been forced to train employees, provide referral services to deal with substance and spousal abuse, facilitate maternity and paternity leave, and provide child-care services—American employers cannot ignore the problems of Mexican workers.

These issues present challenges to management. But few managers take these issues into consideration. In the eighties, as Mexico confronted an economic crisis of daunting dimensions, government expenditures to provide schools, hospitals, and housing for workers employed in maquiladora industries failed to keep up with demand. The result has been the emergence of deplorable slums near state-of-the-art facilities, creating a stark and disturbing juxtaposition that many Americans find appalling. Giants of corporate America operate facilities in Mexico where workers live in cardboard shacks without electricity or running water. Despite greater outlays in the second half of the Salinas administration, and despite provisions in NAFTA, the explosion of maquiladoras offers continuing challenges that the Zedillo administration may not meet adequately.

For corporate America, the importance of conducting business in a socially responsible manner continues to grow. The American public—whether shareholder or customer—expects a certain level of decency. Indeed, opponents of NAFTA argued that unless the Mexican worker's rights were protected, the standard of living of American workers would also suffer. Many critics pointed out that the United States had no business entering into a free trade agreement with Mexico, which showed such contempt for its own people and which failed to provide safeguards and the minimum acceptable protection. Ross Perot made infamous his claim of a "giant sucking sound" as the United States lost jobs to Mexico. While there may be sucking sounds in Mexico as NAFTA unfolds, these are not associated with the displacement of American jobs. To be sure, maquiladora jobs in Mexico have grown tremendously—from a mere 67,000 in 1975 to over half a million in 1992—and with few exceptions these have not been the relocation of existing American jobs south of the border. As NAFTA is implemented, however, the growing number of maquiladoras will exacerbate worker conditions, which will present corporate America with both employee relations issues in Mexico and a public relations problem at home.

THE UNSKILLED SKILLED LABOR

The office I occupy is in a new building, which is probably why it took almost two years for the leak in the ceiling to be repaired. In another new office building across town fissures appeared down a wall within a year of the building's completion. American tourists in trendy resorts like Cancun and Acapulco face the challenges of poor executions of beautiful designs everyday. Indeed, at the landmark Sheraton María Isabel on Paseo de la Reforma in the heart of Mexico City, the elevators are not properly aligned when the doors open. The same holds true for bridges and highways, airport terminals, and seaports. The quality of construction is inferior, a reflection of the training of the engineers and architects, the construction managers, and the standards employed.

Buildings and roadways are easily seen. The same level of mediocrity, however, prevails in other aspects of Mexican life. It is seen in the training of doctors and in the capabilities of attorneys, accountants, bankers, and other professionals. It is evident in the intellectual caliber of public debate and in the derivative nature of contemporary Mexican artistic endeavor. It is seen in an impoverished intellect, an underachieving professional class, and substandard preparations in the most fundamental workers. It is this failure to have an educated working and professional class that undermines the ability of corporate America to nurture Mexican managers readily. The strategic objectives of a long-term presence in the Mexican market, however, necessitate the development of capable Mexican managers. American managers, who are oblivious to the cultural rivalries between Cubans and Mexicans—Cuba has long resented Mexican imperialist designs while accepting Mexican foreign aid—need to be aware of the friction that exists. Now, in the age of free trade, Mexican arrogance is not easily reconciled with the fact of life that Cuban-American professionals are better educated and better prepared to negotiate a modern economy than the Mexicans themselves. In the short term, therefore, despite the cultural difficulties already discussed, corporate America's ability to get their Mexican counterparts up to speed depends on the expertise and sophistication of Cuban-American professionals.

The challenge that corporate America faces with the Mexican labor force is not unique. For two decades, corporate America has been concerned that the American public school system was issuing high school diplomas to functional illiterates. Indeed, many firms spearheaded efforts to teach basic skills to American youngsters. What proves to be problematic in the United States, is catastrophic in Mexico. In the office I occupy here in Mexico, employees stream in on pay day to receive their wages. Because the vast majority of Mexicans cannot afford the minimum required for opening a simple checking account, wages are paid in cash. Each worker signs the payroll, acknowledging receipt of his or her wages. There have been occasions when, looking over the list, I noticed that a few employees affix their thumb prints next to their names; some members of the janitorial staff are unable to sign their own names. There have been occasions when, after the Bank of Mexico replaced the peso with "new" pesos, several workers asked me to "explain" the value of the new bank notes. A great deal of diplomacy is required to handle these situations without offending people. American managers need to be aware that Mexican workers cannot write their own names or read bank notes, or that Mexican workers are unable to drive vehicles and are terrified at taking the responsibility to make a decision. That these kinds of incidents are unexceptional in Mexico in the nineties is an indication of the challenges that corporate America confronts in assessing and implementing long-term strategic goals.

The lack of education among Mexicans is a taboo subject, however, and extreme discretion needs to be exercised. The surprising truth is that it has been the policy of the Mexican government to limit the educational opportunities of the Mexican public as a way of exercising influence. In a country where there is one-party rule, authoritarianism requires the subjugation of the public. Knowledge is power and by restricting access to education, the Mexican government, which is to say the ruling party, has been able to manipulate the Mexican public. This is not a unique development in human history. Writing of Czarist Russia in the nineteenth century, the French nobleman Marquis de Custine observed that "in Russia, to converse is to conspire, to think is to revolt: thought is not merely a crime, it is a misfortune also." In Mexico, to think has threatened the ruling party, which is why only the bare minimum has been tolerated. The result, of course, now becomes apparent in the age of free trade: Mexicans are at a marked disadvantage in competing internationally, which is nowhere more evident than in the continuing deterioration of Mexico's trade balance since the implementation of NAFTA.

Of alarming concern, moreover, are the developments of the past few years, in which current-President Zedillo played a crucial role. Under the De la Madrid administration, Mexico entered GATT; the process of the opening up of the economy began that was accelerated under the Salinas administration, as evidenced by the conclusion of free trade agreements. The opening of the economy created great debate and dissension among Mexico's ruling elite, for an economic opening implied an opening of the political system as well. Christened "Salinastroika" by Mexican liberals, after the famous "perestroika" campaign initiated by Mikhail Gorbachev, the hopes were dashed that Salinas would deliver on his promise and hold free, honest elections. Instead, a concerted program to undermine the Mexican educational system was begun by the Salinas administration. Indeed, under Ernesto Zedillo, the secretary of education who served President Salinas, Mexico's literary rates, especially among Native Americans and rural dwellers, began to decline. The process of "rendering ignorant" the most disenfranchised segments of the Mexican population became the official policy of the Salinas administration. The reason for this is obvious enough: The illiterate voter can be more easily manipulated. Thus, while the ruling party suffered setbacks in urban centers during the 1994 presidential elections, it comes as no surprise that the contested election results that brought Ernesto Zedillo to power was only possible by massive, and improbable, support for the official party from rural areas.

The ultimate price of this kind of political expediency is seen in the continuing problems that Mexicans face in competing in world markets. On a visit to Cancun, one can see Mexicans building a new hotel: Hundreds of men converge on a site, carrying sacks of dirt to be used as landfill. It is a vision out of an MGM film in which an army of slaves is raising a pyramid for a pharaoh, which is not without its irony, since the hotel that the workers are building is also shaped like a pyramid. On a visit to Acapulco, one can see multitudes of Mexicans, on their hands and knees, "constructing" the new Acapulco–Mexico City highway. This is the Mexican labor force: Multitudes of men crawling on their hands and knees, pounding rocks together, using Stone Age technology to build the Mexico of the twenty-first century.

American managers, however, must bear in mind that there is an opportunity in this tragedy. Mexicans long to learn, are anxious to teach, and are wonderful students because they have such enthusiasm. The initial frustrations of American managers arriving in Mexico disappear when they see the progress that Mexican employees make. A Mexican friend who owns a couple of American fast-food franchises recalls the American managers sent to train his staffs. After a three-week course, despite the language barrier, the corporate officers were so impressed with the professionalism of the Mexican employees and their complete dedication to learning their jobs, that one manager wanted to take a couple of the Mexican employees to the company's headquarters in Miami to show other trainers the level of proficiency that could be taught to their employees.

To be sure, Mexicans are acutely aware of their substandard education, and most are embarrassed and ashamed; but what they bring stands to compensate, for they bring an enthusiasm and work ethic that renders them ideal candidates for learning skills and for exercising the discipline necessary to foster a corporate cohesion and loyalty that is far too rare in corporate America itself. This is not to diminish the arduous task at hand—training the unskilled and "unskilled skilled" labor forces in Mexico— but the political forces that have rendered Mexican education substandard are changing, as part of the general forces at work transforming the economic landscape of the country.

A casual perusal of the job applications filed away in an office here is revealing. One of the questions is, "What is your goal in life?" What astounds is the consistent answer: "Superarme," which means "to become better." This is where the evil of the Mexican State is most evidently seen: The manipulation of the Mexican people through the destruction of their dreams. In the countless Mexicans I have interviewed for jobs, the ambition, the eagerness, the willingness to please is breathtaking in scope—but, unfortunately, so is the monumental lack of skills, or competency, to perform their jobs. Under the educational system in place in Mexico, Mexicans have been taught to read and write and to add and subtract, but not to think or to understand; there are, after all, no Mexican rocket scientists. Mexicans are great at parroting numbers and statistics; but ask them what these figures mean, and they are lost.

For corporate America, this ignorance represents a monumental challenge, as compelling as anything else to be encountered in Mexico. The dark irony, then, resides in the struggle of the Mexican worker. The ambition, the desire, the dreams are all there, but the opportunities have never been; and it will take at least a generation to get into the workforce Mexicans who can handle the requirements of a modern economy.

On a personal level, the frustration that an American manager faces in Mexico is enormous. There is little use for professionals who aren't professionals or for workers who don't work. To be sure, Mexicans want to rise above their mediocrity. Mexico has engineers who want to engineer, architects who want to design, doctors who want to cure, businessmen who want to be as successful in New York as in Acapulco but who are frustrated by their lack of preparation. This is why, strolling around Mexico's finest boulevard, everything looks so shoddy: Buildings are monuments to the mediocrity engendered by the Mexican political system that has managed to survive only through the exploitation of the Mexican people.

This is—Mexicans and Americans alike hope—all history. The implementation of NAFTA signals a defining moment. Indeed, the corporate forces unleashed by NAFTA, the growing complexities of the more competitive international marketplace, and the requirements of the emerging North American trading bloc—all put renewed pressure on institutional factors to discard the political machinations of an authoritarian regime in favor of the needs of a modern democratic state. If knowledge is power, the horizontal structure wherein knowledge is dispersed and accessible via modern telecommunications and technology, it is no longer possible to keep a nation in ignorance, and democracy follows. For the Mexican government, perhaps the most exasperating dilemma has been to educate the Mexican people enough to create a modern economy, while sufficiently ignorant to enforce a cruel authoritarian regime. As secretary of education, it was Ernesto Zedillo's task to ensure that the masses of rural and "Indian" Mexicans could be manipulated by the ruling party when election time came. That a man of such demonstrated cynicism as Zedillo emerged as president is proof of the ruling party's ability to snare innocents, as well as evidence of the patriarchal solicitude of the Mexican political system. Such atrophied imperialist aspiration, however, may not be enough to derail efforts to bring up to an international level the quality of Mexican education—or thinking. Thought in Russia may have been a crime in the nineteenth century, according to the Marquis de Custine, but it is a requirement in the emerging Mexico of the twenty-first century, regardless of who rules the nation.

A corollary caveat is the nature of employee relations in Mexico, which is not unlike those in other paternalistic societies. In Latin American philosophical thinking, Indian fatalism is a constant theme of haunting dimensions. The West finds it difficult to accept the idea of surrendering free will. There is, undeniably, randomness in life—a randomness that delights at times and that devastates at others. But the progression of Western civilization has been the struggle to diminish chance and to exert control over our lives.

While randomness—a chance meeting an earthquake, the winning lottery ticket—is undeniable, Westerners are not willing to accept the idea that an individual is at the complete mercy of chance. Western civilization demonstrates the history of the evolution of control. We define as progress the act of enclosing more and more things within our control. When we can control our leaders, we are achieving democracy. When we can control chemical reactions in our laboratories, we are moving toward finding cures for physical ailments. When we can control our education, we are moving toward economic independence. When we can control our right to marry and divorce, start or end pregnancies, we are moving toward individual freedom.

We can't control chance encounters or jetliners crashing, any more than we can control things such as the weather or aging. This isn't to say that Westerners have no desire to seed clouds or arrest the ravages of time on their bodies with fluids from Lancôme (Paris) or correct these ravages with scalpels. So the notion of surrendering control—denying it is possible in any capacity—is not only alien to us, but downright bizarre. We simply refuse to believe that anyone can turn over his life with complete abandon to whatever happens to happen, with total disregard.

Indian fatalism is a body of thought that attempts to treat in a rational manner what Westerners define as irrational. It is an attempt to reconcile with Western logic the worldview prevalent among the Native American peoples. It fails miserably. In this life, as the Victorian stoics reminded us in the nineteenth century, you are not going to get what you want, so you might as well learn to like what you get.

This is a most offensive idea, one of complete resignation, turning on its head the course of Western civilization. To the peoples of ancient Mesoamerica, like the indigenous peoples and many Mexicans today, the lesson of that story is clear: One must abdicate control of one's life to the forces of Fate. The cult of fatalism suffuses Mesoamerican intellectual thought, and the resignation of the individual to the will of others is a valued trait. That the cultural history of the Native American civilizations that inhabited what is now Mexico were based on military conquest and imperialism contributes to this importance of fatalism. The Aztecs, for instance, ruled in an imperial fashion, subjugating other Native Americans into submission through brutal military conquest. In ancient Mexico, all roads led to the Aztec capital, which today remains Mexico City. The Spaniards identified with this philosophy instantly, because it was also their own. Indeed, the notion of the surrender of free will also has a compelling history in European thought. As Paul Tillich said, "The Greek skeptics retired from life in order to be consistent. . . . Another consequence of this skeptical mood was what the Stoics called *apatheia* (apathy), which means being without feelings toward the vital drives of life such as desires, joys, pains and instead being beyond all these in the state of wisdom."[3]

These ideas are poetically expressed in the mythologies of the ancient Americans. Indeed, their oral histories capture the thinking of the fatalistic perspective rather nicely, and it offers insights into their philosophies and world views. What the Spaniards—and we today—deplored as passive acceptance and a fatalistic view of life, terrifies us because, in our own histories, philosophies, and thinking, these are the ideas of defeatism, of failure.

When the first Europeans arrived in New Spain, they encountered this same kind of thinking, and they could not understand it. It was similar to the irrationality that the Spaniards had encountered in the reconquest of the Iberian peninsula. As they pushed the Moors back into northern Africa, and as the emerging nation that we call Spain today began to come into existence, the Spaniards kept encountering peoples whose manner of thinking, reasoning, and logic was incomprehensible to them. The Berbers and the Moors, along with the many north African peoples, were frustrating to the European mind-set.

The reverberations of the clash between the European and non-European mind-sets were felt throughout the entire Iberian peninsula. The idea of reasoning—of reasonableness, of rationality—became an obsession in the Spanish-speaking world. Language reflected these concerns and these preoccupations. In Spanish, when one agrees with someone one says, "Tiene razón," which means "You are right," but which literally means, "You have reason." This idea of having reason became a standard by which all thoughts were measured. One's rationality, then, depends on one having reason in the first place.

PEOPLE OF REASON AND THE ADULT CHILD

The arrival of the Spaniards in the New World fueled this obsession with reason and rationality, especially after the encounter with the civilizations in the geographic expression called "Mexico," with its millions of peoples and dozens of ethnicities. As a consequence, another linguistic expression came into widespread use, a code phrase for understanding the incomprehensible. In Spanish the expression "gente de razón," meaning "people of reason," became a code phrase for understanding the kind of mentality with which one was dealing. An individual's reporting that in a certain town in the valley there weren't any "gente de razón," for instance, conveyed a message: prepare to despair.

Historical documents from colonial Spanish America, therefore, are littered with references to "reason"—who has it, who doesn't, where it's found, where it isn't. The Spanish encountered a world where conversations went round and round in circles, never moving forward, or accomplishing much. The secular authorities of what was becoming New Spain despaired; their searches for "people of reason" across the varied landscape proved futile.

The history of New Spain is the struggle to reconcile two different mind-sets: people of reason living among people without reason, and vice versa. That they managed to pull it off is reasonable, perhaps an attribute of the inclusive nature of Catholicism. Reasonable or not, officials in Madrid and Rome decided that these humans had souls and had therefore to be included in the living body of Christ. The English in New England, by comparison, weren't interested in integrating native peoples into their society. Perhaps some English communities entertained such notions, but apart from individual "converts" there was no wholesale incorporation of native communities into the English ones.

The Spanish and Portuguese, on the other hand, were successful in this endeavor. The reason lies in pushing the right buttons. Just as each generation produces certain pop stars who know which buttons to push to create a scandal in their own time, the Spanish of New Spain quickly learned that it is possible to negotiate an advantage if one pushed the right buttons.

The administrators of New Spain soon learned that the native peoples valued their honor and would capitulate to anything if their dignity was spared. The modern Mexican state is built on the belief that there are two kinds of people in this world: *gente de razón* and *gente sin razón*. It is further built on the moral principle that it is the duty of people of reason to take care of people without reason. In the same manner in which parents assume the financial obligation of taking care of their children and in the same way in which society provides institutional support for this endeavor, the Mexican state takes upon itself the duty of providing for its multitudes of marginalized people, *gente sin razón*.

Parents assume responsibility for their children for one simple reason: children have no money. The assumption is that children lack the maturity—which is to say, the sense—to make money, to understand its value and to use it reasonably.

Modern Mexican institutions duplicate the parental relationship between *gente de razón* and *gente sin razón* through paternalism. It is the kind of political philosophy that would drive the likes of Ayn Rand crazy, would infuriate libertarians, and would create enormous resentment among America's already burdened middle class whose members believe that they tolerate an unfair welfare state that solves nothing and satisfies no one. It is an offensive political arrangement that is condescending in nature, encouraging the individual to surrender responsibility for himself or herself, perversely legitimizing a fatalistic view of life and engendering dependency. It is ideal for Mexico.

Paternalism fosters dependence, constitutes patriarchal solicitude, and creates an atrophied society. Nothing takes on a life of its own and becomes entrenched as forcefully as a political institution that has control over the lives of its citizens, and nothing becomes as uncontrollable and unaccountable as a bureaucrat drunk on power. Mexican paternalism thrives precisely because it gives a sense of purpose to Mexican politicians and bureaucrats, and it allows the state to intervene in the development of the nation's economy, further enhancing bureaucratic control, personal résumés, and bank accounts.

Thus, over the years vast armies of bureaucrats in an ever-growing number of agencies have implemented programs that, if not constituting a "safety net" per se, represent massive redistribution programs designed to maintain an acceptable standard of living for as many people as possible without handing over the independence that money offers. Instead of money for food, there are *price controls*. Instead of money for homes, there are *housing programs*. Instead of money for doctors, there is *a free medical health care system*. Instead of money for tuition, there are *free universities*. Instead of money for savings, there are *forced saving programs*. Instead of freedom, there is *dependence*. Dependence on the kindness of bureaucrats as a model for social development.

Indeed, the traditional view of the worker by the Mexican government is akin to that of a parent to an irresponsible child. Therefore, in the same manner in which a child's discretionary money must be controlled, the Mexican government seems to say, so too must the money that the *gente sin razón* (whom are commonly referred to as the "disenfranchised") have at their disposal. It is therefore the national policy of Mexico to minimize wages while maximizing benefits. It also prevents the working poor from squandering their money, like America's poor do by purchasing newstand tabloids, sweets, and lottery tickets.

Few Americans understand the logic behind organizing society as if its members were incapable of making mature, informed decisions using ordinary, everyday common sense. The American assumption is that all men are endowed by their Creator with the use of reason: American revolutionary literature appealed to reason, to common sense. No argument there, provided, of course, that the reader himself or herself is reasonable (and can read).

What if he or she is not? the Mexican State asks. Is an adult child the same as a childish adult? Mexican technocrats, so smug in their self-assured assumptions, think so. If one is not a person of reason, then one is as senseless as a child. Mexican labor laws, prior to NAFTA, had been organized around this assumption. Mexican labor laws extend low monetary wages but offer rich benefits in health care, housing programs, price controls and subsidies on basic foods, maternity and vacation leaves, retirement savings programs and severance compensation. American workers by comparison are entitled to a minimum hourly rate, and that's all (in Mexico, a bureaucratic paradise, there are currently 264 minimum wages). Consider the writings of Richard Rodriguez, one of the most prominent American thinkers of Mexican ancestry, who deplores Mexican wages as exploitation: "There is complicity between businessmen, hands across the border, and shared optimism. . . . What American capitalism has in mind for [Mexico] depends on the availability of great numbers of the Mexican poor; on the willing acceptance of Third World wages by the Mexican poor; on the poor remaining poor."[4] Third World wages? The poor remaining poor?

The Mexican State assumes that the Mexican people are adult children, with the emphasis on the word *children*.

Children have no money. Are children poor? The appeal of this kind of political economy is undeniable: Spare a poor person's dignity, while creating a loyal constituency for a bureaucrat's ambitious career plan. The Big Daddy of the Southern plantation and the Patron of the Hacienda can only envy the power and prestige of the modern Mexican technocrat.

Old women kiss the Mexican president's hand when he, like an apparition, arrives at their dirt-poor villages, filled with dust, cacti, and wandering, hungry mongrels. *Gente sin razón* kiss his hand in gratitude for a power line, or a phone line, or a water line. *Gente sin razón* kiss his hand for doing what the world assumes a government should do. *Gente sin razón* kiss his hand because in Mexico when the government does what it is expected to do it is nothing short of a miracle in their eyes. Old women kiss the president's hand in gratitude for his benevolence, for his kindness in remembering them, for his saintliness.

Then again, old women kiss *my* hand. On the way to an archaeological dig a few years back, I planned to take a shortcut through a small town of Sotuta in the state of Yucatan. (Some time prior to this, we had spent some time there, buying soft drinks, resting from a long and tiring drive through bad jungle roads, taking the opportunity to take a walk around and stretch our legs. At that time, an old Indian woman who sold us drinks whined on and on about how expensive and impossible it was to get fresh milk.) Months later, as I was about to set out on an appointment, I remembered the old Indian lady. Fortunately for her, Hurricane Gilbert had displaced some cattle, and I was able to secure a heifer that I thought I would just give her for the sake of kindness. When I arrived in Sotuta and had the calf lowered from the pickup truck, the woman's eyes lit up, swollen with tears and disbelief, and she kissed my hand. She crossed herself, blessed me, and promised to pray to me—not *for* me, but *to* me. Thus baptized with an old woman's kiss, I joined the pantheon of minor Maya deities.

What is one to make of this? Is this what the Spanish of New Spain encountered—people without reason who embarrass us in such unexpected ways? What is an average American manager to make of attending the opening of an office in Mexico—which is only "officially" open for business after a religious ceremony in which a Catholic priest sprinkles holy water on the front door? How does one report back to the home office in Anywhere, U.S.A., that the office staff has requested permission for a day off to organize a pilgrimage to some religious site or other? What is one to make of a makeshift altar to honor pagan deities that the cleaning staff has set up in a back room?

In *Harper's*, Walter Russell Mead protested against the free trade agreement: "If NAFTA is signed, Ford and GM will move their factories to Mexico, and hire cheap Mexican labor, and then sell their cars in the United States. But the freedom is not symmetrical: Mexican workers will not be able to simply cross the border and sell their labor at U.S. rates."[5]

American assertions about the Mexican labor market or the dynamics of so-called "cheap" labor are always sentimental tirades deriding the "slave" wages and the immorality of corporate America that profits from the poverty and misery of defenseless workers, abandoned by callous and corrupt governments and manipulated like expendable pawns in international agreements and deals that are finalized in closed-door meetings in New York and Washington. A grim description, and it would indeed be grimmer if it were true in fact. It isn't. American ethnocentric assumptions are wrong. Mexico is not a mirror image of the United States where people happen to speak Spanish and happen to be poorer: Americans never reflect on the paternalistic nature of Mexican society that results in workers being compensated in a calculated combination of wages *and* benefits.

A brief introduction to the institutional organs of the Mexican State for direct subsidies to Mexican workers include health, housing, and price control agencies. In Mexico every full-time worker is entitled to benefits from the Instituto Mexicano del Seguro Social (IMSS), a national health care program. Unlike America's own Social Security, which is a retirement and disability program, Mexico's IMSS is open to all authorized wage earners and their families. Everything from flu shots to chemotherapy is provided free of charge. Workers are encouraged to participate in a housing program run by the state agency known as Infonavit. Almost two hundred thousand housing units were delivered to Mexican workers in 1992. This was not enough to meet the demand for worker housing, but what was provided is substantial. Mexico has elaborate price controls on the "essential" staple food supplies that consist of thousands of items, operated through an arrangement of "voluntary" price controls negotiated by the government between producers and the private sector in an arrangement called the Pacto. It is not uncommon to see consumer items bearing the "Precio de Pacto," meaning "Pacto Price," on the price sticker. Outright price controls are mandated on hundreds of items, including the staple food products: milk, eggs, flour, bread, tortilla, beans, rice, and so on. To implement subsidies to inefficient rural farmers, called peasants in English, the state agency Conasupo pays a farmer $2 for something it sells to the public for $1, the loss being absorbed by the state.

These are the fundamental approaches, but the IMSS, Infonavit, Pacto, and Conasupo are but the umbrella organizations under which dozens of agencies and subagencies flourish in an alarming alphabet soup of acronyms. The humblest of villages has a "Conasupo" market, "IMSS" state health clinics and hospitals almost everywhere; the "Pacto" is stamped on thousands upon thousands of consumer goods; and large billboards herald new Infonavit residential communities, as do constant advertisements in newspapers and magazines—in none of the hundreds of articles I have read in the United States concerning various aspects of NAFTA, or those that cross my desk, have I ever seen any of these agencies, or any other, mentioned once.

In contrast to all this, the American approach—food stamps, welfare checks, housing projects—offends Mexican sensibilities because these redistribution schemes offend the recipients' dignity. I have seen embarrassed women in the United States hand over food stamps, knowing I am behind them observing in the checkout line. Mexico is reluctant to create a system in which a poor person can be humiliated. Instead of parading one's poverty by handing a checkout clerk food stamps, as obvious as a scarlet letter of shame, Mexico chooses to subsidize basic food stuffs. The richest of the rich and the poorest of the poor can buy a dozen eggs at a government-controlled price.

Mexican social institutions rest on the assumption that *gente sin razón*— referred to as "Indians" and "gente sin cultura," meaning people with little formal schooling—are incapable of taking care of themselves, of understanding money, of being anything more than adult children. For the ruling elite, this, then, is their raison d'être. And this requires an army of bureaucrats and technocrats and politicians and know-it-alls to invent and implement institutional bureaucracies that are the envy of the world— among bureaucrats perhaps.

Bureaucracy is power, and power feeds upon itself—especially so in a paternalistic society. This is true the world over. Americans will remember that it was Jimmy Carter who created the Department of Education. Ronald Reagan, who sat is the Oval Office for two terms immediately following Jimmy Carter, from day one, wanted to shut it down. It was ironic, he believed, that for two hundred years Americans had learned reading, writing, and arithmetic without the intervention of the federal government and now, especially now, that there was a cabinet-level secretary of education, well, American high schools were turning out so many illiterates that instead of granting diplomas they had begun to issue "certificates of attendance," which indicated that the holder might have attended twelve years of schooling but there was no guarantee he or she had learned a damned thing.

Ironic, perhaps, but no less so than the Reagan administration's inability to shut it down. How could a bureaucracy become so entrenched in less than four years that even the president of the United States was unable to get rid of it? By the very nature of bureaucracies, of course. The Department of Education became a new venture in pet projects of a pork barrel nature, if nothing else, by both members of Congress and the executive branch. It became a source of employment opportunities of great use in rewarding political allies and backers and in protecting favored causes. The Department of Education became a bureaucracy with the authority to intervene in the affairs of states, counties, and cities. Such temptations prove irresistible for mere mortals—mere mortals who will fight to protect their spheres of influence, or at least their ability to meddle in the business of others. In just three years the Department of Education was able to create a constituency that would ensure its survival. Everyone who benefited in some way from this new department had an interest to defend. So Ronald Reagan in eight years was unable to dismantle something so new.

This is not to criticize the Department of Education. The intention is to demonstrate how quickly bureaucracies take on lives of their own. In Mexico where bureaucracy is paternalism made manifest, government agencies transcend the mortal. Consider just one example to understand how the Mexican political economy has evolved. Let us say that IMSS is a health care program created to protect the nation's workers and their families. Let us boast that by its very mission it is a public institution open to all segments of society. It is, therefore, not very exclusive an institution. State workers wondered if, say, individuals whose work is noble in nature, such as serving society, shouldn't have a more indulgent, exclusive health care system. State workers seemed to think so. Thus was born the Instituto de Seguridad y Servicios Sociales para los Trabajadores del Estado, known as ISSSTE, a health care and service bureaucracy designed to meet the more demanding health care needs of state and federal employees. Better doctors, better hospitals, and better medical attention, all free of charge, for that selfless class of human beings we call bureaucrats.

Why stop there? If state workers are entitled to an exclusive health care system, shouldn't they also be entitled to exclusive stores where they can buy household products, appliances, and groceries at specially subsidized prices? Why not? Thus, Issste Tiendas, or "ISSSTE Shops," were created where state workers could buy everything from Campbell's soup to General Electric refrigerators at below-market prices. Before anyone knew it, a health care agency was in the supermarket and major appliance business. But why stop there? If state workers are entitled to special health care and special shops, why not, say, special vacations? Bureaucrats are entitled to indulge themselves—we know how hard they work. So it is, to bureaucrats at least, a grand idea to start a travel agency that will subsidize economy vacations. Thus, an internal travel program was begun to permit state workers to go on holiday to Disney World and Paris at subsidized rates.

The wisdom of such programs is immaterial. It is a question of power accumulating more and more power, of paternalism distributing benefits in return for loyalty, of giving people a stake in a system in order for that system to perpetuate itself. What bureaucrats did for themselves, they also did for the charges in their care. The state-owned oil company, Pemex, for one, duplicated every program conceivable, from housing to health care, for oil workers. Some smart bureaucrat at the federal housing program, Infonavit, asked, "What good was a house without furniture?" and promptly created Fonacot, a program to help workers buy furniture.

On and on it went, relentlessly. The state-owned oil company was purchasing disposable diapers by the millions; housing department administrators were compiling reports comparing table service in the restaurants of Cancun versus the restaurants of La Jolla, California, officials from the agriculture department spent days picking out lamp shades and kitchen curtains, tourism officials were placing orders for cough medicines, administrators of the state-owned airline were evaluating grain subsidies, and officials at the health ministry were test driving new jeeps. Everyone was on holiday in Los Angeles, Houston, New York, or off somewhere in Europe. If Ronald Reagan thought it inconceivable that he was unable to shut down a department that Jimmy Carter had just created, imagine the task of trying to dismantle a paternalistic political system imbedded in the national economy in such a ubiquitous, suffocating manner.

The growth of these bureaucracies became uncontrollable—and for a very good reason: Each new program benefited someone who became part of an enfranchised constituent with a stake in the continued survival of the system. In extending the imperialist designs of Mexico City on the rest of the political landscape of the country, bureaucratic control became political control, especially if patronage was to be dispensed to reward loyalty. If you asked bureaucrats if they thought subsidized vacations were a good idea, what bureaucrat would say no? If you asked oil workers if free medicine for their families was a good idea, who would deny it? If you asked minimum-wage workers if subsidized housing was a good idea, who would say no? If you asked anyone, "Is something for nothing a good idea?" very few would say no. That was the promise of Mexico's ruling party: something for nothing. Well, not exactly—it was subsidized bread and tortillas in exchange for one thing: freedom.

Economists are fond of mentioning, of course, that the problem with the poor is that they have no money. The implication being that direct transfer payments are the most efficient manner of redistributing purchasing power. The second most efficient manner is through programs like the ones in America, and the most inefficient strategy consists of across-the-board subsidies. Mexico has chosen the most inefficient manner to protect the dignity of its citizens. Inefficiency is not as important as someone's dignity. But the price of such inefficiency astounds. The Mexican political system has created a nation of adult children, a nation of people who are incapable of taking care of themselves, of thinking for themselves. The result is a nation of perpetual adolescents—and the consequences are monumental.

Mexico is a society atrophied in the commodity fetishism of childhood. American executives arriving in Mexico City cannot help but be taken aback by the adolescent mentalities of the Mexicans. Everyone one turns, there they are: adult men and women reading comic books, an entire economy geared toward soft drinks and fast foods, masses consuming candy, television programming filled with insipid shows—clowns, slapsticks, vaudeville—aimed at adults and children, an obsession with toys and gadgets, as if the entire consuming public of Mexico consisted of immature twelve-year-olds. From a political point of view, however, manipulating adult children is not a difficult matter and is one that the ruling party has managed to do with great flair.

This is all instructive. This allows American managers to understand where Mexicans are coming from and what their expectations happen to be—how the Mexican mind-set seeks to be taken care of, to be protected. An adult child is merely a childish adult, and this is a sad, but accurate, characterization of the Mexican worker. To be an employer in Mexico is to be a "patron"—which is, in fact, a substitute parent. The American discipline in leaving personal problems outside the workplace is an alien notion in Mexico. As a consequence, Mexican employers become involved in the personal lives of their employees, offering advice, making personal loans, intervening if necessary. At one of the firms with which I am familiar, there is a fund set up for employee loans, which are later discounted from paychecks, interest free. I have had to help intervene with police authorities in employee problems, and many times meetings have centered on how to best assist so-and-so with his or her personal problems. Whereas American managers would look with surprise at workers asking to use company premises or sponsorship for the annual pilgrimage in honor of the Virgin of Guadalupe, to deny such a request is to invite ill will. It is not uncommon to see the faithful assemble under banners bearing corporate logos. In the same way that many firms sponsor local events in their communities across America, such as United Way fundraising drives, in Mexico firms sponsor religious pilgrimages.

To be sure, as pressures have increased in America, more and more employees have turned to their employers to provide or facilitate employee referral services to assist in personal problems—from finding babysitters to helping overcome drinking problems. In Mexico, however, these take on a familial relationship, and the employer becomes personally involved in helping his employees get on with their lives—from making a personal loan to overlooking absences. At times, these unsolicited responsibilities embarrass: The wives of several workers have approached me and requested that their husbands' wages not be given to them, as a way of preventing these employees from squandering their paychecks on alcohol. This puts employers in uncomfortable and conflicting positions, but American managers must be aware that this is normal in Mexico.

The implementation of NAFTA, however, is nothing short of a philosophical revolution in Mexico. The nature of paternalism, the worldview of manipulating people deemed incapable of being responsible for themselves, the burdens placed on employers and the inculcation of dependency among the workforce are no longer appropriate. State-controlled programs of social engineering are unnecessary when dealing with adults. NAFTA is a blueprint for turning the Mexican people into responsible adults. The economic and political dislocation occasioned by the dismantling of Mexico's paternalistic social structure is causing tremendous pressures within Mexican society. Social unrest and a crisis of self-doubt now plague the Mexican worker, unsure of his or her place in the world and the demands of a modern economy. The frailty of the Mexican identity is explored at length in the next section. For American managers, however, the realization that these revolutionary changes within the Mexican world-view represent risks as one way of life is replaced with another.

What alarms is the utter paternalistic arrogance that is required of employers in Mexico. The Mexican worker, by design, is an adult child, and the employer—el patron—becomes a substitute parent who becomes intimately involved in the life of his worker. An American businessman who set up shop in Cancun, for instance, was surprised by how easily his employees related their personal problems to him and requested assistance—from "loans" to visiting sick relatives to "donations" of things that would otherwise be discarded—and slowly he found himself acting more and more as a paternal figure. The clear-cut distinctions between "personal" and "business" life that is found throughout corporate America made little sense in Mexico, where employees consider their employers to be part of the extended family.

The patriarchal solicitude that then emerges has a self-fulfilling aspect to it that is a grave consideration: To do business in Mexico means to perpetuate a system that fosters dependence. The tragedy has been, and remains, one of cruel tautology. The docile worker is required to maintain a vertical social order, which has been replaced by a horizontal one in which networking equals modernity. Mexican aspirations for modernity require the destruction of the political hegemony on which the nation is built. This, however, shouldn't surprise, for one of the greatest lessons of the twentieth century is the capacity of economic necessity to overthrow ideological machinations based on fantasies. The profoundly unforgiving demands of modern economic systems reveal the irredeemable nature of closed development models. The follies of Mexico, however, exact demands on the American employer who has inherited a Mexican labor force engaged in a North American economy. For the time being, then, history repeats itself. The paternalism reminiscent of the American South is being duplicated south of the border.

NOTES

1. Gary Clyde Hufbauer and Jeffrey J. Schott, *NAFTA: An Assessment* (Washington, D.C.: Institute for International Economics, 1993), p. 21.

2. Ibid., p. 43.

3. Paul Tillich, *A History of Christian Thought: From Its Judaic and Hellenistic Origins to Existentialism* (New York: Simon & Schuster, 1968), pp. 4–5.

4. Richard Rodriguez, "Across the Borders of History," *Harper's*, March 1987, p. 47.

5. Walter Russell, "Bushism, Found: A Second-Term Agenda Hidden in Trade Agreements," *Harper's*, September 1992, pp. 40–41.

Part II

Understanding the Mexican Persona

6

The Surrender of Economic Sovereignty

On August 5, 1982, Mexican President José López Portillo was forced to devalue the Mexican peso, freeze dollar accounts, suspend foreign exchange operations, and declare a banking holiday. The international debt crisis was thus launched.

In short order, other debt-ridden Third World countries confronted crises, and the International Monetary Fund and the World Bank began a huge effort to stave off disaster. For Mexico, the ensuing months created an enormous political crisis. In December of that year, Miguel de la Madrid was sworn in as Mexico's president, and he undertook a massive effort to save the Mexican economy, which characterized his entire administration. The Mexican Revolution had officially failed once the IMF and the World Bank intervened; when foreign organizations have virtual veto power over a nation's federal budget and outlay, does the notion of "sovereignty" exist any longer?

Miguel de la Madrid was forced to begin a program that would surrender Mexico's economic sovereignty to foreign interests, which was a requisite for the approval of loans and bailouts. At the same time, Mexico was required to abandon its historical nationalistic-socialistic development model, which culminated in joining GATT.

When Miguel de la Madrid's term expired, his budget director, Carlos Salinas de Gortari, who was responsible for implementing the wishes of foreigners, became president. The American-trained technocrat then embarked on a program of further integration of the Mexican economy into that of the United States and Canada. This historic repudiation of

Mexican isolationism, which had delivered nothing but a nation of disenfranchised people, further accelerated the processes of surrendering sovereignty. President Salinas, convinced that if this new Mexican Revolution was to succeed he would have to do the opposite of what his contemporary, Mikhail Gorbachev, was doing on the opposite side of the globe, concentrated on economic reform first, then on opening the political system. Carlos Salinas was convinced that Gorbachev had erred in a fundamental way by opening up the political system without having a firm economic foundation upon which democracy could be built and was determined to get Mexico's economic house in order first, then introduce democracy.

To accomplish this, he embarked on negotiations that resulted in NAFTA. The idea was, and remains, that if Mexico's economy is irrevocably linked to that of the United States and Canada, it will be impossible for Mexico's backward political structure to resist reform. While Mexico has been more successful than the former Soviet Union, the emergence of armed rebels, a wave of political assassinations, the escalation of kidnappings and abductions, and the growing unrest in various parts of the country have detracted from President Salinas' claims to having been completely successful. There are many critics in Mexico who denounce NAFTA for what it is—caving in to the wishes of the United States. This, an accurate description of the situation at hand from an analytical point of view, begs the question: Why has Mexico surrendered its sovereignty?

There is no single answer to this question. There are, however, undeniable historical factors that have shaped the Mexican psyche and identity and that offer clues to the convoluted notion of self that Mexico and Mexicans harbor. As Octavio Paz has said, "Even now . . . no one can explain satisfactorily the 'national' differences between Argentinians and Uruguayans, Peruvians and Ecuadorians, Guatemalans and Mexicans."[1]

Corporate officers who want to succeed in Mexico need to understand the fragile psyche of the Mexicans. What follows is a cultural overview that offers insights into the Mexican psyche. Only in understanding the cultural inhibitions, fears, and insecurities of a nation of people who, for various historical reasons, instinctively feel inferior, can a firm learn what buttons to push for the desired responses.

The origins of what we understand as Mexico lay in the meetings of two distinct cultural traditions—the Native American peoples who inhabited the geographic landscape that the Mexican nation now occupies, on the one hand, and the Christian traditions that the European settlers brought with them on the other. The convergence of histories astounds in the resulting society that continues to emerge after these centuries.

AN ENCOUNTER OF TWO CIVILIZATIONS

Mexico is not a Spanish-speaking version of the United States. American managers must have a historical understanding in order to have a context from which judgments are made, decisions reached, and strategies designed. A cultural and social context is vital if a long-term presence in the Mexican market is to be realized. At the same time, it is important that the peculiar Mexican sensibilities, which are present in the business environment, be understood. This does not mean that a manager has to agree with the Mexican point of view, but rather that he or she be aware of what makes the Mexican psyche tick and of which buttons to push in order to achieve the desired results. For this, it is necessary to start at the beginning, which is before Columbus stumbled onto the Western Hemisphere en route to Asia.

The gods of ancient America have the power of transfiguration. They appear in different shapes and forms. The Maize god is a handsome young man one minute, an old hag the next. In Christianity there are similar transformations. Bread and wine become flesh and blood. A sinner becomes saved. The power of redemption, of transforming, of becoming something else reverberates in the imaginations of both the European and the Indian. In Catholicism, where the underlying assumption is that everyone is a sinner and yet worthy of redemption, such noble notions find their parallels in the worldview of ancient America. The idea of becoming something other than what one is transcends differences among the peoples on either side of the Atlantic, and it compels.

Mexico invents itself, transforming its history to fit an imagined idea. These Mexican myths, the foundation on which Mexico itself rests, are the ideas that the Spanish conquered the Aztecs and that the Mexican people are "mestizo," meaning of European and Indian descent. History is discarded in favor of comfortable fictions. But fictions are not true; and if the essence of something is to be understood, the layers of disguises must be removed, to expose what lies beyond mere words.

This deception astounds with its absorbing, mythic power. Mexico invents itself in order to find its place in the world. The nature of this deception rests in the engendering of the two myths that define "Mexicanness," whatever that may be.

The first myth revolves around the idea of victimization, represented by the story of the Conquest of Mexico. Mexico creates the illusion that this military conflict was the result of a European invasion that descended upon the unsuspecting Aztecs, resulting in the subjugation of the Aztec

Empire and the destruction of their fabulous city of Mexico-Tenochtitlán. The second myth is the notion that the Mexicans are, biologically, "mestizo," meaning of mixed European and Mexican Native American ancestry, creating a "cosmic" race that is singular in the world.

These modern Mexican myths are the core of Mexican identity. They are, however, false notions. The Spanish never conquered the Aztecs: Subjugated Mexican Native American armies, under the *direction* of Hernán Cortés rose in revolt against their hated Aztec overlords. That the Spanish then took credit for this military victory—European males are always taking the credit for the accomplishments of others, it seems— is quite another thing. That the Spanish then proceeded to establish a colonialism based on negotiated accommodation with ruling Native American elites, resorting to violence only when necessary, also undermines the Mexican insistence on her cherished, exalted status of victim.

Mexico, further, nurtures the cult of "mestizaje" as a way of creating a public identity within the community of nations. Throughout the colonial period, for a variety of reasons, great numbers of African slaves were shipped to Mexico to build New Spain. Indeed, Africans far outnumbered Europeans in Mexico for the three hundred years of colonialism, leaving a legacy of haunting silence. Mexico's "cosmic" race, and its vision of itself, excludes its African heritage; the mingling of European and Native American and African, after all, is Brazil's claim to a kind of Mardi Gras fame. The political requirements of the Mexican State's idea of identity, on the other hand, would become needlessly complicated if an African heritage were recognized. Then again, despite Mexico's professed wishful thinking, ironies abound; the Mexican landscape is dominated by African produce in its kitchens and its still lifes—constant reminders of its undeniable African heritage.

The key to understanding Mexico is to understand the nature of its self-deception, its need for both victimization as well as the impulse to deny its African heritage in order to preserve the persona that it cultivates. In this and the following chapter, I will examine these dual myths of Mexican identity and why they are the comfortable lies that Mexico holds dearer than life itself.

The duality of Mexican claims to being "mestizo," at times prurient, at times farcical, creates tensions that shatter with the greatest of ease, exposing the raw, fragile Mexican psyche. The dialectical ambivalence of Mexico's invented identity proves a burden of enormous proportions, creating tremendous insecurity that paralyzes the Mexicans. The essential desire for modernity, then, becomes the zeitgeist to soothe the unbearable self-doubt. Throughout history, Mexico has been judged by the world as a nation of bastards. The label stings, and while Europe delighted in dismissing Mexico and the Mexicans as "half-breeds" in the lexicon of nineteenth-century imperialism, derogatory labels endure in the twentieth century. When other Latin Americans wish to mock the Mexicans, names are in order. When the Cuban diaspora in Miami, for instance, is critical of Mexico's unceasing, generous, and inexplicable foreign aid to Fidel Castro, the Cuban Americans refer to the stupidity, audacity, and recklessness of the rulers of the "Aztec Capital," an indirect way of calling the Mexicans *savage bastards.*

The fragile Mexican identity despairs at these unkind reminders of its uncertain origins, of its lack of pedigree, which other Latin Americans delight in pointing out. Mexicans, therefore, struggle against this pain, masking their sorrow through undying faith in the power of belief, even if the nature of this belief is only a childish make-believe. Indeed, Mexico presents itself to the world as a New World phoenix, rising from the ashes of the vanquished "Indian," with Mexicans emerging as a "cosmic" race, transformed into the noble heir of the achievements of ancient civilizations whose serene wisdom and singular achievements assure Mexico a future as astonishing as its past.

NOTE

1. Octavio Paz, *The Labyrinth of Solitude: Life and Thought in Mexico* (New York: Grove Press, 1961), p. 122.

7

The Meeting of Two Great Civilizations

In this presentation of the Conquest of Mexico, sources quoted are from Native American accounts, which diminishes the distorted views often presented by the victors at the expense of those who are vanquished. It is also politically correct, which is a consideration for American managers working in the United States in the nineties. According to J. Jorge Klor de Alva,

> For almost 450 years the history of the conquest of Mexico . . . was based overwhelmingly on Spanish accounts. These had the effect of creating a series of false images, the most important being that the defeat of the Aztecs of Mexico-Tenochtitlán—always "by a handful of Spaniards"—meant the complete collapse of all native politics and civilization. Traditionalist authors wanted us to understand that Spaniards had triumphed against great odds and had succeeded in bringing about not only military and political conquests but also spiritual, linguistic, and cultural ones. A defeated, silent people, we were asked to believe, and been reduced to subservience and quickly disappeared as Indians to become mestizos, or had simply retreated into rural landscape.[1]

THE CONQUEST OF MEXICO

On the evening of February 27, 1956, an *I Love Lucy* episode, titled "Paris at Last," made its premiere broadcast in the United States. The plot of this episode revolved around the arrival in Paris of the Ricardos and the Mertzes. On her first day in Paris, Lucy encounters a Frenchman who, with disarming friendliness, deceives her into exchanging her American dollars for his counterfeit French francs. Lucy altruistically shares her good fortune with Ethel and Fred, and the three of them set out, spending their francs. In no time, Lucy is caught passing counterfeit money and is, of course, hauled off to jail. Ricky, at their suite at the Hotel Royale all this time, is notified and rushes off at once to save his wife.

Unfortunately, language proves a barrier to saving Lucy from herself. She, after all, speaks only English. Ricky speaks English and Spanish. The French magistrate speaks only French. The solution to this dilemma, however, lies in the presence of a French officer who speaks French and German, and, almost unbelievably, a German who is drunk and sleeping out his hangover but who is fluent in German and Spanish. The delightfully charming translation method employed is pure comic genius. Lucy explains the facts of the matter to Ricky in English. Ricky translates these into Spanish to the drunk. The drunk explains the situation in German to the French officer, who then conveys the message in French to the magistrate. The French magistrate, in turns, asks a question in French, which is translated to German and then Spanish and finally English. Back and forth it goes. The scene is grand fun and rather insightful for the purposes of the present discussion.

A few centuries before this television show was first broadcast, a similar hapless journey on a grander scale, but with an essentially similar plot, took place. It is the Conquest of Mexico. Hernan Cortés spoke Spanish. Montezuma spoke Nahuatl. Cortés and Montezuma were as helpless as Lucy and the French magistrate. How on earth were they to understand each other, when neither spoke Arabic, the scientific and international language of the sixteenth century? How were they to understand each other, or at least ascertain each other's thoughts and intentions?

Hernán Cortés and Montezuma were lucky indeed. Their language problems were resolved through the deliverance of two interpreters by providence. When he sailed from Havana, Cortés landed on the island of Cozumel, which is situated off the coast of the Yucatan peninsula in the Caribbean. While on the island, he learned from the Mayas that there were other white men on the peninsula. Eight years before in 1511, a Spanish galleon had left Darien destined for Hispaniola and was lost at sea. A few shipwrecked survivors washed up ashore on the Yucatan peninsula.

These hapless men suffered various fates. Some perished in the extreme conditions, exposed to the elements without food or water. Others managed to hang on until they were rescued by the Mayas. "Rescued" is perhaps too generous a word to describe their ordeal. The Mayas promptly sacrificed a few survivors to their bloodthirsty rain god Chac and enslaved the rest. One Spanish slave, Gonzalo Guerrero, proved himself a capable soldier and military strategist. He earned his freedom, married a Maya woman, with whom he raised a family, and achieved high status in Maya society. When Cortés' message reached Guerrero, he declined the opportunity to return to his countrymen. He was happy, he explained—so happy, in fact, that he made it clear he would fight his own compatriots should they venture forward.

Another man, Gerónimo de Aguilar, on the other hand, hated the place. He was a slave among savage idolaters, and he was miserable. Upon arriving in Cozumel, Cortés sent out envoys carrying letters and gifts. The Maya owners of Gerónimo de Aguilar were open to the idea of trading him for a few beads and trinkets—a reflection, perhaps, on Aguilar's bad attitude or poor skills as a slave. The Mayas happily kept the gifts and let Gerónimo de Aguilar go to be reunited with his countrymen in Cozumel.

Cortés was delighted to have someone who spoke Yucatec Maya fluently and who had lived among the people of this land. Thus armed with an interpreter, Cortés and his men set sail, hugging the coastline of Yucatan. Well into the Gulf of Mexico, Cortés stopped near present-day Tabasco to get supplies and fresh water and to take a look around and rest before continuing forward. As is often the case in human history, landing for supplies in a distant land would not be complete without a skirmish of some sort with the locals. This was no exception. The Spanish, easily defeating the local Mayas, engaged in dialogue, a dialogue facilitated by Cortés' skillful interpreter.

The Spanish learned that vast riches lay in a far-off land ruled by a savage people, an evil empire of sorts, that terrorized its weaker neighbors. The empire was so powerful, Cortés learned, that even these people, the Mayas of Yucatan, were forced to capitulate and offer tribute—bribes to keep those barbarians at bay. Cortés was told that these people, who called themselves "Mexicas," had tremendous wealth: gold, silver—they had it all. Their city was said to be fabulous, suspended in the mountains, floating in the middle of a lake. Cortés also learned of an obstacle: The language of the Mexicas was Nahuatl, not Yucatec Maya, and Gerónimo de Aguilar would be of no use.

If only they could find someone who spoke Nahuatl that the Spaniards could buy? trade? recruit? As providence would have it, there was! Indeed, having been defeated by the Spanish, the Maya were more than eager to please them. Cortés was presented with a maiden for his pleasure and that of his men. The local Maya lord told Cortés he had the woman available—

a bad investment as far as investments in slaves were concerned. This Maya lord had bought this woman years back and didn't care for her—bad attitude, bad slave.

A deal was struck: Cortés could have this Nahuatl-speaking woman who was fluent in Yucatec Maya in exchange for a few things that struck the Maya gentleman's fancy. The woman, who was called Malinche, joined the Spaniards and was given the new name of Doña Marina. With fresh supplies and linguistic problems settled, Cortés sailed off, ready to find fortune beyond his wildest dreams.

Gerónimo de Aguilar and Doña Marina would be the vital links between Cortés and the Native American enemies of Montezuma, and then between Cortés and Montezuma. The rescued Spaniard would then speak to the Native American woman in Yucatec Maya, who would then communicate in Nahuatl, to either a Native American lord who spoke Nahuatl or to a court translator fluent in Nahuatl and the local language. Nahuatl, which was the language of the Aztec overlords who ruled over much of what is now central Mexico, was the lingua franca in Mesoamerica in the sixteenth century. The response in Nahuatl would be translated to Yucatec Maya and then finally into Spanish.

Cortés was thus able to communicate with just about anyone with a minimum of two interpreters, at times three, and, perhaps on that rare occasion, four. A rather cumbersome manner in which to communicate, no doubt, but it was the best system that could be managed, given the circumstances at hand. This arrangement proved rather effective, for it allowed Cortés to convince Native American leaders to join him in a campaign against the hated Aztec overlords who held the Native American nations of Mesoamerica in humiliating subservience.

Word spread quickly. As Cortés and his ships sailed along the coastline, reports of white men reached the city of Mexico-Tenochtitlán. It was a matter of great concern for two reasons. The Native American peoples of Mesoamerica had been waiting for the return of Quetzalcoatl, known as Kukulkan among the Maya peoples, a god who had left long before, promising to return to rule over the land. The arrival of Quetzalcoatl concerned the Mexica ruler Montezuma in the same manner in which the arrival of Christ would prove problematic for individuals like the pope or the U.N. Secretary General: immediate unemployment. Montezuma was a king, and he wanted to keep his job and not relinquish his power, not even to a god whose arrival was the fulfillment of a prophecy.

At the same time, the initial reports of the sighting of white men must have come as a relief. In recent years there had been omens—comets streaking across the sky, temples being consumed in great conflagrations, inexplicable flooding from Lake Texcoco—that had caused great unrest and anxiety at the royal court of Montezuma. Perhaps the most unsettling omen was the wailing of an old woman heard throughout the city night after night. The woman cried incessantly, lamenting, "My children, we must flee from this city!" or "My children, where shall I take you?" or "O my sons, we are lost!" or "O my sons, where can I hide you?" None of this instilled confidence in the reign of Montezuma.

It was therefore with great anxiety that the court received messengers who informed Montezuma that there were "small mountains floating on the waves of the sea" carrying gods. At a loss as to what to do, Montezuma decided to send these gods gifts, hoping to win their favor. Within his court, however, there was dissension. Some court magicians stated that "the future has already been determined and decreed in heaven, and [Montezuma] will behold and suffer a great mystery which must come to pass in his land."[2] These court magicians were promptly jailed. Montezuma's messengers were on their way to the coast bearing lavish gifts of gold and headdresses made of quetzal feathers. They were charged with greeting and welcoming the returned god Quetzalcoatl. Cortés had the upper hand, of course. As they sailed the coast, Doña Marina explained to the Spaniards the history of this land and the peoples inhabiting it.

When Montezuma's messengers sighted the Spanish vessels, Cortés was ready to go along and pretend to be a "god." The messengers rowed small canoes toward the Spanish vessel, saying, "We have come from the City of Mexico." Doña Marina translated this into Yucatec Maya and Gerónimo de Aguilar then translated into Spanish. Then came the reply: "You may have come from there, or you may not have. Perhaps you are only inventing it. Perhaps you are mocking us."[3] The Spaniards were clearly having fun. The messengers protested their honesty: "If the god will deign to hear us, your deputy Montezuma has sent us to render you homage. He has the City of Mexico in his care."[4] Very well, it was decided, and the messengers were allowed aboard. Cortés was ready for them, sitting in his captain's chair as if he were a king. The messengers presented their gifts to Cortés who, speaking to Gerónimo de Aguilar who spoke to Doña Marina who spoke to the messengers, expressed his displeasure: "And is this all? Is this your gift of welcome? Is this how you greet people?"[5] The messengers expressed dismay: "This is all, our lord. This is what we have brought you."[6] The messengers were seized by the Spaniards. They were chained by the feet and the neck and then as a demonstration of their power a cannon was fired. The messengers who had never seen anything like this were very much frightened, some fainted, all to the amusement of the Spaniards.

They were summoned by Cortés. He handed shields and swords and challenged them to mock battles. They protested. They were royal envoys from the court of Montezuma, not warriors. Cortés was unimpressed. The courage and skill of the Mexica warriors was known throughout the world, he flattered them, even in the kingdom of Castile. Cortés would hear nothing of their protests. He told them to practice and rest up, for tomorrow mock fights would be held on deck. The messengers then were lowered to their canoes and instructed to return the following day.

They had no intention of returning. They were frightened out of their wits and were determined to return to Mexico at once. They made landfall at Xicalanco and immediately departed for the City of Mexico.

At the court of Montezuma, meanwhile, there was great anxiety. Montezuma was despairing, "in the deepest of gloom and sorrow," lamenting to his advisers: "What will happen to us? Who will outlive it? Ah, in other times I was contented, but now I have death in my heart! My heart burns and suffers, as if it were drowned in spice!"[7] Upon their frenzied return to the City of Mexico, the messengers told their fantastic tale, of the marvels of the gods and of the strange animals (horses) they had brought with them. Montezuma grew terrified. The gods he was told were intent on marching toward the City of Mexico.

Upon hearing of these events, the royal court was thrown in complete turmoil. One group of advisers were suspicious. Why would Quetzalcoatl need two interpreters to make himself understood? Could it be possible that these were not gods, but warriors of a foreign people? Who were the "soiled" gods—blacks—who accompanied the strangers? Why would the gods come in two colors: white and black, but not brown? The other group of advisers, including Montezuma himself, believed these were gods indeed.

Gods or not, however, he did not want them in Mexico-Tenochtitlán. He did not even want them wandering freely through the empire. Therefore, Montezuma decided to send out a delegation of wizards, magicians, and warriors to prevent Cortés from advancing. He also sent

captives to be sacrificed, because the strangers might wish to drink their blood. [When they arrived to where Cortés was, t]he envoys sacrificed these captives in the presence of the strangers, but when the white men saw this done, they were filled with disgust and loathing. They spat on the ground, wiped away their tears, or closed their eyes and shook their heads in abhorrence. They refused to eat the food that was sprinkled with blood, because it reeked of it; it sickened them, as if the blood had rotted.[8]

Montezuma's wizards and magicians then attempted to cast spells and invoke evil charms against them in the hopes of making them disappear, or at least of harming them.

When the envoys returned to the City of Mexico and reported these events to Montezuma, they confessed that their power was "no match for them: we are mere nothings!" The complete failure of this delegation was a blow. Montezuma was "distraught and bewildered." That Cortés and his men were immune to the magic of the wizards was proof, some said, that these were gods. Others argued that it merely indicated what fools these wizards were and that they should be killed for incompetence.

Montezuma himself was filled with terror, so much so that he "wanted to run away and hide: the thought of evading the 'gods,' of escaping to hide in a cave. . . . But he could not do it. He could not run away, could not go into hiding. The magicians' words had overwhelmed his heart; they had vanquished his heart and thrown him into confusion, so that now he was weak and listless and too uncertain to make a decision. Therefore he did nothing but wait."[9]

By now Cortés was ready to get on with the business at hand. The Spanish landed on the gulf coast on Good Friday, April 22, 1519. It was there that they founded a settlement and named it Vera Cruz, or True Cross, to commemorate the Christian holy day. It was now that the complex political nature of the Aztec Empire became clearer.

Montezuma was ruler of Mexico-Tenochtitlán, the principal city in the Valley of Mexico, but he was not an absolute ruler. The Mexicas ruled in a triple alliance of the three cities of Tenochtitlán, Texcoco, and Tlacopan. Together, these cities were the "Aztec" empire that ruled over dozens of other nations and subjugated dozens more. The emergence of the Aztecs as a political power was a phenomenal development, astounding in how quickly the Native American people were able to rise to the top. As Mexican historian Miguel Leon Portilla explains:

After a whole series of defeats and humiliations, the Aztecs succeeded in establishing themselves on an island in the lake; the ancient codices state that their city was founded in the year 1325. A little more than a century later, incredible as it may seem, this destitute tribe had been able to assimilate the old cultural traditions and, at the same time, to achieve complete independence. Then they began their career as conquerors, extending their rule from the Gulf coast to the Pacific and as far south as Guatemala.[10]

Indeed, the creation of the Aztec "empire" was at the expense of other sovereign peoples and nations, who spoke dozens of different languages and who had their own histories and identities. As the Aztec Empire rose, other nations and city-states fell, crushed by the advancing warriors. One after another peoples were subjugated: Coyoacan, Cuitlahuac, Xochimilco, Chalco, Tlahuicas, Cempoala, Tlaxcala, Huexotzinco, Cholula, Acolhuacan, Cuauhnahuac, Mizquic and Culhuacan were all enslaved, made to answer to the rulers of Mexico-Tenochtitlán. In a matter of days Cortés became aware of the tenuous nature of the Aztec Empire's power.

Cortés, also, understood very well the unauthorized nature of his adventure. He was in violation of Spanish law and was, in effect, a renegade. The only way to redeem himself before legal authorities in Spain would be to make a tremendous find. In a bold move to seal their fate, Cortés ordered his ships destroyed and set ablaze. Now there was no turning back, nor any chance of a mutiny among his men.

They could only go forward. So they did. The first town at which they arrived was Tecoac, which was inhabited by the Otomies. These people welcomed the Spaniards in battle dress. Native accounts of the conflict that followed indicate that the Spaniards not only defeated the Otomies, but virtually annihilated them, for "not just a few, but all of them, perished in the battle" that subsequently occurred.[11] This was the first recorded incident of genocide on the mainland of the Americas by Europeans.

The neighboring nation was Tlaxcala and the leaders of this nation were terrified at witnessing the fate of their neighbors. They met in special council to discuss the alarming dilemma they faced. One leader is recorded as having pondered: "What shall we do? Shall we go out to meet [the Spaniards]? The Otomi is a brave warrior, but he was helpless against them: they scorned him as a mere nothing! . . . We should go over to their side: we should make friends with them and be their allies."[12] It was then resolved to send a delegation to greet and welcome the Spaniards. The Tlaxcaltecas welcomed the Spaniards and "paid them great honors, attended to their every want, joined with them as allies and even gave them their daughters."[13] Cortés was eager to learn as much about the City of Mexico as he could. How far away was it? How powerful was Montezuma? Was there gold there? How much? What other fabulous wealth was there?

The Tlaxcaltecas, in turn, grew enamored with the promise of vengeance that the Spaniards represented. They entered into a free alliance with the Spaniards and became their fast allies with the understanding that this new friendship would be mutually beneficial. The nature of this Spanish–Native American alliance is described by the Tlaxcalteca in the following manner: "Cholula [in the neighboring nation of Puebla] is our enemy. It is an evil city. The people are as brave as the Aztecs and they are the Aztecs' friends."[14] In short, help us avenge ourselves and we'll help you defeat the Aztecs.

It was a deal that the Spaniards could not resist. They entered into an alliance with the Tlaxcaltecas and the neighboring nation of Cempoala, who were also enemies of Cholula, and this triple alliance agreed upon a military strategy. In short time, preparations for war against Cholula were completed. The Spaniards, the Tlaxcaltecas, and the Cempoalas then "marched out in good military order, with enough supplies for their great undertaking and with many important and famous [Tlaxcalteca] captains."[15]

The people of Cholula were unimpressed. They were excellent warriors and were not easily intimidated. Apart from that, they were confident that their god would protect them unconditionally, and they laughed at the sight of the Tlaxcaltecas and the Spaniards. Native witnesses describe the Cholula taunts: "Let them come . . . we laugh at their stupid delusions. They are fools or madmen if they trust in these sodomites from Tlaxcala. . . . Look at the scum of Tlaxcala, the cowards of Tlaxcala, the guilty ones! They were conquered by the City of Mexico, and now they bring strangers to defend them! How could you change so soon? How could you put yourselves into the hands of these foreign savages? . . . What will become of you traitors?"[16]

The Tlaxcaltecas turned to Cortés and implored him, "Most valiant lord, we wish to accompany you, in order to seek vengeance against Cholula for its insolent wickedness, and to conquer and destroy that city and its provinces." Cortés was only too delighted to impress his allies, and he answered them by saying, "Have no fear, I promise you revenge."

A great battle ensued in which "vast multitudes were slaughtered," and Cholula was destroyed. As news "of the destruction spread through the whole land . . . people were astonished to hear such strange reports, and to learn how the Cholultecas were defeated and slain in so short a time, and how their idol Quetzalcoatl had not served them in any way."[17] As the Spaniards worked their way toward Mexico-Tenochtitlán, their numbers grew and grew, assembling an ever-larger entourage as one Native American army after another joined the Spaniards. Armies assembled, hundreds of thousands of souls, speaking dozens of languages, each with his own list of grievances and hate, some seeking gold and glory, others seeking freedom and revenge.

The ability of Cortés to hold such an alliance together is evidence of the convergence of interests among the various Native American nations. Indeed, despite their differences and disagreements, they united in their hatred of the Aztecs and of the triple alliance that enabled Montezuma to rule as a tyrant. Hate is a powerful mover in human affairs, and this was not lost on Montezuma's court. His advisors realized that these strangers were fomenting a revolt within the empire that constituted an enormous military challenge to Aztec rule. Montezuma immediately dispatched another delegation of envoys, this time bearing gold as gifts. His intentions were to give the strangers enough gold to make them go away. The royal delegation met with Cortés at Eagle Pass, near the volcanos of Popocatepetl and Iztactepetl. These envoys "gave the 'gods' ensigns of gold, and ensigns of quetzal feathers, and golden necklaces. . . . [The Spaniards] picked up the gold and fingered it like monkeys; they seemed to be transported by joy, as if their hearts were illumined and made new. The truth is that they longed and lusted for gold. Their bodies swelled with greed, and their hunger was ravenous; they hungered like pigs for that gold."[18] This rather accurately characterizes sixteenth-century Europeans.

The Spaniards wondered if the leader of this delegation, a gentleman by the name of Tzihuacpopocatzin, might be Montezuma himself. When Cortés asked him if he was, Tzihuacpopocatzin lied, answering in the affirmative. The Native American allies accompanying Cortés, however, were outraged at this ridiculous attempt to deceive Cortés. Native American allies from Tlaxcala and Cempoala responded to Tzihuacpopocatzin by saying: "You cannot deceive us; you cannot make fools of us. / You cannot frighten us; you cannot blind our eyes. / . . . You are not Moctezuma: he is there in his city. / . . . We are coming to see him, to meet him face to face. / We are coming to hear his words from his own lips."[19] The ruse exposed, the Aztec delegation fled, realizing that the Spaniards and their allies would not turn back. As Cortés moved closer to Mexico-Tenochtitlán he realized that controlling the armies he was assembling was of utmost importance. Expectations were high, and failure would spell the end of Cortés and "his" men, whether Spaniard or Native American.

In addition to this delegation bearing gifts, Montezuma had dispatched another group of envoys secretly. These envoys were magicians, wizards, and priests who were to try once more to cast spells and work magic to make the Spaniards go away. The entourage set out to meet the Spaniards who were marching from the coast. They were unable to cast their spells and drive Cortés away. The bizarre reason for this failure, quite simply, was that the god Tezcatlipoca appeared to them and cried out:

Why have you come here? For what purpose? What is it you want? What is [Montezuma] trying to do? He has committed many errors and destroyed a multitude of people. Some have been beaten and others wrapped in shrouds; some have been betrayed and others mocked and derided. . . . Why have you come here? It is useless. Mexico will be destroyed! Mexico will be left in ruins! . . . Go back, go back! Turn your eyes toward the city. What was fated to happen has already taken place![20]

Then the god Tezcatlipoca vanished into thin air. The messengers' report to Montezuma caused panic among the court nobles and advisers. That Montezuma was confronted in his own palace with the words of the god Tezcatlipoca constituted divine damnation. Their blunt report suggests confidence in the promise of protection in some capacity.

Montezuma grew further alarmed at this report. He was at a complete loss, lamenting, "What help is there now, my friends? Is there a mountain for us to climb? Should we run away? . . . What can we do? is there nothing left us? We will be judged and punished. And however it may be, and whenever it may be, we can do nothing but wait."[21] The wait was not long. After considering the significance of these sightings, he concluded, "We will be judged and punished."

While Montezuma was on the verge of despair, Cortés was moving forward, on the verge of entering Texcoco. The city-state of Texcoco was ruled by Prince Ixtlilxochitl, a nephew of Montezuma, who despised his uncle. The prince would do anything to liberate his people, especially since it would mean punishing his uncle.

When Cortés arrived at Texcoco, Prince Ixtlilxochitl was anxiously awaiting these gods. To the people of the sixteenth century, the idea of divine intervention was maintained as fact. Human affairs, to them, moved in concert with heavenly favor. When the Spaniards defeated the Moors a few years before, for instance, it was taken by all as evidence of Christ's favoring the Spanish kings. In ancient Mesoamerica, the same ideas held sway. To almost all of the indigenous peoples, the Spanish victory over Cholula was evidence that the gods of the Spaniards were more powerful than their own. Time and time again, military victory was interpreted by sixteenth-century people as divine intervention. The response after the defeat of Cholula as reported by the Native Americans themselves is revealing: "When the battle of Cholula was finished, the Cholultecas understood and believed that the God of the white men, who were His most powerful sons, was more potent than their own."[22] At times it is hard to understand precisely what must have been the thoughts of the Native Americans. When the Spaniards arrived at the outskirts of the city of Texcoco, Prince Ixtlilxochitl was only too eager to join in armed struggle against his uncle, Montezuma.

Taken by the courtesy extended him, and by the lavish gifts bestowed on his entourage, Cortés, mistakenly, believed that Prince Ixtlilxochitl had been impressed by the power of Christ. Cortés, remembering perhaps that his superiors would be pleased if he could report a conversion or two, tried his hand at spreading the Gospel and told the prince and his subjects that "the emperor of the Christians had sent him [Cortés] here, so far away, in order that he might instruct them in the law of Christ. He explained the mystery of the Creation and the Fall, the mystery of the Trinity and the Incarnation and the mystery of the Passion and the Resurrection. Then he drew out a crucifix and held it up. The Christians all knelt, and Ixtlilxochitl and the other lords knelt with them."[23]

Cortés was impressive indeed, considering that he had to use two interpreters to get his message across. Gerónimo de Aguilar stood next to Cortés translating into Yucatec Maya and mirroring Cortés' gesticulations. Doña Marina stood next to Gerónimo de Aguilar and then translated the Yucatec Maya into the Nahuatl language. However cumbersome this might have been, nothing was lost in the translations apparently, for when Cortés, very much taken by the emotion of the moment, pleaded that they become Christian, "Ixtlilxochitl burst into tears and answered that he and his brothers understood the mysteries very well. Giving thanks to God that his soul had been illuminated, he said that he wished to become a Christian and to serve the emperor. He begged for the crucifix, so that he and his brothers might worship it . . . [and the] princes then asked to be baptized."[24] Several Spanish priests objected, but Cortés would hear nothing of it. Prince Ixtlilxochitl, too, was adamant. Cortés would not deny his request for baptism.

This raised eyebrows, and not just for the Spanish. Prince Ixtlilxochitl, taken by his newfound faith, went to get his mother, Lady Yacotzin, to proclaim the good news and to bring her along, so that she could be baptized also. She, however, would have nothing of it and in fact was livid, replying to her son's euphoric requests by saying that he "must have lost his mind to let himself be won over so easily by that handful of barbarians."[25] Her views, however sensible they might appear, did not prevail. Prince Ixtlilxochitl was determined to engage this new, powerful god in his fight against his uncle. In the days that followed, his mother and sisters all were baptized, taking Christian names. Indeed, "during the three or four days they were in the city, the Spaniards baptized a great multitude of people."[26]

What was precisely the motivating factor behind Prince Ixtlilxochitl's enthusiastic welcome of Cortés? There was great animosity between

Prince Ixtlilxochitl and his uncle, Emperor Montezuma. The animosities between these two men extended beyond the usual politics of two rival city-states. Prince Ixtlilxochitl's Texcoco had been subjugated by his uncle's Tenochtitlán and the prince was determined to do whatever he had to do to end this Aztec domination.

Consider this family for a moment. The king of Texcoco was a gentleman by the name of Cacama. His brother was Prince Ixtlilxochitl, who resented Cacama, who occupied the throne only because Montezuma, their uncle, could manipulate Cacama. Prince Ixtlilxochitl would do anything to oust his brother from the throne, but he could only do that by confronting his uncle Montezuma. To do that would be to revolt against the Aztec Empire, an act that meant certain death. The arrival of the Spaniards on the scene was a godsend. Here was an opportunity to enlist an ally to kill Montezuma, end Aztec domination of Texcoco, and oust his brother. It was an opportunity, however, only if these strangers were truly powerful.

The omens that had preceded the Spaniards were encouraging signs that these strangers were up to the task. While the politics of the day were debated, however, something completely unexpected began to occur. The Native Americans began to fall ill. It was a slight headache at first, followed by fever. Then the victims' condition worsened with strange sores erupting over their bodies as they became bedridden. The strange affliction spread to children and older people first, then the general population at large. Many died. It was an epidemic of completely unknown nature that spread throughout the land with ferocious speed.

To the Spaniards the plague that befell these people was further evidence of God's blessing. By striking these wicked heathens, Christ signalled his approval and, in a very real sense, helped them out by killing potential military adversaries. To the Native Americans this plague was also proof that their own gods were unable to protect them from the new gods. The god of the Spaniards, after all, was so powerful, that they could strike at will and their own gods were rendered impotent to protect them.

It was in this context that the Conquest of Mexico unfolded. In this light, Prince Ixtlilxochitl's unconditional welcome of Cortés becomes clearer. The ambitious prince knew how powerful the Spaniards were against brave and capable warriors. Now he understood how powerful their gods were as well. The prince was prepared to do and say anything and everything in order to allow him to use Cortés.

It is a desperate man who is willing to engage the assistance of virtual strangers. Prince Ixtlilxochitl was such a desperate man, prepared to go to such an extreme, and perhaps Lady Yacotzin had been correct in her assessment of her son's state of mind. But desperate men seldom reason, and Prince Ixtlilxochitl was no exception. He laid at Cortés' feet anything and everything.

News of the alliance between Texcoco and the Spaniards reached the City of Mexico in short order. Montezuma summoned his brother Cuitlahuac and other advisers to discuss these developments. Cuitlahuac was very much concerned about the threat that this represented. It was not the strangers that alarmed him—so few in number that they could easily be killed—but it was their allies: Entire armies were amassing. The empire was threatened, and it could collapse in an instant. He wanted to end the menace quickly by forbidding their entering the city and by striking at them while Montezuma still held the upper hand. Cuitlahuac warned his brother Montezuma by saying: "I pray to our gods that you will not let the strangers into your house. They will cast you out of it and overthrow your rule, and when you try to recover what you have lost, it will be too late."[27]

Not everyone agreed with this assessment. Montezuma was warned that if the strangers were not welcomed, it would be seen as a sign of cowardice on their part. The Mexicas were not cowards. There were also matters of protocol to consider. If not gods, then the strangers were royal envoys from a foreign prince or king. Montezuma could not insult these messengers who would surely report the affront to their lords. Montezuma, a hapless Hamlet, vacillated, unsure of what to do.

The Spaniards had been making good traveling time. They had now arrived at Xoloco, on the threshold of Tenochtitlán. Montezuma, still undecided, was in a panic. He did not want the invaders there, but he had no choice. The politician in him won out: Montezuma would greet the strangers as royal guests. He and his court adorned themselves in their best finery; flowers and garlands and gifts were prepared. Montezuma himself led the procession to welcome Cortés. Montezuma placed flowers on Cortés and his men, presenting them with gold necklaces that he himself fastened on them. All sorts of gifts were laid at their feet, and they were welcomed to the City of Mexico. He turned to Cortés and said:

Our lord, you are weary. The journey has tired you, but now you have arrived on the earth. You have come to your city, Mexico. You have come here to sit under its canopy. . . . [Y]ou have come out of the clouds and mists to sit on your throne again. This was foretold by the kings who governed your city, and now it has taken place. You have come back to us; you have come down from the sky. Rest now, and take possession of your royal houses. Welcome to your land, my lords![28]

Doña Marina proceeded to translate. Then Cortés spoke: "Tell [Montezuma] that we are his friends. There is nothing to fear. We have wanted to see him for a long time, and now we have seen his face and heard his words. Tell him that we love him well and that our hearts are contented. . . . We have come to your house in Mexico as friends. There is nothing to fear."[29] When Doña Marina conveyed the message to Montezuma, Cortés grasped Montezuma's hands in a sign of affection. Thus, two politicians of sublime finesse met.

Cuitlahuac was livid. He knew nothing good would come of this. He knew these were not gods. But there was nothing he could do. He watched and smiled and remained silent as the entourage made its way to the Royal House where lavish preparations had been made for the strangers. When the Spaniards and their Native American allies had been safely installed in the Royal House, they placed Montezuma under guard, not permitting him to leave their presence. Other nobles could come and go as they pleased, but Montezuma was, in essence, under house arrest.

The Spaniards then set up a cannon and fired it off. Chaos descended on the City of Mexico as people, filled with terror, screamed and ran through the streets. The commotion was so great that calm did not return to the street as night began to fall. This delighted the Spaniards and their Native American allies enormously. Their host could only look on in silence, stunned.

The next day a list of supplies was given to Montezuma, who ordered his staff to bring everything that the Spaniards and their Native American allies wanted. Then the Spaniards questioned Montezuma about the Aztecs' weapons and warriors. Montezuma answered all of their questions truthfully. Cortés was pleased with what he heard and then began to ask about their gold. He wanted more than had already been given him. He wanted to know where it was kept. There was nothing for Montezuma to do but acquiesce to his wishes.

With Spanish soldiers acting as personal guards, Cortés and Montezuma set out on foot to a place called Teucalco where vast riches of gold and feathers were stored. The Spaniards and the Tlaxcaltecas were delighted at the vast treasures before them: "The Spaniards immediately stripped the feathers from the gold shields and ensigns. They gathered all the gold into a great mound and set fire to everything else, regardless of its value. They melted down the gold into ingots. As for the precious green stones, they took only the best for [themselves]; the rest were snatched up by the Tlaxcaltecas."[30] Montezuma next escorted them to Totocalco, where his personal treasures were housed. There the "Spaniards grinned like little beasts and patted each other with delight."[31]

During the ensuing weeks, the Spaniards grew familiar with their new apartments in the City of Mexico. They explored the entire capital, surveying its defenses, its layout, and how the people lived.

As time passed, however, access to Montezuma was increasingly controlled. Fewer and fewer Mexica nobles or allied princes were allowed to see Montezuma, and he was always guarded by the Spaniards, who kept him within their sight. All the while the Spaniards and the Tlaxcaltecas, along with some other allies, such as the Cempoalas and Tliliuhquitepecas, sacked the royal houses of Mexica nobles.

A native account of this reports that when the Mexicas saw the devastation and destruction that had been committed in the royal palace, as well as in Montezuma's own, they were greatly disturbed. There was nothing to do so long as Montezuma did not protest. Whether he was able to do so remains unclear.

In the midst of all this looting and sacking, Cortés was notified of disturbing news. Diego Velazques, Governor of Cuba, had sent Panfilo de Narvaez to arrest Hernán Cortés. Panfilo de Narvaez had landed near Vera Cruz and was on his way to the City of Mexico. Cortés assembled some of his men—he would fight Panfilo de Narvaez rather than give up the vast treasures of gold he was determined to keep—and left his deputy, Pedro de Alvarez, in charge.

Precisely what occurred in Cortés' absence remains unclear. The eye-witness accounts are often conflicting and contradictory. What is certain is that the Mexicas celebrated a feast in honor of the god Huitzilopochtli around the same time of year that the Christian Easter is celebrated. Montezuma, who was under house arrest, either asked that his people be allowed to celebrate the feast or was petitioned by a delegation of Mexicas who wanted him to secure permission to hold the traditional feast. Whether of his own volition or to honor his people's request, Montezuma raised the issue with Pedro de Alvarez, who granted permission.

The feast involved elaborate dances and special foods to accompany the celebration. The Spaniards were fascinated by the preparations and were intrigued by all aspects, especially the life-size statue of Huitzilopochtli sculpted from a paste made from ground up seeds. The statue was then dressed in elaborate colors and feathers, fanciful accessories of gold and precious stones. They placed a cloak of feathers over his shoulders. Belts and vests were added, which were elaborately painted with dismembered human parts—skulls, torsos, hands, feet—as powerful icons.

On the day of the feast, a procession of celebrants passed by the statue, placing offerings of food at its feet. Young warriors, in ritual dress, and women who had fasted in preparation for the feast, filled the temple patio. As the Dance of the Serpent began and when the patio of the Main Temple was full, the Spaniards sealed the entrances to the patio and attacked the unarmed celebrants. A massacre ensued in which the Spaniards "attacked all the celebrants, stabbing them, spearing them, striking them with their swords. They attacked some from behind, and these fell instantly to the ground with their entrails hanging out. Others were beheaded: they cut off their heads, or split their heads to pieces."[32] The screams of horror that engulfed the patio were heard throughout the city, and the Mexicas rose in arms to avenge the murder of their warriors. Native accounts report that "the Aztecs attacked with javelins and arrows, even with the light spears that are used for hunting birds. They hurled their javelins with all their strength, and the cloud of missiles spread out over the Spaniards like a yellow cloak."[33] The Spaniards sought refuge within the palace, seized Montezuma, and placed him in chains. With Montezuma a hostage, the Spaniards sought to bargain for their safety.

The situation, however, was soon out of control. The Mexicas began to seal off the palace. A noble by the name of Itzcuauhtzin was instructed to speak to the crowds. He did so, beseeching: "Your king, the lord [Montezuma], has sent me to speak for him. Mexicas, hear me, for these are his words to you: 'We must not fight them. We are not their equals in battle. Put down your shields and arrows. . . . Stop fighting, and return to your homes.' Mexicas, they have put your king in chains; his feet are bound with chains."[34] These words had no effect. The Mexicas were enraged and shouted insults at Itzcuauhtzin. A native account reports that the crowd shouted, "Who is Montezuma to give us orders? We are no longer his slaves!"[35] Itzcuauhtzin was shouted down. The royal palace was now under siege. The Mexicas stopped delivering supplies: They would starve the Spaniards out.

Cortés, having defeated Panfilo de Narvaez, was headed back when initial reports of the troubles reached him. The people of Mexico-Tenochtitlán were rising against the Spaniards, their allies, and their own king. Native American allies informed him that the Mexicas were preparing an ambush to prevent him from returning. It was a race to the City of Mexico then, and Cortés reached the outskirts of the city safely. From a garrison, he ordered cannons fired to assert control over the situation.

The besieged city center was complete chaos. Some reports indicate that the Spaniards and the Tlaxcaltecas ordered Montezuma to address his people, who shouted him down, stoned him, and inflicted fatal injuries. Other reports indicate that the Spaniards and Tlaxcaltecas, realizing their hostage was now a liability, killed Montezuma and Itzcuauhtzin outright. No one knows what really happened, except that both gentlemen were killed.

There was great confusion throughout Mexico. The Spaniards and the Tlaxcaltecas decided to abandon the city altogether and seek refuge among their allies. In an event remembered as "The Night of Sorrows," the Spaniards and the Tlaxcaltecas left the royal palaces at midnight in a light rain. As the Spaniards and their allies made their way through the city, their retreat was discovered. Alarms were sounded and the Mexicas rose in battle: "The warriors leaped into the boats and set out in pursuit. . . . Other warriors set out on foot. . . . The boats converged on the Spaniards on both sides of the causeway, and the warriors loosed a storm of arrows at the fleeing army. . . . The Spaniards and Tlaxcaltecas suffered many casualties, but many of the [Mexica] warriors were also killed or wounded."[36]

There was one more canal to cross but the bridge had been destroyed. The Spaniards, the Tlaxcaltecas, and the Tliliuhquitepecs leapt in the waters of the canal and it was "soon choked with the bodies of men and horses; they filled the gap in the causeway with their own drowned bodies. Those who followed crossed to the other side by walking on the corpses."[37]

They were not yet safe, however. The Mexicas were in pursuit, and the Spaniards and the Tlaxcaltecas continued to flee until the break of dawn. When they reached the outskirts of Teocalhueyacan, the lord of that city, known as the Otomi, welcomed them, offering them food, drink, and refuge. The Otomi "greeted them and offered them gifts of food his servants had brought. . . . He placed these offerings in front of [Cortés] and said: 'My lords, you are weary. You have suffered many headaches. We beg the gods to rest now and enjoy these gifts.' "[38]

The Mexicas needed rest in order to recover. They "gathered up everything the Spaniards had abandoned in terror. When a man saw something he wanted, he took it, and it became his property. . . . They also collected all the weapons that had been left behind or fallen into the canal—the cannons, arquebuses, swords, spears, bows and arrows—along with all the steel helmets, coats of mail and breast-plates, and the shields of metal, wood and hide. They recovered the gold ingots, the gold disks, the tubes of gold dust."[39] They also set about to recover their political leadership. A council met in an emergency session. Cuitlahuac, Montezuma's brother, was chosen to succeed as king.

Then, suddenly, a second wave of pestilence erupted throughout the Valley of Mexico. A Spanish account of the epidemic reports: "during this epidemic, the Spaniards, rested and recovered . . . [h]aving taken courage and energy because of reinforcements who had come to them and because of the ravages of the [Native American] people that the pestilence was causing, firmly believing that God was on their side, being again allied with the [Tlaxcaltecas] . . . began to construct the brigantines that they would need in order to wage war by water."[40]

The Spaniards' natural immunity impressed Native Americans and made it easy for Cortés "to forge an alliance and pact with the lord of Texcoco . . . in order to enlist his help in the war. Not only in Texcoco did he make an alliance, but also with the people of Chalco, with the Chinampanecans, and the Tepanecans, using the Tezcocans as intermediaries."[41]

An indigenous account reports:

> While the Spaniards were in Tlaxcala, a great plague broke out here in Tenochtitlán. It . . . lasted for seventy days, striking everywhere in the city, killing vast numbers. . . . Sores erupted on our faces, our breasts, our bellies; we were covered with agonizing sores from head to foot.
>
> The illness was so dreadful that no one could walk or move. The sick were so utterly helpless that they could only lie on their beds like corpses, unable to move their limbs or even their heads. They could not lie face down or roll from one side to the other. If they did move their bodies, they screamed with pain. . . . A great many died from this plague, and many others died of hunger.[42]

It is believed that the plague in question was a smallpox epidemic. Neither the Spaniards nor the Native Americans knew this; and for the indigenous people, it was beyond anything in their experience. Cuitlahuac had warned against allowing the Spaniards into the city, and now vast multitudes were dying.

What were the people on both sides of the conflict to make of all this? The belief that these pestilences were sent by the Spaniards' god became a "fact" when the new king, Cuitlahuac, fell ill to the disease and died. Cuauhtemoc ascended to the throne upon his uncle's death. This war now became one between men of the same generation: Cuauhtemoc against his cousin Ixtlilxochitl.

The succession of an inexperienced young man to the throne of Mexico was not received very well. It galvanized many other nations to enlist on the winning side and fight against the Mexicas. It remains unclear how the balance of power began to shift within the emerging alliance of peoples and nations coming together on the outskirts of the city. The Spaniards, reduced to about 200 men, led a military force estimated to have exceeded half a million.

Months went by as preparations were made; ships had to be built, uniforms had to be made, supplies had to be secured. Finally, the conquest could move forward. The Mexicas also made preparations to defend themselves. During these months there were numerous skirmishes. The allies would attack, fire cannons, set off a catapult. The Mexicas would ambush and attack the allies. But the Spaniards and their allies had the upper hand. The allies moved closer and closer, advancing on Mexico-Tenochtitlán, accumulating a series of small victories in which they gained more and more ground.

At this point, Cortés may have lost control of the situation. The conflict between Cuauhtemoc and Ixtlilxochitl reduced, in some ways, Cortés to the role of a useful pawn in the realpolitik of sixteenth-century Meso-america. This accounts for the sheer orgy of violence that was unleashed in the Valley of Mexico.

There must have been such joy in those days! There must have been such complete happiness at satisfying such a base instinct—revenge. A Mexica warrior who defended Mexico-Tenochtitlán recalled: "They advanced cautiously, with their standard-bearer in the lead, and they beat their drums and played their *chirimias* as they came. The Tlaxcaltecas and the other allies [such nations as Acolhuacan, Chalco and Xochimilco] followed close behind. The Tlaxcaltecas held their heads high and pounded their breasts with their hands, hoping to frighten us with their arrogance and courage. They sang songs as they marched."[43]

The cherished hate between Sparta and Athens and the senseless wars that they waged, motivated only by revenge, had its counterparts in Mesoamerica. In one astounding incident, the Mexicas surprised the Spaniards and their allies who were

> so astonished that they blundered here and there like drunkards. . . . This was when the taking of captives began. A great many of the allies from Tlaxcala, Acolhuacan, Chalco and Xochimilco were overpowered by the [Mexicas], and there was a great harvesting of prisoners, a great reaping of victims to be sacrificed. . . . The [Mexicas] took their prisoners to Yacacolco. . . . One by one they were forced to climb to the temple platform, where they were sacrificed by the priests. The Spaniards were first, then their allies, and all were put to death. As soon as the sacrifices were finished, the Aztecs arranged the Spaniards' heads in rows on pikes. They also lined up their horses' heads.[44]

This had to be avenged. All entrances to the city were sealed off; the

Mexicas would be starved into submission. It proved effective. A native account laments that "nothing can compare with the horrors of that siege and the agonies of the starving."[45]

The campaign moved forward. A major incursion was made into the marketplace, and the Spaniards set the place on fire, setting off their cannons and plundering the market. The Spaniards set up a catapult in the center of the market, but they encountered technical difficulties and were unable to make it work correctly. The battles moved forward, each becoming more and more brutal than the one before it. The desire for revenge must have been tremendous, a temptation too great to resist. In one account we learn that once the Aztecs acknowledged that they had been defeated and Cuauhtemoc, his allies, the Tlatelolcans, and their courts were escorted to surrender to Cortés, "there arose a great tumult among the [Native American] allies of the Spaniards. They wanted to break in to rob and kill the [Mexicas] and Tlatelolcans within their stockade."[46]

What happened then is unclear. In the original account of this incident, Fray Bernardino de Sahagún reports that Cortés sent his men to free the Mexicas and the Tlatelolcans to guarantee their safety from the mob. In the published 1585 account, Sahagun states that the Spaniards defended the vanquished in their care.

But there was too much hate built up over too long a time. Although the Spaniards had been satisfied by the terms of the Aztecs' surrender, their Native American allies were not. They wanted vengeance, and the wave of violence unleashed was such that Cortés "and his men began to defend the [Mexicas] and Tlatelolcans from being robbed or taken captive by their enemies . . . but . . . [the Native American] allies who helped [the Spaniards in their military victory] rioted again and assaulted the Mexican stronghold. There was killing, robbery, and much confusion on both sides. The Spaniards with their Captain went to make peace and defend the [Mexicas and Tlatelolcans]."[47]

Sahagun's account is revised to reflect the political and religious controversy of his day and therefore discounts the Spaniards' own rampage. In an account given by Alva Ixtlilxochitl, we are told that the fall of Tenochtitlán was characterized by the Spaniards and Native Americans' committing acts of great brutality, "some of the most brutal acts ever inflicted upon the unfortunate people of this land. The cries of the helpless women and children were heart-rending."[48] But then again, vengeance was the order of the day for all. Alva Ixtlilxochitl further states that "the Tlaxcaltecas and the other enemies of the Aztecs revenged themselves pitilessly for old offenses and robbed them of everything they could find."[49]

No matter how it was carried out, however, it is not disputed that it did get out of hand, and the Spaniards soon found themselves in a situation in which they had to protect the people they had defeated from being killed by the Spaniards' own allies.

It was all too much for the Mexicas. They numbers were decimated by war and disease, they had run out of food, their enemies waged a relentless military campaign. The leadership of Mexico-Tenochtitlán gathered to discuss the situation. Cuauhtemoc resolved that the city should surrender to the Spaniards and their allies in order to save as many of the surviving people as possible. He led a delegation to surrender to Cortés and hand over the city. A humiliated Cuauhtemoc stood before Cortés and stated: "I have done everything in my power to save my kingdom from your hands. Since fortune has been against me, I now beg you to take my life. This would put an end to the kingship of Mexico, and it would be just and right, for you have already destroyed my city and killed my people."[50]

This was not enough. The enemies of the Mexicas had waited far too long to be so easily satisfied. In a wave of terror, the Native American allies of the Spaniards unleashed violence beyond belief—killing, looting, and sacking the entire city and its population. The Spaniards, swept up in the frenzy of events, participated in the slaughter and frantic search for gold. An indigenous account tells how "the Spanish soldiers were stationed along the roads to search the fleeing inhabitants. They were looking only for gold and paid no attention to jade, turquoise or quetzal feathers. The women carried their gold under their skirts and the men carried it in their mouths or under their loincloths. Some of the women, knowing they would be searched if they looked prosperous, covered their skirts and rags for blouses; everything they wore was in tatters."[51] Cortés was also interested in the gold. Interrogations with Cuauhtemoc proved unsatisfactory. Despite protestations back and forth and intense questioning between Cortés and Cuauhtemoc and his royal entourage conducted with Doña Marina, who by now had learned Spanish, no concrete information on the gold treasures was forthcoming.

Ahuelitoc, an ally of Cuauhtemoc, confessed to Cortés that it was customary for the Aztecs, meaning the alliance of the Mexicas and Tlatlelocos, to demand that conquered nations and peoples bring them "the tribute we had imposed: quetzal feathers, gold, jade, turquoise and other kinds of precious stones, as well as birds with rich plumage. . . . All these things were brought here to Mexico-Tenochtitlán."[52] This meant that vast quantities of treasures had to be hidden in the City of Mexico. Cuauhtemoc was taken into custody, and word of his surrender immediately spread through the city.

Prince Ixtlilxochitl was only too delighted at this turn of events and reportedly "was eager to grasp Cuauhtemoc's hand." He had defeated his cousin; he was triumphant. He then instructed that Cuauhtemoc's queen and the ladies of her court be taken to his kingdom of Texcoco under guard. It was over. Prince Ixtlilxochitl had managed his coup, destroying the empire that his uncle had controlled. When it was all over, a Native American account puts the number of dead near half a million. Two hundred thousand Native Americans died while fighting on the side of the Spaniards, and over 240,000 Mexica and Tlateloco warriors are estimated to have died. Millions more died from epidemics.

As they surveyed the devastation, Cortés faced a predicament that most of us faced at one time or another: How was he to explain any of this when he got home? Fomenting rebellions and revolutions were not sanctioned activities. The solution was to lie—invent a fabulous story of incredible danger and heroism, of unspeakable odds and divine intervention. Weave a tale of how a handful of Spaniards overwhelmed a civilization of millions—a miracle, no doubt.

The first deception that Mexicans tell themselves is that the Spaniards conquered the Aztecs, a way of romanticizing the vanquished indigenous people and a reason to hold a grudge against their European heritage. It wouldn't do to admit to organizing armed rebellion throughout the Aztec empire. The Spaniards had to claim complete victory against unimaginable odds—solid evidence of divine intervention. What was the alternative? The truth? What would the response in Madrid be to organizing civil wars in foreign lands? The truth would never do. The myth of the Conquest of Mexico is necessary for defending Spanish sensibilities, European vanities.

The Conquest of Mexico creates a cultural context that is most peculiar. American managers who are to be successful in the Mexican marketplace must be sensitive to the enormous insecurities fostered by these historical events. Specifically, it has given rise to racism, the notion of victimization, and extreme prejudice directed at women.

RACISM

"Mexicans" are an interracial people, of Native American, European, and African heritage. Mexicans, therefore, have a very perverse notion of race; feeling inferior, they are racists. To understand the fragile psyche of the Mexicans, consider for a moment how they have been viewed throughout history. When the French occupied Mexico and installed Maximilian as emperor in the nineteenth century, American historian Gene Smith reports that, complaining of the inability to get anything accomplished in

Mexico, "the French said it was because Mexico was a half-breed and mongrel country, lazy, debased, unambitious; but the Emperor and Empress were unable to reach beyond that and say the problem was the result of the people's subjugation by the Spanish and the Church."[53]

At the height of Western imperialism, in Europe, as in the United States, Mexicans were viewed as "mongrels"; and it was the Native American heritage that was blamed for the passive and violent nature of Mexico, as viewed by foreigners. The visceral nature of life in Mexico, so offensive to European ideas, contributed to a feeling of insecurity among the Mexicans that is monumental in its pervasiveness—and that contributes to the biting racism. In Mexico, for instance, the darker one is, the poorer one is. Few societies have such a marked differentiation of economic class.

According to Richard Rodriguez, "*Mestizo* in Mexican Spanish means mixed, confused. Clotted with Indian, thinned by Spanish spume."[54] Rodriguez, a Mexican-American writer, has long commented on the cultural implications of Mexico's peculiar brand of self-hate. It is unfortunate, for people of all races can be attractive or unattractive. The dynamic intermingling of peoples in Mexico should be welcome; few nations can boast of such a delightful range of attractive people and exciting heritage. Mexicans, however, do not see it this way.

The oppression and exploitation of the Native American people terrifies, but it is something that invades all aspects of Mexican life. In Mexican Spanish, to call someone "indio" is an insult, perhaps the greatest insult that can be leveled against a Mexican. The only other society where race was of such consequence in my experience was South Africa, prior to the dismantling of apartheid. In South Africa the differences between a Caucasian and a Negroid individual is clear-cut, whereas in Mexico the mixing of races has produced a rainbow of colors, whereby race becomes a more difficult matter to determine. But, as in countries such as Haiti where light-skinned blacks enjoy privileges over their dark-skinned compatriots, in Mexico the greater one's pigmentation or "Indian" features, the lesser one's status in society.

An American businessman who has been living in Mexico for a quarter-century jokes that to close a deal, he always inquires about his prospective client's family. If he mentions children in their early or midtwenties, he always offers that he has at least one child in the same age range, of the opposite gender. In most cases, his prospective client's face lights up; if one good deal leads to another, the implication seems to be, business relations may become personal ones, and the likelihood of having blond, blue-eyed grandchildren is too great an incentive to pass up. A variation on this story is the high premium placed on "trophy wives" in Mexico and on the obsession with aspiring to the European notions of beauty.

To add irony to this, Mexico officially celebrates its Native American heritage (boulevards, universities, and airports are all named after Native American individuals) while discounting its European heritage (there is not a single monument to Cortés, who conquered Mexico, anywhere in the country). What Mexico does officially, however, is not duplicated in the normal civil social intercourse. American managers need to be aware that race is a taboo subject, that Mexicans will, on the surface, express admiration for the cultural and artistic achievements of the Native American civilizations, but no Mexican wants to claim direct descent from the Aztecs or Mayas: No Mexican arrives at his office after a two-week vacation and shows off his suntan.

VICTIMIZATION

If official Mexico identifies with its Native American heritage, it does so for political purposes. The hierarchical nature of Mexico's political system is built on the broken backs of the masses of the Mexicans. To appease these exploited people, many of whom are Native Americans, meaning disenfranchised multitudes, the Mexican government has created an elaborate mythology to pacify the Mexicans. This mythology, spread through television, radio, and other forms of mass media, celebrates an "Indian" heritage and lays the foundation for creating the notion of "victimization" as a cultural characteristic. Mexican Nobel Laureate, Octavio Paz, for instance, has long been subsidized by the Mexican government to be the official apologist. Indeed, Paz resembles a combination of Bill Moyers and Joseph Campbell in the United States, offering mythologies on public television for the consumption of the public.

According to Paz, "Propaganda spreads incomplete truths, in series and as separate units. Later these fragments are organized and converted into political theories which become absolute truths for the masses."[55] No one understands this more than Paz himself, for the anti-Americanism that, to some extent, continues to characterize Mexico is the direct product of Mexico's political system. American managers must be aware of this tendency and must rise above it. It is not rare, for instance, to hear Mexicans complain about American "imperialism" and the U.S. "annexation" of vast areas of Mexican territory. Long after most people have forgotten what prompted the Mexican-American War, Mexicans still foster resentments, even if they have no basis in historical fact to do so. Consider for a moment

President Zedillo's first public statement after Californians voted for Proposition 187. Decrying this anti-immigrant, anti-Mexican ballot measure, President Zedillo lamented that this was happening in California, "which once was part of Mexico."

An examination of the historical record, however, shows that California was never a part of Mexico. After Mexico declared independence from Spain on June 21, 1822, Agustín Iturbide was crowned emperor of Mexico, which claimed all the territory that constituted mainland New Spain, from the border of present-day Oregon in the United States, east to the Sabine River in the present-day American Midwest, south through all of present-day Mexico, and the whole of what now constitutes Central America, stopping where present-day Costa Rica runs into present-day Panama. This was the same Mexican Empire that was granted diplomatic recognition by the United States a few months after its founding and that collapsed less than a year later when Emperor Agustín was dethroned and banished for life. This was the same Mexican Empire that began to disintegrate from its inception when California refused to recognize Mexican sovereignty and that made it clear that it still considered itself part of New Spain, pledging loyalty to Madrid. This was the same Mexican Empire that further collapsed when what are now the nations of Central America rose up against Aztec domination and Mexican imperialism, declaring themselves an independent federation for the sole purpose of creating future sovereign republics. This was the same Mexican Empire that, upon collapsing, would lead to decades of political chaos that would culminate in declarations of independence by other "republics" within the pretentious empire, specifically Yucatan and Texas; would produce the Mexican-American War, further carving up the Mexican Empire; and would end with an invasion by France's Napoleon, bringing to nothing the Mexican Empire, which lasted two days short of nine months.

California never recognized its annexation by the Mexican Empire, and it took an act by the Mexican Congress, modeled after the U.S. Homestead Act, to entice Mexicans to move to present-day California. The idea was that Mexico could claim California by colonizing it, something which did not sit well with the "Californios," as the Spanish residents of California called themselves. The United States, at about the same time, set about "colonizing" California too, as part of the Gold Rush.

Claims are free for the making, and Mexican claims to California were never substantiated, except in fantasy. If the United States "stole" California, then Guatemalans "stole" Guatemala, and so on. It should be noted that Agustín Iturbide, not one to take dethronement gracefully, foolishly returned to Mexico from exile in the hopes of reclaiming the throne, only to be captured and shot on sight the very day he landed illegally on Mexican soil—or soil claimed by Mexico, in any event.

But the Mexican State has much invested in promoting the cult of victimization, and it has, until NAFTA, done so with great enthusiasm and success: Mexicans have raised entire museums dedicated to recording their exploitation by other nations, and the Mexicans see themselves as David confronting a Goliath of unspeakable strength. There is another aspect to this cult of victimization. The Mexican State's paternalistic arrogance and imperialistic schemes entail the subjugation of the Mexican into believing a mythology in which Mexico confronts a hostile, indifferent world.

This is a profoundly unforgiving assessment of the achievement of the Mexican Revolution, no doubt, but it is an accurate portrait. Mexico, after all, has found out that playing the victim speeds the World Bank loan approval process and produces the blind adulation of a docile people. When France occupied Mexico in the nineteenth century, Emperor Maximilian was saddened by the "passivity" of the Mexican character, one that resulted in the unconditional surrender to the whims of Fate. In the twentieth century, an equally futile worldview has, for the most part, prevailed. Richard Rodriguez observes that "Mexicans speak of the government as something imposed upon them, and they are the victims of it. But the political failure of Mexico must be counted a failure of Mexicans."[56] In the process of extending Mexican imperialism—like concentric circles radiating across the Mexican landscape from Mexico City—an industry in the cult of victimization has been necessary. Octavio Paz, as the high priest in this temple of doom, presides over the dissemination of misinformation and propaganda to benefit the interests of the ruling party.

The bankruptcy of Mexican intellectual thought in this century, then, is the recognition of the expediency of the fascism of the Mexican State, where Mexicans are silly children whose personal aspirations for freedom and democracy are evidence of their status as irresponsible creatures incapable of taking care of themselves. The sociopolitical stratification of Mexican society—the darker your skin, the emptier your wallet—is based on the denigration of the "Indian" heritage of the Mexican nation, which is perverse: victims victimizing victims, creating a labyrinth of claims to status to claims of who, among the Mexicans, is the greatest victim. The ideological constructions of Max Weber and the lessons of European—not to be confused with Mexican—imperialism have produced a nation that is dominated by ideological constructions that confound Americans who attempt to understand the surreal and perverse machinations found in

Mexico. Indeed, Mexico's greatest lament is that it is irrelevant within its own sphere of influence: Central America looks past Mexico to the United States, and Cuba only lavishes empty praise, in return for free oil. Not even Mexican acts of indulgence—financing public relations offices in downtown Mexico City for, say, Salvadoran guerrillas or subsidizing Cuban terrorism in the area—are enough to earn Mexico the respect and adulation owed to an imperial power, as Emperor Iturbide once envisioned, and to which vainglorious Mexican presidents aspire.

Market economies, however, have no room for victims. Things work, or they don't. It is the marketplace—not impossible ideologies—that determines success. The refuge of victims—handouts from international organizations and conscience money from the First World—does not constitute a development plan, by any stretch of the imagination. If Mexico is to be integrated in the emerging North American economy, the impulse to claim special status as victim—the most annoying manifestation of which are the tired accusations of "gringo imperialism"—have to give way to a sensible worldview. The impossible ambition of Mexican imperialism is folly; the philosophical bankruptcy of twentieth-century Mexico has become a self-evident truth.

A few years ago in a televised conference addressing "democracy in Latin America," held unironically in Mexico City, Peruvian writer Mario Vargas Llosa, sitting across a table from Octavio Paz, stated that it was ludicrous for Mexico to be holding a forum on democracy when Mexico was nothing but "a perfect dictatorship." Octavio Paz, shocked that the emperor had been pronounced naked, stumbled, and the television cut to a commercial. When the program came back on, the only thing Octavio Paz could manage to say was that Mexico was "a perfect hegemony," not a perfect dictatorship. But in Mexico, to speak the truth is to invite retaliation; the next day legislation was introduced in the Mexican Congress to expel Mario Vargas Llosa from the country and to give Octavio Paz a sturdier chair, to keep him from almost falling from his seat should the obvious catch him off guard in the future.

MISOGYNY

Mexico's most severe critics are her children. American businessmen who have been in Mexico for a while are struck by the self-denigrating humor used by their Mexican associates and clients, which is only evident once ongoing relationships are in place and friendships have been established. Mexicans, in fact, put down Mexico through compliments laced with wicked double entendres. This form of self-degradation surprises in how pervasive it is, as is the general misogynism of Mexican society, for Mexico is female. In fact, Mexican contempt for women is an insidious manifestation and degrades both men and women. According to Paz, "Women are inferior beings because, in submitting, they open themselves up. Their inferiority is constitutional and resides in their sex, their submissiveness, which is a wound that never heals."[57] This repugnant Mexican misogyny has its origins in the myth of the Conquest of Mexico. Rodriguez writes that "the most famous guide in Mexican history is also the most reviled by Mexican historians—the villainess Marina— "La Malinche." Marina became the lover of Cortés. So, of course, Mexicans say she betrayed [Mexico] for Europe. In the end, she herself was betrayed, left behind when Cortés repaired to his Spanish wife."[58]

Mexico remembers Doña Marina as "La Malinche," the betrayer of Mexico itself. It is a view nurtured over the centuries by male historians. It is an argument made possible only by the willful censoring of certain facts. Mexican children learn, for instance, that she was Cortés' interpreter—but no one explains how she learned Spanish in the first place. Mexican children are taught, additionally, that she freely joined the Spaniards— but the fact that she was given to Cortés by her Maya lord is ignored.

Make no mistake about it. Doña Marina is not just a Benedict Arnold in a dress. She is Mexico's Eve, a woman responsible for Mexico's fall from grace. Mexican shortcomings and failures must find a scapegoat. Mexican misogynists must find a raison d'être. Doña Marina fits the role perfectly. According to Paz, "Woman is a domesticated wild animal, lecherous and sinful from birth, who must be subdued with a stick and guided by the 'reins of religion.' . . . Thus it is impossible for her to have a personal, private life, for if she were to be herself—if she were to be a mistress of her own wishes, passions or whims—she would be unfaithful to herself."[59] Doña Marina, indeed, is unfaithful to herself. A villain as delightful as this requires greater scrutiny. A villain this perfect has to be invented. And so she is.

Over the centuries, the cult of Doña Marina, called "malinchismo," apart from meaning the preference for foreign goods solely for their foreigness, has evolved into an instrument to oppress women, stifle political criticism, and legitimize "machismo." Doña Marina has been transformed into a creature that has little resemblance to her person. Patrick Oster observes that "her name is synonymous with betrayal of what is Mexican."[60]

Doña Marina, then, is evil incarnate for Mexico. She is the reason why everything that has gone wrong has gone wrong. That she is a woman goes a long way in understanding her enduring appeal. Ever since Eve enticed Adam with that apple, women have been blamed for everything. But in the case of Doña Marina, fortuitously, documents absolve her of the gravest charge levied against her: treason.

The role of women in the Conquest of Mexico has long been denied by Mexican historians. This denial dismisses recorded facts, which reveal that women played a significant role in the actual fighting—on both sides— of the conflict. More importantly, there is strong evidence that suggests Doña Marina came into her own as a leader in this war of liberation to free the peoples of ancient Mexico from Aztec domination.

Historical documents reveal a woman who was no mere interpreter for a group of renegade Spaniard scoundrels. In a document identified as Manuscript 22, housed in the National Library in Paris, there is a native account of the conquest written in the Nahuatl, the Mexica language, circa 1528, which shows the crucial role that Doña Marina played in mobilizing the struggle against the hated Aztecs. She commands: "Come forward! The Captain [Cortés] wants to know: what can the chiefs of Tenochtitlán be thinking of? Is Cuauhtemoc a stupid, willful little boy? Has he no mercy on the women and children of his city? Must even the old men perish? See, the kings of Tlaxcala, Huexotzinco, Cholula, Chalco, Acolhuacan, Cuauhnahuac, Xochimilco, Mizquic, Cuitlahuac and Culhuacan are all here with me."[61] The *men* are with *her*? Isn't she merely a guide, an interpreter, a concubine?

Who's in charge here? Where is Cortés anyway? Isn't this supposed to be a *European white male* conquest? Is it possible that a *woman* is directing the enemy *kings* of the Aztecs? Paz would have us believe that "the Mexican woman quite simply has no will of her own. Her body is asleep and only comes really alive when someone awakens her. She is an answer rather than a question, a vibrant and easily worked material that is shaped by the imagination and sensuality of the male"[62]

Cortés, her man, is nowhere in sight, and the business of conquering the Aztecs has been left to her direction. The enemy kings of the Mexicas are with *her*. Only after she is through does a man—some king or such thing—who was with her, speak up, issuing a stern warning, "Why should the Tlatelolcas feel sorry when the people of Tenochtitlán bring a senseless destruction on themselves?"[63]

It is to no avail, the Mexicas refuse to surrender. Galvanized around Doña Marina's leadership, the enemies of the Mexicas push forward. Fighting resumes again, a fighting so intense that "the women of Tlatelolco joined in the fighting. They struck at the enemy and shot arrows at them."[64]

The role of women on the battlefield proves riveting. Doña Marina emerges as a capable leader in her own right, which is a fascinating transformation from a slave to interpreter to principal. The sixteenth century, arguably, offered fast-track career paths for women of ambition under certain circumstances. While so-called intellectuals like Octavio Paz pontificate on the inferiority of women, Mexicans are comfortable ignoring philosophical questions that Doña Marina's life raises. Sold into slavery by her people, for instance, raises the question of what one's moral obligations are to a society that treats one in this manner. The question of morality and ethics, of loyalty and duty—as compelling, for example, as Antigone's—are ignored in Mexico. It is enough to label women as "domesticated animals" and ignore the role that women played in the Conquest of Mexico, which, as this brief overview demonstrates, requires significant revision. Doña Marina's ambition and abilities—and success—go a long way in understanding why she is so reviled in misogynist Mexico.

The Marquis de Custine observed that "the political state of Russia may be defined in one sentence: it is a country in which the government says what it pleases, because it alone has the right to speak."[65] In Mexican society, women receive no right to speak, or toleration, except that which their fathers, then their husbands, and, finally, their sons see fit to grant them. This oppression of women from cradle to grave is the most offensive form of "machismo," made possible through the cult of "malinchismo."

The Mexican woman, Mexican intellectuals never tire of reminding us, are the only creatures who are beyond redemption, for the Mexican woman will never be able to compensate for Doña Marina's betrayal. None of this surprises. Men have always been rather shortsighted where women are concerned.

What should neither surprise is the poverty of Mexican intellectual thought, political construction that requires mediating the world through a perverse paradigm. The ignoble construction that requires the invention of the systematic oppression of women—which limits the effectiveness of female executives working in Mexico—serves to betray the insecurities of the Mexican male and lays bare his fragile psyche and sense of self-worth. The vulnerable nature of the Mexican notion of identity is the mind-set of the manipulative ideologies; Mexican males have never been able to be masters of their own destinies, and, as such, their only hope is to control the lives of women. The Mexican woman, according to Octavio Paz, "is shaped by the imagination and sensuality of the male," not a free agent with a right to her own life.

American managers in Mexico are in for surprises. The kinds of activities that would result in a sexual harassment complaint in the United States are the most ordinary events in the Mexican business environment. It is not uncommon for companies in Mexico to provide "uniforms" for female employees, uniforms which are not only uncomfortable but inappropriately sexual in their design. To make matters more discomforting, male executives routinely have affairs with their secretaries; everyone, it seems, who is anyone, has a mistress—or two. Meetings and luncheons consist of small talk filled with more sexual innuendoes and jokes than in the United States or Canada. Sexism in the corporate office resembles more closely the norms of, say, France and Italy, than of Germany or England. It is not uncommon for Mexicans to father children out of wedlock, and conversations about women are reminiscent of my college days in a fraternity house. This kind of business environment offers certain challenges, particularly for female executives of American companies on business in Mexico. When confronted with a woman of equal standing, Mexicans are unsure of how they should conduct themselves; a profusion of manners—American female executives have more doors opened, cigarettes offered, and chairs pulled for them than imaginable—is a charming tactic employed under these circumstances. This is of small comfort, for the general conclusion is rather dim: women are objects, not to be taken seriously, and rarely occupy positions other than those through which they can be manipulated.

American businesspeople need to be aware that the land mines of racism, victimization, and misogyny dot the Mexican landscape, and can be detrimental to doing business in Mexico if one does not display the proper sensitivity to these issues or know how to gracefully move around them. Being conscious of these traits of the Mexican character is enough to recognize a difficult situation before it arises or before one becomes entangled in a no-win situation. American executives also need to understand that their Mexican colleagues and clients are not attempting to be offensive when they bring up these issues or make comments that would, in the United States, raise eyebrows. The cultural forces that shape how people think—and the ideas they hold—are powerful; Mexicans have a tendency to fall back on worldviews that are inconsistent with the needs of modern economic development and political democracy. American managers, however, should bear in mind that while being slapped with a sexual harassment suit in Mexico never happens, being slapped in the face does. The prospects for female executives, sadly, remain dim. Although the sexist ideas in Mexican society are changing, change is slow, and the ideas remain ubiquitous precisely because they remain an integral part of the Mexican persona.

NOTES

1. Miguel Leon Portillo, ed., *The Broken Spears: The Aztec Account of the Conquest of Mexico* (Boston: Beacon Press, 1990), p. xi.

2. Ibid., p. 14.

3. Ibid., p. 24.

4. Ibid.

5. Ibid., p. 26.

6. Ibid.

7. Ibid., p. 29.

8. Ibid., p. 33.

9. Ibid., p. 35.

10. Ibid., p. xxxii.

11. Ibid., p. 38.

12. Ibid., p. 39.

13. Ibid.

14. Ibid., p. 40.

15. Ibid., p. 43.

16. Ibid., p. 44.

17. Ibid., pp. 48–49.

18. Ibid., p. 51.

19. Ibid., p. 52.

20. Ibid., pp. 53–54.

21. Ibid., pp. 54–55.

22. Ibid., p. 48.

23. Ibid., pp. 58–59.

24. Ibid., p. 59.

25. Ibid., p. 60.

26. Ibid., p. 61.

27. Ibid.

28. Ibid., p. 64.

29. Ibid., p. 65.

30. Ibid., p. 68.

31. Ibid.

32. Ibid., p. 76.

33. Ibid., p. 77.

34. Ibid., p. 78.

35. Ibid.

36. Ibid., p. 85.

37. Ibid., p. 86.

38. Ibid., p. 88.

39. Ibid., p. 89.

40. Fray Bernardino de Sahagún, *Florentine Codex: General History of the Things of New Spain*, trans. from Nahuatl into English by Arthur J. O. Anderson

and Charles E. Dibble, 12 vols. (Santa Fe, N.M.: School of American Research and the University of Utah, 1950–1982), p. 103.

41. Ibid., p. 104.

42. Portillo, *Broken Spears*, p. 92.

43. Ibid., pp. 105–6.

44. Ibid., pp. 106–7.

45. Ibid., p. 109.

46. *Florentine Codex*, p. 136.

47. Ibid.

48. Portillo, *Broken Spears*, p. 122.

49. Ibid.

50. Ibid., p. 123.

51. Ibid., p. 118.

52. Ibid., p. 121.

53. Gene Smith, *Maximilian and Carlota: A Tale of Romance and Tragedy* (New York: William Morrow, 1973), p. 87.

54. Richard Rodriguez, *Days of Obligation: An Argument with My Mexican Father* (New York: Viking Penguin, 1992), p. 2.

55. Octavio Paz, *The Labyrinth of Solitude: Life and Thought in Mexico* (New York: Grove Press, 1961), p. 68.

56. Rodriguez, *Days of Obligation*, p. 15.

57. Paz, *Labyrinth of Solitude*, p. 30.

58. Rodriguez, *Days of Obligation*, p. 22.

59. Paz, *Labyrinth of Solitude*, p. 36.

60. Patrick Oster, *The Mexicans* (New York: Harper & Row, 1989), p. 229.

61. Portillo, *Broken Spears*, p. 135.

62. Paz, *Labyrinth of Solitude*, p. 37.

63. Portillo, *Broken Spears*, p. 57.

64. Ibid., p. 58.

65. The Marquis de Custine, *Empire of the Czar: A Journey through Eternal Russia* (New York: Doubleday, 1989), p. 531.

8

The Nature of
Mexican Nationalism
and Culture

If self-deception and wishful thinking constitute the conscious key to Mexico, the remaining keys are subliminal, existing in the collective memories of the inhabitants of contemporary Mexico, transmitted across the centuries in dreams and myths from both ancient America as well as ancient Europe. The legacy and worldview constitute a cultural heritage that endures across the ages in stories and ideas, in language and faith—all of which shape the thoughts of the living, influencing their lives. In their blood and in their heritage, Mexicans carry an exciting legacy that combines traditions of several great civilizations, which often-times clashed with one another. The Native American civilizations that inhabited what is now Mexico produced societies of tremendous achievements and sophistication. The Europeans—mostly from the Iberian peninsula—who migrated here also brought with them the legacies of a Mediterranean world, one which had contact, and conflicts, with Islam.

Therefore, it is only appropriate that before we can begin to understand how pre-Columbian Mesoamerica and Renaissance Europe would evolve to become Mexico, it is vital to understand precisely the worldviews of these different peoples. Before there was a "beginning of Mexico," there were existing cultures and peoples from both sides of the Atlantic. The ideas, thoughts, beliefs, and notions that they held in their heads, about themselves and about the world, became the essence of what was conceived on the battlefield in the Valley of Mexico.

Spaniard and Native American fought side by side, for the same objective, so common among human societies regardless of culture, history or traditions: conquest. Aztec imperialism was to be replaced by another imperialism—that of Europe. The natural evolution and convergence of the European and Mesoamerican worldviews, patriarchal arrogance, and belief systems account for the remarkable vitality, strength, and unique character of what we think of as "Mexican." In much the same way that Italy was considered a "geographic expression" throughout the nineteenth century, so, too, what we consider as "Mexico," in fact, consists of lines on a map, denoting recognized international borders, but not a definite "nation."

According to Octavio Paz, "The history of Mexico is the history of a man seeking his parentage, his origins."[1] In the beginning there were peoples scattered across the landscape of "Mexico." These peoples spoke different languages, were part of fascinating and sophisticated cultures, had histories of great antiquity, and were as varied and diverse as are, say, the peoples that populate the face of Europe. This more dominant ones— Aztecs, Mayas, Olmecs, and Toltecs—are easily recognized and conjure up familiar images. There were dozens of other, smaller nations as well. The names of some of these—the Lancondones, Tarahumaras, Tzetzals, Coras—are more obscure, but remain very important, for each exists as a people.

However diverse these ethnicities were, they shared common mythologies, in much the same way in which most of Europe is familiar with the dramas of the Greek and Roman gods, and now with the Judeo-Christian mythologies. Morals conveyed through mythologies constitute a world-view. The philosophical perspectives instilled through storytelling is one way in which each generation understands life and imparts a way of looking at life to the following generation. The peoples of what is now Mexico were no different. Through their stories and mythologies, lessons are taught, a way of looking at life is described, and a definite philosophy about human beings and their relationships to others and the universe emerges.

The same processes, of course, have been at work wherever humans exist. The Europeans (and Africans) who arrived in the New World brought with them a wealth of mythologies and religious ideas. The lessons learned from the Bible or from the adventures of pagan gods shaped a singular worldview with definite ideas of what life was all about and what a person's purpose was on this planet. The peoples of the Iberian peninsula who developed into what we now call "Spanish" were, for the most part, peoples obsessed with exactitude, by which is meant clearly defining philosophical ideas. This was both a response to and a legacy from the Muslim presence on the Iberian peninsula for the better part of eight centuries. The Christian Iberians were most definite in their ideas about the Muslim Iberians, whom they called "Moors" and whom they expelled after prolonged warfare. It is not without irony, then, that the cultural and intellectual achievements of the Moors have influenced the Spanish worldview.

The quiddities of the Mexican worldview are found in the mythologies of the indigenous peoples, and three lie in the philosophical and religious ideas of the Europeans who arrived in Mexico after the sixteenth century. To understand the psychology of the Mexican consumer, colleague, and business associate, it is necessary to understand the collective mythologies that enfuse Mexican society. For this purpose, a discussion of poignant Native American myths is presented; for in understanding the meaning of these myths, greater understanding of the Mexican psyche is possible.

A MYOPIC MAN

Consider a Native American myth that explains the origins of humanity.

In the beginning, the gods were lonely. Nothing is more tragic than lonely deities. To alleviate the pain of solitude, the gods decided to create beings who could worship them. These gods were vain gods. The first humans were made of clay. There were problems, of course, with humans made of clay. They were quite mindless and couldn't learn how to pray. They also dissolved in the rain. The gods' efforts had come to nothing.

The gods were now lonely and dismayed at their ineptitude. They resolved to try once more, this time carving humans out of wood. These wooden humans had their wits about them, but they moved stiffly. Worse yet, they had no hearts and were incapable of loving. What use are prayers from those who do not feel? The wooden humans were also mean. They didn't take care of the things that the gods had given them. They destroyed their utensils, and they beat their dogs. They were cruel and cold—and the gods grew restless, displeased with their creation.

Then, in a great flood these wooden people were destroyed, but not entirely. Since they were made of wood, they were able to float, and some clung to the tops of the trees in the jungles. When the food waters receded, the wooden people who were clinging to the trees were transformed instantly into monkeys. This is how monkeys originated.

The gods brooded over their predicament. They resolved to try one last time. This time they would make people from corn so that they would be nurturing beings, capable of worshipping and understanding what it meant to pray and praise. These people of corn would be life-givers, capable of remembering and feeding the gods. The people of corn would cherish the gods in their hearts and would also have emotions, thoughts, and an intellect.

So it was. The people of corn, which is to say mankind today, were smart and capable.

This very success, however, resulted in an unexpected problem. People of corn were, perhaps, *too* smart. They were so smart, in fact, that they threatened the gods. People of corn could conceivably become godlike. This worried some gods—and one god in particular. Huracan, who is the Heart of Heaven and who had dominion over the winds, decided to act on his own to end this potential threat.

Huracan blew a powerful mist into the faces of humans, a mist as powerful as a hurricane. (The English word "hurricane" comes from this Mesoamerican deity.) Since that time, people's vision has been clouded. What is near to humans is seen clearly, but what is far away remains a blur. People of corn, blinded by god's selfishness, stumbled about, in a manner reminiscent of Plato's allegory of the cave. Since that day, humankind has been myopic, enlightened fools who stumble about, unable to see for any great distance with clarity or purpose.

In European history, the idea that this line of thinking engendered is that of transcendence. Paul Tillich wrote that "the idea of transcendence, that there is something that surpasses empirical reality, was prepared for Christian theology in the Platonic tradition. Plato spoke of essential reality, of 'ideas' . . . as the true essence of things . . . [which resulted in] a trend toward the devaluation of existence. The material world has no ultimate value in comparison with the essential world."[2]

This is the similar lesson for the people of ancient Mexico. Further, the moral of this myth is that people are best off when they concentrate on what is close to them—family, friends, village—and do not bother with peoples and villages far away in distant lands. The same holds true with time: Why bother about yesterday? And tomorrow is always one day away: Live for the moment, live for today.

The lesson is that a person's proper focus in life is on what is immediate, within his or her reach, close at hand—one's family, friends, and village. It is futile to be concerned about what is far away, either in time or in distance.

This "myopia" reverberates throughout Mexican society in unexpected ways and has produced four Mexican cultural peculiarities that delight in their power. The first way is the tendency to reflect on the immediate, which creates a strong regionalism that undermines the abstract notion of "nationhood," which is to say, "Mexicanness." In a landscape populated by dozens of ethnicities, where nations and traditions and languages differ across a geographic mosaic, people are clannish and close-knit, further strengthening these distinct regional identities. The second way is the Mexican predisposition to indulge in exquisite manners as a way of dealing with people whom the Mexicans—what the world calls their fellow countrymen—cannot stand: one another. Manners are therefore used to dismiss, to insult, to distance.

What one can do to an alleged countryman, naturally, one can certainly do to women. Mexican "machismo," offensive as it is pervasive, is intrinsically linked to Mexican "malinchismo," which is the unique Mexican predisposition to ridicule and mock Mexico. *La patria*, Mexico, is, after all, *feminine*. Thus, "machismo" and "malinchismo" are the final two Mexican traits that have their origin in this myopic worldview, generated by a patriarchal society that strives to dominate the female, however manifested. Each of these tendencies reinforces the other, resulting in a society of polite hypocrites, who deride their own country as enthusiastically as young men degrade women in locker rooms.

The impulse to be myopic, of course, is the tendency to delight in instant gratification. The consuming habits, and the general market of the Mexican economy, is geared to satisfying this impulse; immature consumer purchase decisions are made at the point of sale. The creation of a nation of adult children, with an accompanying consumer preferencing, while devastating to the creation of a mature market, nonetheless is very much in keeping with the worldview of the ancient peoples of Mexico. The failure of the Mexican Revolution, the pathetic state of the Mexican nation, the inability to become developed—all evidence the veracity of the myopic nature of the human being. This legacy of frustration, albeit in a more indirect way, shows the madness and futility of conquest, no matter what form it takes. The history of Mexico is a succession of quick fixes and of the disappointments inherent in these measures.

When Cortés returned to Spain, Charles I asked him, "What is that land like?" Cortés crumbled a piece of paper and threw it on the floor. "This is what Mexico is like."

Charles I knew exactly the headaches that lay ahead. In the same manner that the conquest of the Iberian peninsula had been arduous, so would the establishment of a New Spain in the geographic expression radiating from the city called "Mexico." The creation of "Spain" had been complicated by the very diversity of the people who inhabited the nooks and crannies, valleys and seasides of that varied landscape. Cortés had found another geographic expression, and it would be a struggle to coalesce the different nations that inhabited that landscape into a unit, into a single colonial possession.

The defeat of the Aztecs, after all, was only possible because there were dozens of nations subjugated by them that rose against their hated overlords. The mountains and valleys of the Mexican landscape were occupied by many different nations speaking different languages and with diverse traditions, histories, and cultures. It was impossible to journey for a day before one encountered still another nation—one that, in all likelihood, was its neighbors' rivals.

The myopic lesson of mythology was inward looking: Turn your back on your neighbors and focus your attention on your people.

But turning your back on your neighbors didn't mean ignoring them. In a world where skirmishes served to settle scores, and to harvest sacrificial victims and slaves, the constant threat of violence loomed near. The advent of the Spaniards, and the imposition of a peace, served to suspend hostilities for a while, but history is not easily forgotten. If for thousands of years the people from the neighboring valley had been on the warpath, raiding under cover of darkness, how could such memories be forgotten?

But minding your own business is an important lesson. Minding your own business also renders one inward looking, resisting the call to a united "nationhood." Regional rivalries throughout "Mexico" exist to no end. People from one part of Mexico mock people from another part of the country, often telling the cruelest jokes about one another. Everyone despises people from Mexico City. There is venom in their voices when they speak of their hated Mexico City overlords. This animosity stems from the tenuous reality of "Mexico," a contrived identity that never quite satisfies entirely.

After 500 years of the first European's arrival in what is now Mexico, an American of Mexican ancestry visits his parents' village and is quoted in an American magazine as complaining: "Listen, he says. I went back to my mother's village in Mexico last summer and there was nothing *mestizo* about it. Dust, dogs, and Indians. People there don't even speak Spanish."[3]

The myopia of the ancient people of Mexico is evident in the modern people of Mexico. There is strong regional pride in being who you are, first and foremost. This isn't to say that in the past two decades the government of Mexico has not made great strides in convincing the Mexicans that they are Mexican. But this has been neither easy nor cheap. It has required enlisting mass communications, expensive public relations, and advertising firms in New York and London, as well as many buckets of paint to cover the country with the word "Mexico." Still, this is not enough. For many Mexicans far from the capital, "Mexico" only intrudes through the television set. But so does America, in the form of *I Love Lucy* and *Love Boat* reruns and continuous broadcasts of MTV and HBO.

Can "Mexico" capture the imagination as a Marilyn Monroe or a Madonna can?

National unity, the act of forging—or is that forcing?—a national identity, however, has a long way to go. More Mexicans identify with Coca-Cola than with "Mexico," by which I mean more Mexicans have an understanding of what Coca-Cola is all about, than what "Mexico" means. As Richard Rodriguez observes, "Perhaps Mexico's tragedy in our century, perhaps Mexico's abiding grace thus far, is that she has no political idea of herself as compelling as her [faith]."[4] More Mexicans identify with their regional ethnicity, with their masochistic interpretation of Catholicism, with their physical and metaphysical geography, with anything at all, than with any national (prepackaged) notion of themselves, clever commercials on television notwithstanding.

The history of Mexico's struggle to transform itself from a geographic expression into a nation is a history of the resilience of the human will in the face of coercion, to strike a balance of power among the competing ethnicities, to placate divergent interests, to keep a wave upon the sand. In the same way in which the Soviets were unable to erase the identities of the peoples of the Baltic republics (as well as other nations, among them Georgia, Ukraine, and Byelorussia), so have Mexican bureaucrats been unable to crush the identity of people who, while physically living in what the world recognizes as the boundaries of the republic of Mexico, are not Mexican at all. Indeed, in the discussion of corruption later on, "malinchismo" plays a pivotal role in the Mexican tendency to exaggerate Mexico's "depravity" as a way of dismissing Mexico itself.

Can the tendency to parochialism, the myopic turning of one's back to neighbors, which has undermined the creation of nationalism, be reversed, or is the implicit market segmentation a foreshadowing of dismemberment?

THE IMPORTANCE OF AN INDIVIDUAL'S DIGNITY

The stoic resignation to fate requires a corollary: Surrendering one's self to fate entails relinquishing ambition. In a country where people lack basic material comforts, where the disparities in income distribution are enormous, the political economy of the nation is designed to engineer subsidies that do not offend the individual. Mexico is a country where, while on the way to a hotel for a meeting with a Fortune 500 company eager to open a representative office, one is likely to negotiate a sidewalk crowded with "Indian" peasants selling traditional handicrafts and where one can attend a private dinner at which an exiled Persian princess is holding court. The social contrasts are more distinct than in New York or Los Angeles, and class status is more guarded than in London or Buenos Aires.

In a day, one is likely to encounter individuals occupying the extremes of human society as a matter of course; an illiterate gardener needs to be told what to do in the morning before heading out to meet with a visiting scholar from Harvard. Mexican society recognizes the paradox of this mode of life and strives to create a society in which the most disenfranchised members of Mexican society save face. Thus, the noble ideal of facing life with dignity, no matter what, underscores an acceptance of passivity that is unbearable. If the individual has no will of his own, there is no sense in even attempting to exert control over one's life, to say nothing of the external world. Indian fatalism is the acceptance of the randomness of fate with grace, the refusal to be an active agent in one's own life. Like leaves drifting through the gutters, one ends up wherever the wind takes one.

Now pity the poor colonial administrator charged with the impossible task of making his little corner of the New World into Christian Europe. It was a herculean effort, one that was not made easier by independence in the nineteenth century. In *Maximilian and Carlota*, by Gene Smith, for example, the ill-fated Maximilian, who resembles a regal Rousseau, is met with nothing but frustration in the face of fatalism:

> For a time the Emperor had thought the Indians would be his officials. But slowly he was forced to realize what could happen if Mexico was ruled by men who had never had responsibility and did not understand it. There was what he and the Empress called "a nothingness" about the masses of the Mexicans, which found them passive in the face of bandit raids against their villages and made difficult the procurement of men willing to do anything for the Empire or for anything else.[5]

"Understanding responsibility," expresses the frustrations that Europeans encountered with people who had no reason. Without a linear thought pattern, intelligible decisions cannot be made, and the "nothingness" in the character hints at the acceptance—if not resignation—of the randomness of life, the absence of control.

Some assessments were not as kind as the emperor's. The *Times* of London, commenting on the defeat of the French reported near disbelief that this was possible, given that the French's adversaries were a "cross-bred . . . castes . . . which combine the vices of the white man with the savagery of the Indian."[6] Nineteenth-century racism aside, there are valid issues at hand. If, in the name of cultural diversity, indigenous communities are to be subsidized through price control on foods, free medical attention, public schools, and funding of cultural activities, what of the individual?

There is something charming about the consistency of human nature that transcends philosophy. Over the centuries, many have come to "change" the "Indians" and save them from themselves. The French, particularly, took it as a personal affront that they were unable to "change" Mexico for the better, remaking it into a land of reason, of Enlightenment. What the French failed to consider was this: What if people don't want to change? What if people are content?

This is a difficult proposition for Westerners to accept: contentment and fulfillment. It is our nature to be restless, searching for something, always, unendingly, with enthusiasm. It is impossible for us to believe that there can be a soul that is content with what he or she has at hand, with no desire to progress. That such individuals are to be pitied somehow is an arrogant approach. Great arrogance, however, is a Western indulgence as well.

Vladimir Lenin held in contempt the superstitious babushkas who dotted the landscape of Russia. He predicted that once atheism became the official faith of the new Soviet State, ancient mysticism and superstitions would die with the babushkas, and the women he sneered at would be the last generation of women loitering around the churches, crossing themselves and saying their prayers. Ironic place, this world, for there is still a generation of old women saying their prayers in Russia today, even as busts of Lenin are being put in storage and the official religion of communism relegated to the "History" section of libraries everywhere. The Europeans of the Old World and the children of the transplanted Europeans in the New World after half a millennia have failed to transform the *gente sin razón* into *gente de razón*.

The absence of reason also encompasses the idea of an absence of ambition. The morals of Mesoamerican mythology revolve around the resignation to destiny, however it unfolds. This resignation, then, requires an individual to become a passive agent in his own life, to deny the idea of control, of power over things. It requires, in short, the absence, denial, or suppression of ambition.

This is how Gene Smith describes the nature of the Mexican:

Mestizos possessed the quickness of mind and drive of the Spaniards but they also had learned from their Indian mothers the silent, joyless ways that suddenly and impulsively could be broken by a terrible mindless violence. There lived in them something of the Indian reticence to speak of emotion, feelings, thoughts—Indians communicate through gesture, through attitude of body, hints instead of statements, or through things said to third parties—but there were also in the mestizos wildness and great ambition. It showed in the fiery fiestas, the guns fired into the air, the boasting speech-making which suddenly gave way to self-effacement, the smiles to answer threats.[7]

Notice how the mestizo inherited Europe's "great ambition." The implication being that "Indians" lack such an ambition. Now consider the reflections of Richard Rodriguez on the nature of "mestizaje": "No one in my family had a face as dark or as Indian as mine. My face could not portray the ambition I brought to it."[8] And later on, when discussing an American Native American, Richard Rodriguez remarks: "I never saw him without the current issue of *The New York Review of Books* under his arm, which I took as an advertisement of ambition."[9]

Throughout the centuries, the question of "ambition" is a constant theme, almost a quiddity, that distinguishes, if it doesn't forthrightly define, what is "non-Native American" in nature or character. In the nineteenth century, the French deplored the "Mexican" character, which they characterized as "lazy, debased, unambitious." The French must have associated "Mexican" with "Mexica," which is to say "Aztec," or indigenous; for "mestizos," we are told in the same book, were "ambitious," like their Spanish and European fathers.

The colonial administrator in New Spain needed definite answers; there was work to be done, and he could not indulge the luxury of idle speculation. The linguistic evidence suggests a Spanish obsession with the idea of reason. This fascination, however, was not exclusive to the Iberian peninsula. In the fifteenth and sixteenth centuries in Europe, certain ideas began to circulate and hold currency. What was it to be human? The argument that the ability to reason was a defining essence of humanness became increasingly compelling. In future years these ideas would congeal into a philosophical outlook and would eventually be known, by later generations, as the Age of Reason.

In speaking of Mexico, Octavio Paz observes that "our territory is inhabited by a number of races speaking different languages and living on different historical levels. A few groups still live as they did in prehistoric times . . . a few epochs live side by side in the same areas or a very few miles apart, ignoring or devouring one another."[10] In the years before the

Age of Reason blossomed and in the years since, the mission of, first, New Spain and then Mexico has been to integrate floating populations of indigenous peoples in some sort of social order that is comprehensible to the Western world. When thinkers lament the fatalism of the "Indians," what they are lamenting is their lack of ambition, their willingness to drift through life in a state of contentment, their insidious ability to make us, reasonable people, bend to their will and, playing on our sense of guilt, establish a political economy based on paternalism, engendering dependency, rendering millions of human beings "adult children" who need to be taken care of as surely as black slaves needed their masters and as peasants needed their *patrones* (the plantation and hacienda owners).

This grand achievement of insidious intent, rests on the proposition that an individual's honor and dignity must be respected. It rests on the chivalric principle that a gentleman never reminds someone of his poverty. In this purpose, Mexico has triumphed without a doubt. The creation of a vast paternalistic society, so enmeshed with the communal practices of pre-Columbian societies and European vanities, has fostered a society of noble dependence, subsidized by oil export revenues, but unsustainable in the modern economy. This is where Mexico must make a break with her past, which remains to be seen.

COMING TO THE AMERICAS

Of the millions of people who came to the New World, each had his own reasons that compelled a journey to an unknown life. Many had similar reasons for coming to the colonies of New Spain. Many came to advance careers by serving the colonial administrators, civil and religious, of New Spain. Many more came to make their fortunes. Few anticipated spending their entire lives here. New Spain was an opportunity, not a final destination.

The difference between the settlers of the United States and Mexico lay, not in their religions, but in their sense of purpose. England saw New England as a safety valve, a dumping ground for dissidents and entire *families* of dissidents. Indeed, entire Protestant *communities* were encouraged to leave (Papist persecution) and transplant themselves across the ocean, establishing new lives. Spain, however, saw things differently. New Spain wasn't an empty landscape of vast stretches of territory to be filled; it was a populated world that had to be converted to Christianity, a world of great riches to be exploited. The Spaniards viewed their New Spain as a brutal, dangerous frontier, but one filled with opportunity for the ambitious and the brave. The Spanish who came to New Spain came to make their fortunes. They would come, work, grow rich—and then return home. Or so they thought (some did, but most did not).

Of the millions of men who came to New Spain over the centuries, few fulfilled their dreams of making their fortunes and returning home. Tempered by experience, by the realities of this strange new world, by the limits of life, they lowered their expectations. Passage back was an expensive commodity; besides, was there anything better awaiting one back in the Old World?

Decent livelihoods could be acquired here. Decent lives could be established here. Few would become rich, but building a life is more important than building a fortune. Most could fare better in New Spain than they would if they returned to their peasant lives in villages and towns, large and small, that dotted the European landscape. In the face of this reality, once the idea of staying, of settling down, of living one's life in New Spain took hold, this new world looked different. This was no longer an adventure, it was about to become "home."

Of course, it bears remembering that there were three kinds of men sent to New Spain. The religious orders charged with various functions were filled with educated men. The civil authorities were hand-picked by the court and were men of privilege. Together, the religious and civil authorities constituted an elite. The remaining men—the vast majority of those who made the voyage—were illiterate men from humble backgrounds who had nothing to offer, save their labor. The vast majority were what Europeans called peasants.

Richard Rodriguez states that "whereas the United States traditionally has rejoiced at the delivery of its landscape from 'savagery,' Mexico has taken its national identity only from the Indian, the mother. Mexico measures all cultural bastardy against the Indian . . . equates barbarians with Europe, beardedness with Spain."[11] Indeed, the historical documents from these early decades are filled with complaints and grievances. The religious authorities time and time again complain to the Crown and the Vatican of the "low character" of the arriving Spaniards and of how these Spaniards are "corrupting" the "Indians" with their lewd behavior and their drunkenness.

What kind of role model is a drunken man from Salamanca who is passed out on the street, choking on his own vomit as his friends, also drunk out of their senses, laugh on?

Apparently not the kind to which the "Indians" should be exposed. It is striking how many petitions were made by the religious authorities, especially the Franciscans, requesting protective measures. It must have been appalling, for the Council of the Indies granted exclusions time and time again. The Europeans were not permitted into certain towns, they could not fraternize with the "Indians," they could not dispose of "Indians" without consultation with the priests. The Franciscans, who aspired to utopian schemes of creating genuine "Christian" communities of "Indians," were unyielding in their efforts to safeguard the "Indians" from the corrupt, sinful European colonials.

To what extent this dim view of the colonials was influenced by class issues—priests and administrators were educated men of rank and privilege while the colonials were mere peasants—is uncertain, but the suggestion is quite strong that the religious and civil colonial elite was anguished over the influence that Europe's white trash would have on the noble savages under its care. The moralistic self-righteousness, however, disguises imperialist intent, whereby the Native Americans are considered "children" who must be taken care of, who must look to their new fathers for guidance, and who, should they protest their status, confirm the suspicion that children are often silly and ignore what is best for them.

The civil authorities also had a litany of complaints and grievances forwarded back to Spain. The priests refused to let Indian women attend dances. They were unsympathetic to their lonely situation. A few complaints submitted before the Council of the Indies requested that part of the frustration lay in the inability of certain priests to understand that, well, men *like* women—something certain clerics wouldn't understand. Thus, Spain was constantly trying to remind everyone to be reasonable— and to play nice.

These humble European men who sailed for New Spain, peasants in origin for the most part, were adventurers, fortune seekers, and dreamers who soon realized that they would be remaining in New Spain. There are limits not to one's liking in this life. When one accepts the circumstances one faces, the world looks different. These millions of men began to abandon illusions of returning to their hometowns, and they began to turn their attention to their new homes. Once this happened, love entered the picture. Indeed, whether it was the love for another or the love of work or the love of money, there lies the essence of commitment, the determination to make long-term commitments.

THE MEDITERRANEAN CHRISTIAN LEGACY

In the same way in which Native American peoples have left a rich legacy, so has European thought, which, by virtue of its hegemony in Mexican society, is evident. Modern Mexico is a child of Europe, more than a continuation of Native American states. In turn, the south of Europe's historical processes have resulted in a worldview that differs from that of northern Europe. Mediterranean Christianity, for instance, is enamored with the notion of forgiving our frailties. The commonality of our human predicament bonds the individual to his community. This fits in nicely with the all-inclusive nature of Catholicism, which embraces communalism more than it does individualism.

In Christian mythology, this idea was one of the catalysts for what we call the seven deadly sins. Consider this for a moment. Gluttony, apart from being one of the deadly sins, is also a natural indulgence among humans. From the "burden to bear" perspective, an individual who is overweight is tested by God through the natural inclination to overindulge, and he or she must resist this temptation, which is also a test of faith. If he or she succeeds, so much the better. But if he or she fails, it doesn't mean that overweight persons are damned to hell, but that they were unable to resist temptation—and, while unfortunate, it is not damning.

In the Spanish-Christian worldview, life is filled with such "burdens" and "crosses" that an individual must overcome and bear. That each of us has his or her own set of imperfections, which constitute his or her own series of "tests," lends itself to great tolerance on a social level. The Spanish-speaking world, consequently, is tolerant to a remarkable degree.

But if "tolerance" is the recognition that humans face obstacles in life, then each one of us has temptations to resist.

These "crosses" and "burdens" are not always public, however, In this philosophical worldview, an individual who must resist gluttony (and fails) is easily identified, whereas the person who must fight avarice may do so undetected.

This religious construction complements rather nicely the philosophical worldviews expressed linguistically. The idea of private shames, in essence, has the effect of confirming that each individual has his or her own "scarlet letter" known to him or her and visible only to God. It engenders an unspoken understanding that collectively, as well as individually, great acceptance must be exercised. Social tolerance, then, becomes societal forgiveness. Society must forgive in the same way in which Christ forgives sinners. Whereas in the United States, for instance, there are groups working toward greater "social acceptance" of overweight people (whom we are reminded suffer discrimination), there is no need to open a Mexico City chapter.

A key to understanding why Mexico is the way it is lies in understanding that the Mexican government, for seven decades, chose, as its cross to bear, those people called "Indians." It is a historic commitment that has its origins with the nature of "otherness." In their failure to accept the commonality of the human spirit, the Spaniards engaged in a program of segregation initially. The indigenous people would govern themselves wherever and whenever possible. This was not born out of benevolence; it was a product of pragmatism. Self-government was the only reasonable response to an overwhelming consideration: too few Spaniards governing too many indigenous peoples and nations.

In a striking convergence of interests almost too delicious to believe, the Spaniard and the Native American elite became allies. Spanish recognition of the Native American elites as elites resulted in a political and military alliance: In exchange for official Spanish recognition of the Native American existing power structure, Native American rulers pledged allegiance to the Spanish king. The result, Robert Haskett, one of the leading authorities on colonialism in New Spain, describes in this way: "The status of [the Indian elites] . . . was proved by their descent from an earlier hereditary elite whose ascendancy had been recognized by the all-powerful Spaniards."[12] With unintended irony, the Spaniards legitimized Native American culture and society through recognition and official sanction.

The result was one of manifest divine right. Native American elites could, throughout the whole of New Spain, rationalize the new social power structure by recognizing that the Aztecs had been defeated by the Spaniards; instead of paying tribute and loyalty to their former Aztec overlords, the same tribute and loyalty was now owed to the Spanish. The imperialism of Aztec society had been replaced by European imperialism. For the many subjugated peoples that inhabited the geographic region called "Mexico," it made little difference if the ruling oligarchs spoke Nahuatl or Spanish: Servitude is servitude.

Who could argue with that? Thus, native cultures accommodated their new relationship with the Spaniards. For many peoples, it was a question of replacing their Aztec overlords with the new Spanish ones. The difference, in practical terms, was that while the new overlords demanded conversion to their religion, at least this new faith did not include human sacrifice.

Robert Haskett observes that "the notion that Spanish culture was 'victorious' over its indigenous counterpart . . . has become mixed up with the so-called . . . 'Black Legend' of Spanish conquest. . . . Yet if the Legend is completely true, if the indigenous people were unable to withstand the rigors of invasion, why is it that so much 'Indian' culture can still be found co-existing with other elements in places such as central Mexico?"[13] There are "Indians" dressed in their traditional clothes walking around downtown this morning, going about their business. On the other hand, there are no Seminoles casually strolling down Biscayne Boulevard in downtown Miami, no Cayuga spending an afternoon shopping in the Ithaca Commons in upstate New York, or any of the now-extinct Native Americans spending the day at the beach or seashore in northern California. To see a Native American in the United States requires planning a field trip day, making a day trip of it. To *not* see a Native American in Mexico is almost impossible. Even at resort enclaves such as Club Med, there they are: Mexican Native Americans serving drinks and fluffing one's pillows.

Of course, not everyone is pleased about this. An Iranian friend in Mexico, who claimed to be fascinated by all the "Indian" cultures of Mexico, was distraught at the thought of so many "Indians" running around unsupervised all over Cuernavaca. Another member of the deposed Persian despot's court, who had been enjoying a few beers, interrupted our conversation, turning to me and noting with derision disguised as wit (reeking of condescension and not a little alcohol), "Mexican Indians are worse than Visa—they're everywhere you want to be, and everywhere you don't want them to be, too!"

The nature of Spanish rule during the colonial period sometimes seemed tenuous at best, or worse—like Europe's flattering itself by pretending that Charlemagne, not chaos, did in fact rule over most of the continent—an outright fabrication. Consider that in the vast region that was given to Cortés and that became known as the Cortés Marquesado del Valle, "no Spanish municipality was ever established in the area during the colonial period. Instead, the region's [native towns] continued to be ruled by indigenous councils."[14] What? After 300 years of colonialism no Spanish municipality was founded? All those *siestas* add up to one long coma apparently. Is it any wonder, then, that 500 years later there are so many people in Mexico for whom Spanish is a foreign tongue, rather far removed from their daily lives.

The most important question remains unasked. What if the "Indians" in that village are happy with just dust, dogs, and themselves? What if, like many other indigenous peoples around the world, the Indians of Mexico are content with their lot, indifferent to material possessions, which is the standard by which they are judged? Of the Bajau, a people who live in the Philippines, James Hamilton-Paterson has written: "They are mostly unconvinced by the idea of education, so are often unwilling to send their children to school. Nor do they seem keen to learn new skills. And as for taking part in any social or political activity, it has proved almost impossible to interest them. They suffer, in short, from an admirable lack of ambition."[15] What if the Indians of Mexico are satisfied with their "admirable lack of ambition"?

This point of view is unacceptable to most Mexicans, almost all Americans, and too many officials at the World Bank and United Nations. On a fact-finding trip to a small Indian village in the Mexican highlands, Patrick Oster reported: "I found this to be the case when I visited San Bartolomé Quialana, a tiny Zapotec hamlet in the state of Oaxaca. All of San Bartolomé's *jacals* ("huts") had dirt floors. None had electricity, sinks or bathrooms. Only one person in this town of three thousand spoke Spanish."[16] Thus the dilemma of modern Mexico, seen firsthand.

> Some Mexican writers argue that Indians were a burden on Mexico, that they should be snatched out of their primitive existences for their nation's good. . . . Others countered that Indians should be left alone to develop in natural, dignified ways that respected their unique culture. . . . The political debate over what to do about the "Indian problem" rages on. Some anthropologists argue that the reservation-style life of some Indians is the equivalent of putting them in zoos. They are nothing more than guinea pigs for research conducted by light-skinned university professors, they charge. Leftists politicians, perhaps seeing the potential of all those millions of Indian votes, insist that cultural isolation is a ploy to block the "proletarization" of these poor masses. They favor integration of Indians into the economy in terms of language and jobs. A third wave argues that Mexico should be recognized as a multiracial society that allows Indians to live as Indians, with autonomy over their lives and without cultural integration.[17]

Whatever autonomy is exercised presupposes the existence of free will. This is why "Indian" is a state of being. "Cuando fuí indio"—meaning "When I was an Indian"—one hears people say.

When I was an Indian . . . what? Well, when I was an Indian . . . I could not read. When I was an Indian . . . I could not write. When I was an Indian . . . I had no ambition. When I was an Indian . . . I had no future. When I was an Indian . . . I did not reason. But now I can read and write. Now I have ambition and a future. Now I can reason. *I am no longer an Indian.*

"Peasant," like "Indian," is state of mind. The problem, however, is that states of mind affect one's behavior. Not unlike counterculture Americans who "drop out," the failure of entire communities of people in Mexico to participate in modern market economies exacerbates the problems that Mexican society faces—if nothing else, in a diminished tax base. Resentment from the taxpaying members of society is only natural.

Intellectual possibilities are constrained by economic limitations. However much we would like to subsidize indigenous people, money is a consideration. There are, of course, a few societies fortunate enough to be blessed with a small population and a marketable commodity. Saudi Arabia comes to mind. This is a country where the costs of producing its chief export—oil—is relatively inexpensive. Its profit margins are higher than for other countries. Compared to Britain's costs of drilling in the North Sea, Saudi Arabia enjoys a tremendous profit margin, which is guaranteed because the price of its commodity is set on an international market and is not subject to local production costs. At the same time, Saudi Arabia has few people. Thus, the kingdom can indulge in the luxury of subsidizing its citizens and providing a surprisingly high standard of living.

Money for nothing, unfortunately, is not Mexico's situation. To be sure, the state-owned oil monopoly does provide substantial revenues to the state; but there is not enough oil, and there are too many people. Discrepancies are evident everywhere. The state of Alaska is able to *pay* its residents, whereas the state of New York levies considerable taxes on its residents to finance its expensive operations.

For a time, Mexico thought that it could be like Saudi Arabia—or, at the very least, like Alaska. In the early seventies, vast new oil discoveries were made, making Mexico a major player on the world scene, and the prices of crude were soaring. When oil reached $30 a barrel, Mexico was sure that it would be another Alaska. Analysts the world over expected the price to move an additional $15 per barrel. If it did that, then Mexico would be another Saudi Arabia. But it didn't happen. The price of oil did move $15 per barrel—but down, not up. Mexico was—and is—in no position to provide livelihoods to people who do not participate in a market economy or who are unemployed and head either to the border maquiladoras or, better, to the United States.

Richard Rodriguez notes that "Mexicans imagine their Indian part as dead weight: the Indian stunned by modernity . . . because the purpose of the world has passed him by."[18] Mexico pretends to be concerned about its indigenous peoples for exclusively moral reasons. It is the inclusive nature of Catholicism that mandates a reaching out and embracing of all people. To this day, the message remains the same. Pope John Paul II has visited the far corners of the world precisely to make this point: Catholicism, meaning salvation, is for everyone.

A more compelling reason, however, is more sinister in nature. Mexico exalts indigenous people because it cannot resist turning to the United States and noting, with feigned surprise, America's *loss* of her Indians.

Americans come to Mexico to stand in awe of the achievements of the ancient peoples of the Americas, to buy their textile blouses and ceramic pots, to photograph those Kodak moments—an Indian woman who is breastfeeding in the park, an old Indian who is balancing a basket of fruit on his head, stamping feet that are dancing noisy dances, slightly under-nourished Indian children with stupid grins on their faces, idle natives who are whiling their days away in the main plazas.

Mexico knows Americans long for these things, perhaps out of remorse, out of guilt. Mexico understands America's weaknesses and biases, because they are her own. Mexico understands that the people of the Third World exist exclusively for the entertainment purposes of anguished Western intellectuals.

The continued integrity of existing indigenous social structures after the conquest is unremarkable. Outside Mexico-Tenochtitlán, which became Mexico City, the center of European government, and the Valley of Mexico, entire Native American peoples and nations were left to live their lives as they saw fit. According to Robert Haskett, "Most members of the surviving indigenous elite continued to pursue their lives and their careers within the indigenous world. . . . Continuous documentary references to their elevated social status make it clear that ruling legitimacy rested on traditional definitions of status."[19]

This is not to diminish the negative effect of the conquest, however. But it is important to distinguish between accommodation and evolution with outright destruction.

Richard Rodriguez muses: "The Spaniard entered the Indian by entering her city—the floating city—first as suitor, ceremoniously; later by force. How should Mexico honor the rape?"[20] Perhaps, but it bears remembering that Montezuma tried in vain to keep Cortés out of Tenochtitlán, and the warriors engaged in "force" were the Aztecs' enemy, reducing the Spaniards to the supporting role of general leadership and overall choreography. That the Spanish "conquered" the Aztecs is as much a myth as it is an instrument of political expediency.

The subsequent subjugation was in keeping with the standards of the time, standards which to us, however, seem reprehensible. As Robert Haskett writes of the indigenous peoples of the Cuernavaca area,

Conquest and colonization are never gentle. . . . But the Spanish onslaught was neither as monolithic nor successful as it is sometimes still pictured to have been. . . . The indigenous elite, given a surprising amount of autonomy at the local level, accepted the fact that they would have to accede to the new system, but they did not embrace the notion that this would inevitably lead to the wholesale abandonment of tradition.[21]

Debate about "Indians" at the close of the twentieth century centers on the demands of modern economies and the need to make people productive members of society. This is a similar concern for San Franciscans who want—desperately—to transform the deadheads into productive members of society. In both the United States and Mexico, "productive members of society" for the most part means "taxpayers."

The social transformations now underway are challenges that Mexico is confronting remarkably well. Although political violence has increased and a historic power struggle within the ruling party is unfolding, social stability, for the moment, remains a given. This is not to say that the political "opening" that accompanies economic liberalization will be peaceful. In the last century, Mexico descended into chaos when economic reforms were introduced. Gene Smith observes that

> In the country which had been New Spain chaos reigned supreme. . . . In a country larger in size than France, Austria, England, Ireland, Scotland, Italy, Holland, Portugal and Belgium put together, there was not a road that was safe from bandits, hardly a business that was not in the hands of a foreigner . . . the Acapulco-Mexico City road was impassable for any wheeled vehicle, and it took a good horse or mule to travel it; and the road to Vera Cruz was so dangerous that it was not uncommon for a diligence to arrive at its destination bearing passengers who had been robbed by one band after another.[22]

In the sixteenth century, the Aztecs ruled throughout the Valley of Mexico and subjugated the nations and peoples throughout much of what today constitutes Mexico. Not unlike concentric circles made by a stone dropped in a pool, the Aztec capital was the epicenter of power, whose influence radiated outward across the landscapes of the empire. All roads, therefore, led to Mexico. The Spaniards were thus spared the bother and expense of constructing new roads. They merely improved on what existed and they raised the capital of New Spain amid the rubble of the pagan city of Mexico-Tenochtitlán. Centuries later, Mexican patriots chose to occupy the same city, making it the capital of the new independent country and the center of what, they hoped, would become a nation as well.

Authoritarianism is the glue that holds Mexico together. What, then, happens when decentralization is introduced?

According to Richard Rodriguez, "Catholics are children."[23] This, now, is the essence of understanding how Mexican society has been organized throughout history. If Catholics are children, as Rodriguez proclaims, then Mexicans are children. Thus, Mexican society has striven to duplicate the parental relationship between the government and the people. It is evident that Mexican bureaucrats earlier this century found inspiration in the arguments of Max Weber:

> Rational calculation is manifested at every stage [of bureaucratic organization]. By it, the performance of each individual worker is mathematically measured, each man becomes a little cog in the machine and aware of this, his one preoccupation is whether he can become a bigger cog . . . it is horrible to think that the world could one day be filled with these little cogs, little men clinging to little jobs, and striving towards bigger ones . . . this passion for bureaucracy is enough to drive one to despair.[24]

Bureaucracies are systems of organizing human activities that are necessary for the execution of complicated tasks. These tasks can be economic or social. In economic terms, the requirements of industrial and advanced activities require sophisticated organizations capable of delivering systems whereby economic objectives can be met. In political terms, the complex nature of the modern nation-state necessitates the organization of activities to ensure the viability of the nation-state.

In both economic and political instances, bureaucracies can be interpreted as systems for the dissemination of information, authority, and power, which are required for the execution of objectives and goals as identified. (It is important to note the recent origin of our contemporary understanding of "bureaucracy." The word itself has its origin in "bureau," which is French for "desk." The implication, therefore, is that bureaucracies are systems of activities of a sedentary nature, where organization is the primary objective. This "organizational" activity can be of information, authority, activities. The "bureaucrat," therefore, is a professional organizer or agent through whom information, authority, or other activities deemed desirable are performed.)

By its very nature, political bureaucracies define tasks and delineate authority to the individuals within the organization. "If organizations are the form of our modern condition, one cannot help but note that this is frequently represented less as an opportune or benevolent phenomenon but more as something which is constraining and repressive."[25] The effect, then, is a segmentation of tasks throughout the organization, not unlike its industrial equivalent where functions are relegated to a very narrow definition within a factory, whose efficiency rests on discipline and economies of scale.

In colonial Mexico, the bureaucratic structure of Europe was transplanted to create a system of social organization. New Spain duplicated the European social order in a rather disingenuous manner. Paul Tillich's description of Chartres, in France, is instructive:

> Take a medieval town, the town of Chartres, for instance. Not only its cathedral is important—which you must look at to understand the Middle Ages—but also the very way in which it stands on the hill in the middle of a small town. It is a tremendous cathedral, overlooking the whole surrounding country. In it you find symbols of the daily life— the nobility, the craftsmen, the guilds, and the different supporters of the church. The whole daily life is within the walls of the cathedral in consecrated form. When people went into it, their daily life was represented in the sphere of the holy; when they left it, they took with them the consecration they had received in the cathedral back into their daily lives. This is the positive side of it. The negative side is that all this is expressed in superstitious forms of poor pictures, sculptures, relics and all kinds of holy objects.[26]

Take a Mexican colonial town, and it is a mirror image of Europe. Thus, the process of introducing a bureaucratic state into the Mexican equation in this century became an easier task.

But the limits of social control became evident as the limits of the nation-state also became obvious. One criticism of industrial production— and capitalist society in general—remains the alienation in the workplace. This is understood as the dehumanization of the worker, who is relegated to a narrow task whose constricted nature impoverishes aspirations and demoralizes the spirit. The most effective criticism, leveled by Karl Marx, was very definite in its contempt for economic organizations that reduced men and women to sprockets in a bigger wheel. Indeed, criticism of this fact of modern life—alienation caused by the industrial workplace— characterizes the modern era. In his work, Charlie Chaplin ridiculed the factory and its dehumanizing effect on humans.

The Industrial Revolution, as is clearly evident, has been taken to task by political writers and thinkers precisely because the means of production of industrial societies rest on rote systems of labor, on the differentiation of tasks, on the segmentation of activities, on the division of human activities through a system of rank and privilege, authority and power. The autonomy of the worker is diminished, and alienation becomes inevitable.

Weber argued that these distinctions in power resulted in alienation of the human spirit and in a stratification of autonomy inherent in the differentiation of authority within an organizational system. To his way of thinking, the same critiques of the modern factory applied to the modern bureaucracy. The very act of segmentation, it can be argued, constituted an act of psychological rape: The human is deprived of his or her individuality and is reduced to the function that he or she performs. "The morality of bureaucracy lies in its implicit promise to treat each person according only to their status as an organizational member, irrespective of any other aspects of their identity."27 Then again, proponents of bureaucracy can, with delicious irony, point out that this fulfills Marx's vision of utopia: to each according to his need, from each according to his ability.

Weber, in contrast, found horror in this vision. The stripping of the individual of his or her identity was an Orwellian nightmare. Far from liberating, it imprisoned. The modern bureaucracy of the organization, whether economic or political, becomes a prison, a constrictive armor that imprisons the individual. Weber mourned this and saw the future as a horrific nightmare in which men and women were reduced to functions, not individuals. He was not alone in fearing such a future. Aldous Huxley, the British author and social critic, warned of a future without hope. He predicted a totalitarian state in which the dignity of the individual no longer existed. The rise of fascism in Europe—Hitler and Stalin—was cited as evidence that this vision of the future would come to pass. The twentieth century, many believed, would herald the beginning of the enslavement of mankind, not its liberation.

The promise of revolution—industrial inventions that foreshadowed a future of leisure and plenty—was turned inside out. Instead of freedom, the individual would become enslaved to machines and the requirements of bureaucracies (economic and political) that were necessary to run Industry and the State. The oppressive nature of these human relationships—many people on the bottom and middle levels of a hierarchical organizational pyramid are necessary so that the few at the top can enjoy authority and power—held no promise of hope.

Weber believed that the designation of tasks, with its defined parameters of restricted autonomy, created "iron cages." A compelling and lovely metaphor, Weber's "iron cage" poetically described the future then unfolding: Modernity would result in the enslavement of humankind. Thus, "Disenchantment meant an end to ultimate values and to sacred meanings. . . . [Bureaucracy] limited freedom by imposing an ethic of calculation, as a totally objective rationality, upon this freedom to act."[28] The irony, for Weber, as for Marx before him, lay in the oppressive nature of technology and the impersonal character of the modern economy and nation-state. The horrific nature of the world wars, the relentless advance of industrialization, the deteriorating conditions of the human condition, and the proliferation of bureaucracies painted a bleak future.

That bureaucracies were the means by which power—that is to say, freedom—was dispensed in the modern era contributed to the haunting nature of the task at hand. This became the intellectual background against which the modern Mexican nation-state emerged. The ruling party and the state became one and the same, which is similar to such totalitarian regimes as the Soviet Union and the People's Republic of China. The idea, then, is to direct the development—political, economic, social, and cultural— of the "nation" in an effort to consolidate the aspirations of the Mexican Revolution and accelerate the economic development of the new nation-state.

If factories were the means of production through which economic goods would be produced, then the nation-state would be the means through which political and social ends would be delivered. Both would rely on disciplined, hierarchical bureaucracies to achieve their goals.

These objectives, and the methods by which they were to be achieved, happily coincided with the traditional communalism of the indigenous peoples of what had now become "Mexico." To understand communalism, which can be interpreted as the surrender of the individual to the interests of the group, it is necessary to examine the mythologies of the Meso- american peoples. Nations that had lost their written history relied on oral traditions, in much the same way in which the ancient Mediterranean peoples relied on stories and mythologies to preserve a cultural heritage and historical memory. The ancient Mesoamericans did likewise, and it is in the body of their mythologies that we find tantalizing clues about their worldview.

For contemporary Mexico, however, the grim realities of this unfortunate combination of historical factors are all too evident. Every time that I leave for Mexico for a prolonged period of time, I end up breaking the same promise to myself. I always promise myself that I will socialize exclusively with Mexicans, but, over time, without meaning to do so, I drift and begin to associate more with non-Mexicans. The utter madness of the Mexican development model in this century is that it has produced a docile, uneducated nation of people who are—boring. The most fascinating people in Mexico are foreigners who happen to be in Mexico. That the Mexican people are subordinate to the imperial designs of their nation, that the subjugation of multitudes depends on the sequestering of knowledge within the elite, that the Native American peoples (scattered throughout Mexico) who maintain their traditional cultures are the only "Mexicans" who have not atrophied spiritually or intellectually—all conspire to make of the Mexicans a nation of rather unaccomplished and uninteresting people. Few countries depend on the social associations of foreign nationals for intellectual and cultural stimulation as much as Mexico does.

Free trade, however, mandates free thinking. The unbearable burden of thinking is dialectically opposed to the essence of paternalism. Free trade exposes the contradictions within the prevailing Mexican worldview, which is now torn asunder by the unwelcome intrusion of market realities. Free trade requires that the individual become responsible for himself or herself. It is only natural, then, that the most egregious resistance to free trade and Mexico's integration into the world economy is found among the entrenched political bureaucracy that has governed Mexico with impunity for almost seven decades. The members of this ruling party elite, who see themselves as emasculated, destined for extinction by an unforgiving future that has arrived and that is far different from what they had expected, resist the economic and political reforms that NAFTA implies. A wave of political assassinations—most spectacularly the assassination of Luis Donaldo Colosio, who had been handpicked by Carlos Salinas to be the next president—threatens the stability of the country.

But the future is here, and it is undeniable. The success of political bureaucracies that are horizontal (democracies), the success of economies whose corporations foster the autonomy of the worker (Microsoft), contrasts with the monumental failure of "iron cages," such as the fiasco of the political structure of the Soviet Union or the economic disaster of Cuba.

It is also important—and exciting—to see experiments of every kind underway. The People's Republic of China is engaged in a daring and ambitious experiment: to develop a horizontal economy while maintaining a vertical political hegemony. (To a lesser extent, Mexico is participating in a similar program—and with alarming parallel developments: in both China and Mexico, economies produce television sets at the cost of armies opening fire on unarmed students who are protesting the absence of democracy, which, of course, results in massacres that we can see on television.) The success or failure of the Chinese will be an outcome that tantalizes in its promise of producing evidence to bolster arguments.

None of this was ever anticipated by Marx or Weber. None of this is encompassed in any theory of organizational bureaucracies. The future is unpredictable, especially when the world can change so unexpectedly. The

Information Revolution stands to rival the Renaissance in the creative social forces that it unleashes. The world is becoming a different place, where the paradigm described by Weber is as valid as a world in which slavery is the basis of economic development—that is to say, Weber's paradigm is obsolete.

The Information Revolution has rendered the analyses of Marx and Weber obsolete, for the world that they describe no longer exists. NAFTA renders the intellectual raison d'être obsolete. By requiring the end of paternalism, NAFTA undermines the power structure of populist forces in Mexican society, not only the ruling party and its ruling bureaucracy but also the labor unions and the Catholic Church. The facade of civility gives way in much the same manner in which some parents resist the independence of their children who have grown into young adulthood. An individual who has defined himself as a parent is nothing without a child to care for. These unforeseen consequences of free trade are creating political convulsions within Mexican society of historic proportions.

NOTES

1. Octavio Paz, *The Labyrinth of Solitude: Life and Thought in Mexico* (New York: Grove Press, 1961), p. 20.

2. Paul Tillich, *A History of Christian Thought: From Its Judaic and Hellenistic Origins to Existentialism* (New York: Simon & Schuster, 1967), p. 6.

3. Richard Rodriguez, "Mixed Blood: A World Made Mestizo," *Harper's*, November 1991, p. 50.

4. Richard Rodriguez, *Days of Obligation: An Argument with My Mexican Father* (New York: Viking Penguin, 1992), p. 13.

5. Gene Smith, *Maximilian and Carlota: A Tale of Romance and Tragedy* (New York: William Morrow, 1973), p. 186.

6. Ibid., p. 130.

7. Ibid., p. 97.

8. Rodriguez, *Days of Obligation*, p. 1.

9. Ibid., pp. 4–5.

10. Paz, *Labyrinth of Solitude*, p. 11.

11. Rodriguez, *Days of Obligation*, p. 12.

12. Robert Haskett, "Indigenous Rulers: Nahua Mediation of Spanish Socio-Political 'Evangelism' in Early Cuernavaca" (unpublished paper, 1994), p. 24.

13. Ibid., p. 1.

14. Ibid., p. 6.

15. James Hamilton-Paterson, *The Great Deep: The Sea and Its Thresholds* (New York: Random House, 1992), p. 260.

16. Patrick Oster, *The Mexicans* (New York: Harper & Row, 1989), p. 256.

17. Ibid., pp. 254–55.

18. Rodriguez, *Days of Obligation*, p. 14.

19. Haskett, "Indigenous Rulers," p. 11.

20. Rodriguez, *Days of Obligation*, p. 13.

21. Haskett, "Indigenous Rulers," p. 23.

22. Smith, *Maximilian and Carlota*, p. 100.

23. Rodriguez, personal communication.

24. J. P. Mayer, *Max Weber and German Political Thought* (London: Faber and Faber, 1979), p. 127.

25. Ibid., p. 122.

26. Tillich, *History of Christian Thought*, p. 148.

27. Mayer, *Max Weber and German Political Thought*, p. 122.

28. Ibid., p. 109.

Part III

Integrating the Mexican Economy into the Age of Free Trade

9

Integrating the Mexican Economy

It is evident that there are fundamental transformations taking place within Mexican society, in economic and political terms. The requirements of the emerging trading bloc envisioned by North America, Inc., foreshadows the kinds of changes that developing countries must undergo if they are to become integrated into the world economy. The enthusiastic surrender of sovereignty that Mexico chose is a portent of the evolution of the nation-state. American managers, however, need to be sensitive to the revolution that integration into the world economy represents for Mexico. Indeed, the effects of these structural changes are causing tensions of historic proportions that have not been visited upon Mexico since its revolution earlier in the twentieth century. The economic dislocation as NAFTA is implemented—in the first full year of NAFTA foreign investors experienced losses—is being accompanied by political turmoil: armed insurgencies, an affected electorate, a crisis within the ruling party, continuing election fraud. With the preceding analyses and discussion, however, the American manager has a fundamental understanding of the forces in conflict in Mexico and has a broader perspective from which to assess opportunities and risks in the Mexican marketplace. Indeed, the reader, at this point, enjoys a significant competitive advantage, for the majority of Mexicans, caught up in the revolutionary changes engulfing their country, are too close to these changes to have perspective or objectivity.

In contrast, corporate America, mindful of the turbulence unleashed by free markets, is better able to develop long-term strategies for securing significant market shares in key sectors of the Mexican economy. The challenge, then, is to begin or expand operations in Mexico. In this section, a survey of the Mexican marketplace is presented. The information will involve a discussion of the differences in the legal structure of forming companies in Mexico, as well as a discussion of the disturbing facts of business life in Mexico, including the continuing problem of corruption in Mexican society and the prejudices that limit the effectiveness of managers who happen to be African American. There are times when change does not take place fast enough.

A change that has already taken place, and which is of strategic importance for corporate America, is the enthusiastic reception that free trade has received in Mexico. Indeed, the pent-up demand for American goods and the cultural predisposition to favor American products, is accompanied by, of all things, fear. Corporate Mexico, aware of its inability to compete directly against corporate America, is eagerly pursuing alliances with American companies. In the early nineties, the opening of the Mexican market produced a franchise fever; Mexican entrepreneurs were convinced that their best chance of surviving the economic dislocation now taking place lay in competing against one another to bring American companies to Mexico. From laundry to hamburgers, from discount liquor to shipping services, the familiar neon signs of American franchises have blossomed in Mexican cities, changing the urban landscape forever.

This welcome is unlike anything that corporate America has experienced. The ease with which American companies—from the ubiquitous McDonald's to smaller firms, such as Miami Subs—are now establishing significant market shares in their respective areas is remarkable. Historical feelings of inferiority, the cultural "malinchismo" that derides Mexico in the eyes of the Mexicans, and greater value are the factors that contribute to Mexico's voracious appetite for American goods and services. Indeed, in a sense the border has disappeared, and American firms, regardless of size, have an enthusiastic market, anxious to participate in a modern economy, which means the American market.

The question, then, is not whether to enter the Mexican market but how.

The easiest way to enter the Mexican market is to sell to Mexicans in the United States who are purchasing merchandise for their businesses in Mexico. The lowering of tariffs and elimination of nontrade barriers accounts for increased sales by American companies to firms based in Mexico. The border states have witnessed a continuing rise in the number of Mexican businesspeople who are buying merchandise; and the double-digit growth of trucking services, from the United States into Mexico, is evidence of the one-way nature of the trading boom. Firms in cities like

Los Angeles and Houston have reported an increase in sales to clients residing in Mexico, from interior designers to hardware supply stores. The systematic reductions in tariffs and the lifting of barriers is one reason that the United States now enjoys a huge trade surplus with Mexico. It is one thing, however, to have Mexicans travel to the United States and quite another to seek out the Mexican market. For small- and medium-sized companies, there are strategies to enter the Mexican marketplace at once. Indirect exporting and the more aggressive direct exporting offer American companies the opportunity to participate in the Mexican marketplace.

INDIRECT EXPORTING

Mexico is in the process of standardizing its economy to mirror and complement that of the United States. In this process, distribution and retailing systems differ from their American counterparts, and the absence of standardization is a barrier for some firms. An assessment is necessary to determine if the distribution network in place in Mexico is compatible with the one in place in the United States. The nature of the product or service, of course, is an integral part of this analysis; the simpler the product, the more readily it can be introduced into Mexico. Complex products or services, the service required, and the ability to travel to assist clients and customers are important considerations.

For many American firms, the trade-off between entering the Mexican marketplace, on the one hand, and sacrificing control over marketing and sales support, on the other, may be advisable. The use of intermediaries may be an acceptable way of testing the market to determine if the product meets with a favorable response. The drawback with using intermediaries, naturally, is that less information is known about the client, how the product is received, and whether it was marketed in a manner consistent with U.S. practices. Nevertheless, the use of agents and trading companies offers smaller firms the chance to enter Mexico immediately while long-term strategies are defined.

Agents and Brokers

The use of import-export brokers, such as agents and customs, offers the chance to facilitate trade. These intermediaries who coordinate transactions—connecting American sellers to Mexican buyers—receive commissions that reflect the dollar value of the sales that they conclude. Agents and brokers, who have business contacts and working relationships with buyers in Mexico, have a fundamental understanding of the market for given products and are in a position to help promote the distribution of these products in Mexico. Because import-export brokers are commission based, they often keep the identities of their clients confidential. Agents or brokers who are familiar with the Mexican market often provide all the necessary documentation and labeling required to import products into Mexico.

Export Trading Companies

Working on a wholesale basis directly with Mexican distributors and retailers, Export Trading Companies (ETCs) act as international distributors and independent brokers. There companies are the market makers that have extensive knowledge of the product lines that they handle. They can provide American manufacturers instant access to the Mexican market, and are familiar with the Mexican industry in the product line that they represent. The advantage of using ETCs is the complete access to Mexican distribution for a given product, and the fact that ETCs pay the U.S. company directly, reducing the risk of selling to foreign companies.

Foreign Trading Companies

Foreign Trading Companies (FTCs) are similar to ETCs, except that the level of commitment is more defined. They tend to specialize in certain narrow markets, product lines, and differentiated market segments. These companies usually require exclusive distribution rights to a given market or territory, and business relationships are structured as most domestic distribution arrangements are. Expectations are established by both sides; suppliers are expected to provide an acceptable turnaround time, have sufficient inventory on hand, and commit to advertising and marketing, while FTCs establish targets for sales within a specified time frame.

DIRECT EXPORTING

Exporting to Mexico offers greater benefits than indirect exporting, but it also requires a well-defined long-term strategy. The appeal of thinking of Mexico as an SBU is manifold. American companies have greater control over the distribution of their goods and services in Mexico, as well as better controls over the pricing, product availability, marketing strategies, and protection over trademarks and patents. In addition, the firm is able to assess market conditions, analyze customer feedback, and fine-tune strategies to better serve the needs of the Mexican marketplace, which is vital for a sustainable presence. The added investment in human resources and financial commitments associated with direct exporting is often offset by the fact that profits do not have to be shared with intermediaries.

Direct Sales

Selling to Mexican firms and institutions is far easier under the terms of NAFTA. Whereas elaborate contracts, and even government-approved exemptions, were necessary in the past, sales contracts now increasingly require few procedures that are markedly different from those for purchasing agreements that are in use in the United States.

Distributors and Representatives

Mexican firms with distribution networks in place offer the opportunity of dealing with one client who will represent a product or service line in a given market or territory. Rules that permit Mexican companies to import directly have been modified, and it is now an easier procedure. The widespread use of custom brokers in Mexico now allows most established firms to import American goods directly. Criteria for the selection of an appropriate distributor include the size of the company, the time it has been in business, the nature of its distribution network, its track record in the specific market, access to bank financing, pricing policies, and ability to inventory.

Sales Agents

The use of Mexican sales agents is an effective method of reaching end-user customers of capital goods. The agents act on behalf of American companies by soliciting business and concluding sales. An agent receives a commission on the value of the sales that he or she makes. While contracts vary, it is important that the contract define the relationship between the U.S. firm and the Mexican citizen. In the absence of a well-articulated business understanding, the relationship might be construed as an employer-employee one, which would subject the American company to Mexican labor laws. When identifying agents, it is imperative that a friendship be established first, as well as an agreement about which product lines, territories, and customer services will be provided by the agent in Mexico.

FINANCING AND PAYMENTS

In any business transaction, the interests of the buyer and the seller are in direct opposition as far as payment is concerned. It is in the interest of the seller to receive payment as soon as possible, while the buyer would like to delay making payment as much as possible. These natural tendencies are exacerbated in foreign trade, for issues of exchange rates and the ability to collect take center stage. The terms of payment must be negotiated clearly when business transactions are made. Mexico, not unlike many developing countries, poses risks for American companies precisely because it is difficult to evaluate the creditworthiness of a Mexican firm. This is one reason that, in Mexico more than in the United States, business relationships are based on friendship. It is necessary to know with whom one is dealing in order to be able to incur moral obligations on both parties. For Mexicans, the question of honor is important, and keeping one's word to a friend carries great weight.

The risk for Americans who are dealing in Mexico, too, also resides in pressuring a Mexican client. The desire to live up to their obligations may result in Mexican clients' making unrealistic commitments, thus undermining long-term relationships. The risks in establishing parameters for accounts receivable from Mexican operations, therefore, must encompass the personal aspect of business life in Mexico. For American managers, it is necessary to remember that track records are vital in Mexico. A firm that has been in business for a number of years is one that has been able to demonstrate the ability to negotiate through the uncertainty and turbulence that Mexico has experienced over the past decade. A certain level of risk might be required to get a Mexican importer to undertake a contractual commitment. The terms of payment, therefore, are in few cases cash in advance. To some extent, then, credit terms must be considered as a requisite.

Letters of Credit

The most commonly used method for payment of international shipments involves letters of credit. The Mexican importer's bank, known as the issuing or opening bank, issues a letter of credit in which it makes a commitment to forward payment to the bank of the American exporter, known as the beneficiary, once the instructions on the letter of credit have been followed. When the exporter meets the instructions and conditions specified in the letter of credit, the issuing bank is legally required to make payment in full to the exporter's bank. For the U.S. exporter, this itself is an assurance, for the issuing bank will not prepare a letter of credit until it is sure that the Mexican importer has sufficient funds to cover the value of the letter of credit. Once an ongoing business relationship develops, it is usually beneficial to establish a revolving letter of credit; or if the volume of business increases substantially, then perhaps transferable letters of credit may facilitate larger transactions.

Revolving Letters of Credit. A revolving letter of credit facilitates transactions that become regular because it allows for a single letter of credit to cover several transactions, usually with a specified maximum dollar amount for any given period of time.

Transferable Letters of Credit. If the U.S. exporter is unable to finance the shipment of a large order to a Mexican client, instructions in the letter of credit can be specified to designate a portion of the funds to the U.S. supplier. In a practical sense, the Mexican importer extends credit to the American exporter, precisely because it assures the U.S. supplier that the exporter will be able to secure payment for the export order.

Letters of credits are not exclusively the only way of selling overseas. There are other methods that may permit American companies to commence exporting to Mexico. The risks are greater, but these other methods offer flexibility to some Mexican companies who are eager to work with American companies but who either are not able to pay in full at the time they receive merchandise or may be uncomfortable with letters of credit.

Consignment

Selling through consignment is an extremely risky way of doing business. The U.S. firm does not receive payment until the merchandise is sold. This is made more difficult by the fact that upon entry into Mexico the importing company pays customs duties, whereby giving rise to ownership claims if disputes arise. Under Mexican law, the act of paying duties provides documentation that confers legal claim to the imported goods. At the same time, the American company faces enormous challenges in tracking sales and in determining when the Mexican importer received payment for the goods sold. This is further exacerbated by distance, language barriers, and fluctuations in exchange rates. Consignment is discouraged.

Open Account

While less risky than selling through consignment, open accounts offer the limitations associated with legal jurisdictions. In the event that the buyer is unable to make payment, an American company would have to file a suit in a Mexican court. At the same time, open accounts allow a working relationship to develop. Mexican importers can receive a small initial shipment, have thirty or forty-five days to make payment, and subsequently order more merchandise. In this way, both the American firm and the Mexican importer can build up trust and familiarity with one another. The risk of sending an initial shipment may be acceptable if it becomes the means of assessing a market, as well as evaluating the performance of the Mexican importer.

Documents Against Acceptance

Risks are diminished by using documents against acceptance. While using banks as intermediaries is not a risk-free proposition, the use of time drafts and date drafts lessens uncertainty. Time drafts, which specify payment within a certain number of days after acceptance of the draft, and date drafts, which require payment on a specific date, are written orders that instruct the importer, known as the drawee, to make payment of a determined sum to the seller, known as the drawer. An American exporter prepares documentation when merchandise is sent to the importer. This documentation is sent to the exporter's bank, which in turn forwards it to the importer's bank. The importer is then notified that the merchandise has been sent. The Mexican importer is then required to acknowledge receipt of the documentation and acceptance of the terms. Once this is done, the importer's bank releases the documents, which are necessary for the importer to be given the merchandise, which in all likelihood has remained in the possession of customs brokers who were awaiting the documentation prior to clearing customs. The importer's bank then makes payment to the exporter's bank when the terms of the draft have been met, such as payment within thirty days after the shipment arrives in the country or payment on a specified date.

Documents Against Payment

A more convenient method of payment is the sight draft, which provides for payment to the exporter's bank before the merchandise is released to the importer. This may pose financing problems on the part of the importer, who is required to, in essence, pay in full upon receipt of the merchandise. At the same time, it is important to note that not unlike collect-on-delivery shipments, the importer has the right to refuse the merchandise. If this happens, the exporter has to pay to have the merchandise returned, which can entail significant bother and expense.

Once initial sales to Mexican clients has begun, the strategic objectives of the firm's presence in the Mexican market need to be assessed. Mexico remains a highly profitable market and will remain so during the initial stages of NAFTA's implementation. This, coupled with the growing sophistication of American companies with the Hispanic markets, may require establishing a corporate presence directly in Mexico. Indeed, this is very much a requisite if a firm is to achieve a sustainable competitive advantage in the Mexican marketplace.

An area of tremendous risk for businessmen in Mexico is the prevalence of check fraud. Mexican legal statutes protect defendants to a surprising degree. In addition, the more casual business style among Mexicans contributes to an ethics whereby bouncing checks is not seen as something peculiar. Indeed, it is not uncommon for bad checks to be issued on purpose as a way of securing "loans" or "extensions of credit." The problem is exacerbated because Mexican law treats checks issued on foreign—meaning U.S.–based—banks as matters not easily pursued. In other words, if a Mexican company were to pay an American company with a check drawn in the United States and if there were a problem with this, the U.S. company would have a very difficult time prevailing in a Mexican court. The law offers very few remedies for check fraud in Mexico, and it is recommended that only bank-issued "certified checks" be accepted.

10

A General Survey
from the
Mexican Investment Board

The Mexican Investment Board (MIB) is a nonprofit organization jointly sponsored by the private financial community and the government of Mexico. Its mission is to help the foreign investor explore and pursue business opportunities in Mexico. The MIB is located at Paseo de la Reforma No. 915, Lomas de Chapultepec, 11000, Mexico, D.F.

The following is information provided by the MIB on assessing opportunities in Mexico.

Corporate Structures

Foreign investments, regardless of the percentage of ownership, are usually made through Mexican corporations with variable capital (S.A. de C.V.), a relatively flexible form of organization. When the foreign investor wishes to have the Mexican entity qualify as a foreign partnership in his country, the general partnership (S. en N.C.) is used.

Setting Up versus Acquisition

Forming a new Mexican corporation as the vehicle for foreign investment is usually preferred. The new investor does not become liable for existing tax, labor, or other liabilities of a previously existing operation.

Investment Incentives

Investment incentives have been limited as part of the efforts to reduce the federal government deficit and are only applicable in cases of minority foreign participation. However, two major tax incentives are granted to encourage investment: (1) the immediate deduction for corporate income tax purposes of all inventory purchases instead of future deductions for costs of goods sold, and (2) an optional immediate write-off of a substantial portion of the total cost of "new" fixed assets acquired. To avoid excessive concentration and overpopulation, this write-off is not available for assets used in the Federal District, Monterrey, and Guadalajara.

Location of Industries

Mexico City, with its enormous market, was traditionally the most important industrial center in the country. But, as a result of the government's decentralization policy aimed at spreading economic growth more evenly, many other areas of the country offer attractive incentives for the establishment of industries. To avoid excessive concentration and overpopulation, the Mexican government is discouraging the establishment of new industries in the metropolitan areas of Mexico City, Monterrey, and Guadalajara.

Financing

Local risk capital is available for most economic activities but is typically directed to export-oriented industries. The privatization of the banking system, improved government financing, and the increasing return of Mexican capital will tend to increase the availability of local risk capital and bank financing.

Preferential lines of credit can be obtained from international development organizations through Mexican banks to import machinery and equipment. The government has also simplified the paper work involved in obtaining permits and authorizations and has considerably reduced administrative procedures.

Export loans with preferential rates are also available. Investing in export-oriented activities permits investors to take advantage of these rates as well as Mexico's cost-efficient, skilled labor and its proximity to the U.S. market.

Remittances of Capital and Profits

There are no exchange controls or other restrictions on the repatriation of profits. The necessary foreign currency must be acquired on the free exchange market. There are no restrictions on the remittances of initial or subsequent investments. Recent tax reforms have considerably reduced the overall tax levels of investors to those levels comparable to world standards.

Remittance of Dividends, Royalties, and Fees

Payments to nonresidents of dividends, royalties, and technical assistance fees are not subject to exchange controls. Dividends can be paid without limitation as long as there are retained earnings from prior periods from which to pay them.

Tax Planning Considerations

Corporate and individual tax rates are competitive. No special, favorable tax treatment is provided for foreign investors or expatriate personnel working and residing in Mexico. It is advisable to form a Mexican corporation since this receives a more favorable tax treatment than a branch of a foreign corporation. The calendar year is the legal fiscal year that is used for tax purposes.

Professional Advice

Legal and tax advisers should be retained early in the planning stages. This will be necessary in order to obtain government approval, to design the most flexible and desirable corporate structure, to benefit from a smooth start-up, and to ensure compliance with regulations.

Labor and Labor Costs

There is an abundant supply of young, readily trainable, unskilled, and semiskilled labor in Mexico. Skilled labor and managerial personnel are available, and the demand for it is growing. It is universally agreed that the Mexican employee readily accepts and assimilates training. Productivity and quality standards achieved by foreign investors are outstanding examples of this.

Labor costs are low, particularly when converted to U.S. dollars. There are substantial fringe benefits and other labor-related costs but, in spite of this, labor costs remain extremely competitive.

Market Studies

Specific product/market studies backed by investigations of potential partners, locations, sources of supply of inputs, labor availability, distribution, and the estimated costs of production and operation are vital before making an investment decision.

Currency Exchange Controls

Mexico's exchange control laws require the conversion of export proceeds into pesos at a controlled market exchange rate. This also applies to foreign bank loans and to part of the fees from "maquiladora" operations.

Information and Assistance

The Mexican Investment Board, a nonprofit joint venture of the government of Mexico and the private financial community, has been created to assist foreign investors. The board's executives are available to help in every step of the way as foreign investors explore and pursue business opportunities in Mexico.

Background information should be obtained from the foreign branches of Mexican banks, the embassies and consulates of Mexico, and local chambers of commerce, including those of other nations, such as the American, British, German, French, and Japanese chambers of commerce.

Trends

A most important indicator for a potential investor to watch is the trend in the fight to maintain inflation down in Mexico. The success of this campaign appears to be linked to the continued strengthening of the private sector as a whole, the deregulation of the Mexican economy, and the moves to increase foreign trade and investment. The North America Free Trade Agreement is a critical part of this, although Mexico is also pursuing other free trade agreements. Finally, the aggressive policy of reprivatizing state-owned enterprises is making the Mexican economy, as a whole, more competitive.

Investor Considerations

Mexico is not considered a tax haven, but its tax rates are now competitive with those of both developed and developing countries. Although tax incentives have been reduced substantially, incentives do remain in place for two important areas:

1. For investments in plant and equipment (as mentioned before)
2. For export-related manufacturing activities such as allowing duty-free imports of components or raw materials used in the manufacture of export goods and assigning a zero rate of value-added tax (VAT) on exports (exporters are exempt from charging VAT and can obtain refunds of VAT charged by their suppliers of goods and services)

There are no free trade zones, but duty-free import zones exist.

Under new liberalized foreign investment regulations, at least 75 percent of economic activities are now open to 100 percent foreign ownership. Incentives exist for fixed assets investment. Taxpayers may elect to take an immediate one-time deduction at rates specified in the law. These rates are established to represent the present value of future depreciation on the basis of the taxpayer's annual depreciation rates approved by the tax authorities.

Investment Policy

It has been the general policy of the Mexican government to provide tax incentives only on a selected basis, consistent with its economic development plans. Accordingly, the main thrust of Mexico's incentives have been to

1. Maintain or increase employment levels
2. Increase Mexico's share of the international market of manufactured goods, through special tax and nontax incentives offered to entities that export their output, including those with foreign participation in their capital
3. Increase the participation of small- and medium-sized industries in overall economic activity
4. Promote social welfare by providing tax and nontax incentives for construction of low-income housing, production and distribution of basic food products, and expansion of agriculture, livestock, forestry, and publishing

State Incentives

A number of Mexican states promote new investments in their own territories. They typically provide local tax incentives and/or offer industrial sites at little or no cost.

Classification of Restricted Activities

To clearly identify activities restricted for foreign investment purposes, 141 activities were selected from the "Mexican Classification of Economic Activities and Products," prepared by the National Institute of Statistics, Geography, and Informatics and listed in the regulations. This list is referred to in the regulations as the "Classification."

Foreign investors may form Mexican corporations with up to 100 percent foreign ownership to engage in any activity not included in the "Classification." A review of the "Classification" indicates that a very large number of activities are not included. Consequently, corporations engaged in these "unclassified" activities may establish operations without prior authorization from the Commission on Foreign Investment simply by meeting the requirements discussed further on.

Category 1. Activities considered to be "strategic," reserved exclusively for the State (Examples: oil and gas production and the basic petrochemical industry)

Category 2. Activities reserved exclusively for Mexican nationals (Examples: television and radio broadcasting)

Category 3. Activities in which foreign investment is limited to 34 percent foreign ownership (Examples: mining and/or refining ore)

Category 4. Activities in which foreign investment is limited to 40 percent (Examples: secondary petrochemical products and the automotive parts industry)

Category 5. Activities in which foreign investment is limited to 49 percent (Examples: mining and refining precious and metallic ores)

Category 6. Activities in which prior approval is required if foreign ownership is to exceed 49 percent (Examples: construction industry, accounting, and legal services)

New regulations now allow foreign investment in activities such as banking and insurance.

Forming New Corporations with up to 100 Percent Foreign Ownership to Engage in "Unclassified" Activities

The regulations established that, when an activity is not included in the Classification, wholly owned subsidiaries may be formed without prior authorization. The new company must comply with the following requirements.

1. The initial investment in fixed assets during the preoperating stage may not exceed US $100 million. Larger investments will probably be authorized, but prospective investors must inform the authorities about them to make sure all the necessary infrastructure is available.

2. The investment must consist of foreign funds. One exception is for investments made by foreign investors already established in Mexico. They may use funds held in Mexico. Shareholder's equity must be equal to at least 20 percent of the investment in fixed assets at the end of the initial start-up stage.

3. The industrial or manufacturing facilities of the new companies must be located outside zones designated as high-density industrial areas. These comprise Mexico City, Monterrey, and Guadalajara, as well as certain municipalities in the State of Hidalgo and the State of Mexico belonging to Zone III-A, known as Controlled Growth Areas and listed in a decree issued January 22, 1986.

4. Companies must maintain an overall favorable foreign exchange balance during the first three years of operation.
5. Permanent jobs must be created as a consequence of the new investment. Companies must establish continuing training and education programs to promote employee skills and development.
6. The investor should use appropriate technology and comply with environmental requirements.

Forming New Corporations to Engage in "Classified" Activities Where Foreign Investment May Be Authorized to Exceed 49 Percent

In considering authorization of foreign investment in excess of 49 percent in restricted activities, the Commission on Foreign Investment asks whether the proposed investment will

1. Complement domestic investment
2. Show a positive balance of payments and promote exports
3. Create jobs and improve employee earnings
4. Contribute to the development of zones or regions where economic improvement is of high priority
5. Bring in new technology and contribute to the development of local technological research

Acquiring Existing Corporations

The rules regarding the acquisition of stock in existing corporations have been liberalized. Authorization is required only when, as a result of the acquisition, foreign ownership exceeds 49 percent. Under NAFTA provisions, requirements are changing according to the treaty's time schedule.

Expansion of Existing Foreign Investments

The rules have been liberalized concerning the opening of new establishments, changing corporate domicile, engaging in new activities, and introducing new product lines. The new foreign investment regulations apply—and therefore no authorization is required—provided that the existing foreign investment meets the following criteria:

1. The investment is made by an in-bond processing plant ("maquiladora") or by export-oriented companies.
2. There is a merger.

3. The establishment agrees to invest in additional fixed assets an amount
   equal to at least 10 percent of the net value of its current fixed assets and
   to meet the requirements applicable to new foreign investment in the
   "unclassified" activities discussed previously.

Temporary Investments through Trusts

The foreign investment regulations further liberalize the rules on foreign
investment by allowing temporary majority foreign ownership through
twenty-year trusts or when companies are engaged in the following
activities:

1. Gas distribution and domestic air or maritime transportation normally
   reserved for Mexican nationals
2. The mining, secondary petrochemical and automotive parts industries
   normally restricted to maximum minority foreign ownership (34 percent,
   40 percent, and 49 percent), provided that
   (a) the investee company requires new capital investment to increase
       exports and production capacity, to introduce new products, or to
       modernize operating technology
   (b) alternatively, the investee company has experienced a drastic reduction
       in sales or is in a precarious financial position because of foreign
       currency indebtedness
   In either case, the investment may be made by injecting fresh funds or
   capitalizing existing liabilities.

Real Estate in Border and Coastal Areas

The foreign investment regulations authorize the establishment of
renewable thirty-year real estate trusts. These allow foreigners to hold and
use real estate for industrial or tourism purposes within 100 kilometers (62
miles) of the border and within 50 kilometers (31 miles) of the coastline.

Temporary Investments by International Development Agencies

International development agencies, such as the International Finance
Corporation or the Inter-American Development Bank, can invest directly
in the stock of new and existing corporations engaged in "classified"
activities. The maximum holding period—namely when such agencies
must divest themselves of their shareholdings—is now extended from ten
to twenty years.

"Neutral" Investment Trusts

In order to permit publicly traded Mexican corporations to have access to foreign capital markets, a public placement of trust "participation certificates" can be authorized. These are issued by thirty-year trusts specifically formed to acquire and hold the stock of the Mexican corporation.

These certificates entail ownership, but not voting rights, over the shares held by the trust. A special series of shares may be issued specifically for the placement, to be acquired only by the trust.

Expeditious Processing of Applications

The foreign investment regulations establish standards for speedy processing of all applications for authorization by the Commission on Foreign Investment and other authorities. They also require that all cases be resolved within forty-five business days. If no reply is received from the commission within that period, the application is automatically approved.

National Commission on Foreign Investment

The National Commission on Foreign Investment, as required by the foreign investment regulations, is the centralized authority that approved foreign investment in new or existing companies. It is responsible for new establishments and the use of existing foreign investment in either new economic activities or product lines. The commission operates through an executive secretary and an experienced staff.

National Registry of Foreign Investment

The Law Regulating Foreign Investment established a National Registry of Foreign Investment, an office of the Ministry of Trade and Industry. Under the foreign investment regulations, the following information is gathered by the registry:

1. Foreign individuals or corporations who make investments within the scope of the law
2. Mexican companies whose capital stock is wholly or partially owned by foreigners
3. Trusts in which foreigners participate

Persons or companies required by the foreign investment regulations to register should file the applications within forty business days following the date on which they become subject to registration. Duly registered Mexican corporations, wholly or partially owned by foreign investors, must periodically furnish detailed information by filing the appropriate forms, showing economic, financial, and balance-of-payments information.

Choice of Corporate Structures

Several options for corporate organization are open to both domestic and foreign investors in Mexico. A corporation (S.A. de C.V.) is the most commonly used entity for a subsidiary or a foreign corporation. A general partnership with unlimited liability (sociedad en nombre colectivo) also may be used, especially if the Mexican entity is to be treated as a foreign partnership for tax purposes in the investor's home country.

Forms of Business Enterprise

The different organizational structures for businesses operating in Mexico are regulated by the General Law of Mercantile Organizations (Ley General de Sociedades Mercantiles) and the Civil Code (Código Civil). The principal forms are summarized below:

Sociedad Anónima (S.A.) and Sociedad Anónima de Capital Variable (S.A. de C.V.), or corporation and corporation with variable capital, respectively (These two are the forms most commonly used by domestic and foreign investors.)

Sociedad de Responsabilidad Limitada (S. de R.L.), or limited liability company (used occasionally)

Sociedad en Nombre Colectivo (S. en N.C.), or general partnership (This is rarely used by foreign investors because of its unlimited liability, unless they want it to qualify as a foreign partnership in their own country.)

Sociedad en Comandita (S. en C.), or limited partnership (rarely used)

Sociedad Civil (S.C.), or civil partnership, that is, of a noncommercial nature (used for administrative service units, educational institutions and by professional practitioners)

Asociación en Participación (A. en P.), or joint venture contract

Sucursal de Sociedad Extranjera, or branch of a foreign corporation

Empresa de Persona Física, or sole proprietorship (A foreigner must qualify as a permanent resident, or "inmigrado," to be able to do business in this way.)

Asociación Civil (A.C.), or civil association (used by charitable and other nonprofit organizations)

Corporate law is federal in nature and applies throughout the country. Although civil law is established by the states, the different state civil codes are practically identical when concerned with the formation of entities of a civil nature.

Formation Requirements

Minimum share capital for an S.A. or S.A. de C.V. is $25,000 in pesos, or about $6,500 in U.S. currency, and the corporation must have at least five shareholders. After all necessary authorizations have been secured, the charter and bylaws must be formalized in a public deed executed before a notary public.

Government Approval

Prior authorization from the Ministry of Foreign Affairs is required to form a corporation and any business entity. This is also required to amend the charter or bylaws of a business. Depending on the type of activity that the proposed corporation will be engaged in, prior authorization may be required from the National Commission on Foreign Investment.

Intellectual Property and Protection

A new law, called the Law for the Development and Protection of Industrial Property, became effective June 28, 1991, and replaced the former Patent and Trademark Law of 1976. Amendments to the Copyright Law took effect on August 16, 1991. NAFTA mandates further standardization of Mexican legal protections.

The Law for the Control and Registration of Transfer of Technology and the Use of Patents and Trademarks was repealed in 1991. The prior approval and registration contracts for the use of patents, trademarks and trade names and for providing technical assistance or know-how are no longer necessary.

Patents

Patents are generally issued for a nonextendible term of twenty years from date of filing. Patents can be obtained for inventions that are new, nonobvious, and have industrial application. Patents are available in all fields of technology, including chemicals, pharmaceuticals, alloys, food and beverages, biotechnology, plant varieties, and microorganisms.

Compulsory licensing, when the patent granted is not used, is notably restricted to exceptional circumstances. Importation of a product constitutes use of the patent and therefore precludes the issuance of a compulsory license.

Increased protection is provided for trade and industrial secrets. Severe penalties are established for their unauthorized disclosure.

Trademarks

Under the law, trademarks can be registered for a ten-year term and are renewable for an indefinite number of additional ten-year periods. Proof of actual use of a trademark is not required; it is sufficient to submit a simple affidavit of such use upon renewal. No previous use in commerce is required for registration of a trademark. Three-dimensional and collective marks can be registered.

Franchise agreements, including the licensing of trademarks, together with the transmission of technical managerial know-how, are registered without any requirement for formal approval. The law stipulates minimal disclosure requirements for the franchise.

Copyrights

In order to protect authors or owners of exclusive rights to software, video and sound recordings, books and other intellectual or artistic works, such property must be registered with the Copyright Department (Dirección de Derechos de Autor) of the Ministry of Public Education. Protection is granted in all cases for a term of fifty years.

For commercial use of copyrights, individuals or companies using the copyrighted materials must demonstrate ownership of the rights. Infringement is subject to criminal prosecution, and both the unauthorized copies and the equipment used for reproduction are subject to confiscation.

MISCELLANEOUS INFORMATION

Visitors' Visas

Persons visiting Mexico to plan, supervise, or carry out business operations need a nonimmigrant visa to enter the country. This applies both to visitors employed by a foreign company and to self-employed persons who will not receive remuneration from Mexican sources. Such visas are obtained from Mexican consulates throughout the world.

Non-Mexican citizens (expatriate employees) living and working temporarily or permanently in Mexico must also have the proper nonimmigrant or immigrant visa (FM-3 and FM-2 forms, respectively) to be able to work in Mexico.

Exchange Controls

All currencies may be freely held, transported, or traded by anyone. Some exchange controls relate to certain types of transactions, principally exports, imports, and bank financing.

Time Zones

Most of the country is on the U.S. Central Standard Time (U.S. Eastern Standard Time minus one hour, or Greenwich Mean Time minus six hours). The far northwest of Mexico is on U.S. Mountain Time and the Baja California peninsula is on U.S. Pacific Time, one and two hours earlier, respectively. Daylight Savings Time was adopted by a number of northern border states in 1988. In those areas, clocks are moved forward one hour between April and November.

Business Hours

Business offices are normally open for an eight-hour working day from 8:30 or 9:00 A.M. until 6:00 or 7:00 P.M., with one or two hours for lunch. The two-hour lunch period is almost universal outside Mexico City.

Legal Holidays

The Federal Labor Law establishes the following obligatory holidays throughout the country: January 1, February 5, March 21, May 1, September 16, November 20, and December 25. December 1 is an obligatory holiday every six years for the inauguration of a new president. Religious holidays are also observed by most business offices, banks, and large stores. These holidays include the Thursday and Friday of Easter week, November 1 and 2, and December 12. These and other holidays may be agreed upon in collective labor contracts.

Weights and Measures

The metric system is used uniformly in Mexico. There is, however, a good working knowledge of the English system in technical circles and among the workforce.

Dates and Numbers

In writing dates, the day is usually placed before the month, and Roman numerals are often used to indicate the month, that is, 10/VI/89 or 10/6/89 for June 10, 1989. A decimal point is used to denote fractions of the monetary unit. Commas indicate thousands, millions, and so forth.

Local Customs

Business relationships tend to be somewhat more formal than in the United States. The use of first names, particularly outside the northern border zone, is not widespread. Meetings with customers and advisers are often held at breakfast or lunch. A luncheon meeting may be quite lengthy.

11

The Limitations on African-American Executives in Mexico

In the past twenty years African Americans have made tremendous progress in advancing their careers in corporate America. African Americans, in greater numbers, are taking their place in all areas of American society and are making significant contributions that serve to enrich American life. As a consequence of these continuing advances, African-American executives participate in all areas of life in corporate America, which implies that there are many capable African-American businesspeople who can contribute to the establishment of successful SBUs and business operations in Mexico.

It is therefore unfortunate to have to issue a caveat about Mexican views of blacks. It is both embarrassing and shameful that a discussion such as this one has to be included in a business book as the twenty-first century approaches, but it should serve as a reminder that the struggle for equality in human societies remains that—a struggle.

Blacks are invisible in Mexico for they are a secret shame of Mexico. The idea of blacks in Mexico itself surprises. The Mexican people, we are told, evolved from the intermarriage of the indigenous people and the Spanish, as well as other Europeans, who migrated to the New World. Mexico calls itself a "mestizo" nation, that word being a colonial name for an individual of Native American and European ancestry. What the world considers "Mexican" is taken to be the natural evolution of Native American and European peoples, cultures, and societies.

Mexicans deceive themselves into a kind of wishful thinking, an unconscious attempt to see themselves and their histories as what they would like them to be. This is a natural human trait, similar to the way in which Americans overlook a great deal of unsettling in the settling of the West. "The only good Injun is a dead Injun," shatters the romantic notion of American expansion across the continent. And in Mexico the myth of "mestizaje," or of being mestizo, is an equally powerful myth. As Richard Rodriguez has written, "Miscegenation was a sin against Protestant individualism."[1]

By the end of the sixteenth century, there were three times as many Africans as Europeans in New Spain. The number of black slaves exceeded 20,000 while the number of whites barely reached 7,000.

For Mexico to be a "mestizo" nation would require an impossible feat. Each European male would have had to father 375 children by 375 different Indian women, and every black in New Spain would have to have been celibate.

The census figures allow no other possibility, but the probability that this happened at all is rather dim. But fiction, like propaganda, has little to do with facts. And for Mexico, the creation of a national identity mandates that Mexican people are "mestizo," meaning that the blood of Europeans and Native Americans run through their veins.

With the same ease, then, that a sinner is transformed into a state of grace, so too have historical facts been edited, erased, and manipulated to conform to political ideas. The "Día de la Raza," or "Day of the Race," after all, is an official holiday celebrated on Columbus Day.

This myth endures because it is comfortable, successful. Indeed, Mexicans honor the image of Spaniard and Aztec in battle, a new people emerging from their union. It is a rather simple, if not simplistic, view of history. Unfortunately, Mexicans deceive themselves into pretending that blacks never played a role in the development of "Mexico." It is a historical—and biological—fact denied by one and all. Richard Rodriguez writes: "Europe has been accustomed to playing the swaggart in history—Europe striding through the Americas, overturning temples, spilling language, spilling seed, spilling blood."[2] And through this "spilling" of seed, "in Mexico the European and the Indian consorted. The ravishment of fabulous Tenochtitlán ended in a marriage of blood and the generation of a 'cosmic race,' as the Mexican philosopher José Vasconcelos has called it."[3] This would certainly be news to José Vasconcelos. It would be news to him because his writings were literary love letters born from his sojourns to South America. It was while in South America that José Vasconcelos grew excited at the vitality of Brazil and, in profound admiration, he contemplated a future in which the nations of the Americas would lead the way, inventing a seemingly effortless society of European, Native American, and *African* peoples.

His writings were wishful thinking of what Mexico's future had the promise to become: Mexico's blood might become as rich and splendid as Brazil's— an attempt to redeem Mexico's African legacy. It was an attempt that failed.

The Mexican state, enamored with José Vasconcelos's generous philosophical construction, appropriated his arguments for Mexican political objectives—philosophical ammunition to justify its actions. "Cosmic race" does have a rather nice ring to it. Thus, José Vasconcelos's argument became edited, blacks falling by the wayside while Mexico's intellectuals enshrined the idea of Indian and European miscegenation.

The official version of history would be repeated over and over by people in Mexico and abroad in a manner so convincing and with such authority that it has become accepted as fact. But upon close scrutiny— marriage, birth, and baptism records of the Mexican Inquisition— historical documents reveal more African seed was spilt than European. Yet, blacks have no place in Mexican history.

From the very beginning, there were blacks in Mexico. When Cortés arrived, he was accompanied by blacks; and after orchestrating the defeat of the Aztecs, he set about establishing European institutions to carry out the business of Europeanization. Many of the indigenous nations were rather indifferent. To them a "foreign" Spanish King replaced an Aztec emperor, and a "foreign" god, Christ, replaced Huitzilopochtli, the Aztec god of war. To them, essentially, tribute, subservience, and military occupation remained the same. The Spanish weren't any crueler than the Aztecs—in fact, at first, they were benevolent: The Aztec gods required human sacrifice, the European god did not. But there was a remarkable continuity in many ways: the Aztecs defeated, enslaved, and used the indigenous people, and so did the Spanish.

In the process of establishing European society in New Spain, the Spaniards went about establishing a caste system. Those born in Europe were at the top. Individuals born in New Spain of European parents, known as criollos, were next. At the bottom were the indigenous peoples, whom they referred to collectively as "Indians." But there were two problems. First, mostly men came to the New World. The Spaniards left their women behind. In the natural course of things, Spanish men began fathering children born of Indian women. For the Spanish colonial administrators, these interracial children were labeled "mestizos," and their rank was above that of "Indian" but below that of "criollo." The other problem was one of efficiency: the Mexicas, Mixtecs, Zapotecs, Oaxacans, and other ethnic peoples in the Valley of Mexico were terrible slaves. Slavery was, of course, common among the indigenous civilizations of Mexico, but there was a fundamental difference. In the New World, slavery was a temporary condition, used as a source of labor and as a prelude to being sacrificed to the gods—and probably to being eaten. In the Old World, slavery was permanent; slaves were full-time workers, not a source of protein.

The Spaniards were dumbfounded. They were here to find their fortune, to put in their years in a savage land, and return home rich. (This viewpoint was the major reason that the Spaniards didn't bring their women to Mexico. They were not immigrants like the English who would migrate to North America in less than three centuries. After their adventures they all wanted to return home, leaving their priests behind to civilize what they perceived to be barbaric peoples.) But if they were ever to return home rich, the Spaniards would have to establish a profitable colony. That the "Indians" didn't understand what was expected of a slave—namely, work—only frustrated their plans. Worse still, the "Indians" fell ill to European diseases and died in droves.

In no time, the Spanish administrators were faced with an acute labor shortage: The "Indians" lay sick and dying, and it would be impossible to enslave the mestizos. Although the mestizos were "bastards," their Spanish fathers felt a moral obligation to them; they would be the future heirs and administrators of New Spain, not the workhorses. Therefore, to amend the labor crisis, it was decided that "real" slaves, black slaves, were necessary to work the fields, to labor in the silver and gold mines, and to carry out the tedious work of erecting European cities.

Thus, the colonial caste system was expanded and modified as follows: Europeans, criollos, mestizos, "Indians," and blacks. Blacks proved to be much better laborers than "Indians," and New Spain prospered: The fields were tended, gold and silver were mined, and cities were built. Blacks didn't get sick, and they had a "better" work ethic. The Spaniards, ever so efficient, kept importing more and more blacks with greater and greater enthusiasm.

It was, at first, a gradual process that accelerated with alarming speed. Basil Davidson recounts:

> By as early as 1501, only nine years after the first voyage of Columbus, the Spanish throne had issued its initial proclamation on laws for the export of slaves to America. . . . These slaves were white—whether from Spain or from North Africa—more often than black; for the black slaves, it was early found, were turbulent and hard to tame. . . . The Spanish Governor of Hispaniola, Ovando,

complained to the Spanish Court that fugitive African slaves among the [Native Americans] were teaching disobedience, and that it was impossible to recapture them.[4]

Despite the initial ban on the export of African slaves to New Spain, however, the discovery of Mexico changed all that. There was an empire to expand, much work to be done. None of this, however, could be accomplished with these "shiftless" Indians. Thus, according to Davidson,

> African labour in Mexico early took the place of "Indian": no wonder, for the "Indian" population was cut down by more than half in little over a century. As early as 1570 there was said to be as many as twenty thousand African slaves in Mexico. In 1584 the king of Spain passed to his vice-regal council in Mexico an order that "the Indians, a weak people, be left to their own business, and that the labour of the mines, construction, fields and mills be undertaken by mulattoes, negroes and mestizos." And so it was.[5]

With perhaps too much enthusiasm, for what occurred was peculiar indeed. The religious settlers, who were intent upon establishing a Franciscan utopia in New Spain, were allowed to establish communities apart from the emerging Spanish ones. The civil authorities, were only too pleased to have permission for the wholesale importation of Africans.

The results were impressive. Between the years 1570 and 1650 there were over three times as many blacks as Europeans in Mexico. And the blacks began to take their proper role in "spilling seed"—more so, by virtue of their numbers, than any band of conquistadores. Basil Davidson again reports that

> the careful records of the Inquisition in Mexico, records that were kept as part of the process of "safeguarding Christianity" by ensuring baptism, show that the land was fertilized by many African peoples. . . . The Mexican Inquisition archives mention at least two of the East African city-states: Melin, presumably Malindi, and Mozambique. . . . And other victims came from places still farther afield: the Mexican records tell of slaves from Burma, Malaya, Java and even China.[6]

But it was the slaves from Africa who far outnumbered all other slaves. More importantly, too, as disease ravaged the indigenous peoples and as quarrels between the ecclesiastical and civil authorities raged on, the administrators of New Spain resorted to increasing their importation of African slaves to provide the manpower necessary to construct the cities and mine the minerals of Mexico.

The arrival of so many blacks in Mexico benefited the economy tremendously. As a colony, New Spain prospered. Mexico, Guadalajara, and Veracruz were growing cities, Spanish women began to arrive in greater numbers, the transformation of Mexico into Europe's image had begun. But there were now other issues to address. Some issues were easy to resolve. Black slaves were of lower rank than "Indian" slaves. Others were more difficult. The Native Americans of Mexico were already fearful of the blacks. Their legends told of the benevolent Quetzacoatl, a fair-skinned, blue-eyed, bearded god, so to them the fair-skinned Spaniards were the stuff of myths. But blacks? The indigenous peoples of Mexico had never seen blacks before. Nothing in their lives or their myths had prepared them for blacks.

To compound the racial tensions, as the Spanish went about the business of Christianizing the natives, some peculiar ideas about the Bible were taught. Among these was the belief that black people were the descendants of Cain. The descendants of Cain, furthermore, were dark-skinned as punishment for Cain's murder of his brother, Abel, who was a good son. At the same time, as with the Spaniards, mostly black males arrived in Mexico; they were there to work and "strengthen" the native stock, not to establish black communities.

To the "Indian" peoples, what had been an initial fear—taller, dark-skinned men whom they had never seen before—was exacerbated by two additional concerns: Blacks were damned by God, and "Indian" women had to be protected from them. The Spanish colonial administrators were indifferent to the concerns of mere slaves and Indians. (This was a source of friction with the religious authorities.) They secretly wanted the blacks to father children in order to make the "Indians" stronger and to produce more slaves and mullatta concubines, who were highly valued by the Spaniards. But they also wanted to be sure that their own European women were safe. The same fear that American plantation owners sowed throughout the South about the "danger" and "threat" of black men was sown by the Spaniards to frighten the already-fearful "Indians."

But blacks were a fact of life in colonial Mexico, and their presence presented the Spanish bureaucracy with a dilemma: Five categories were no longer enough. An individual of black and white parents became "mulatto," and an individual of "Indian" and black parents became a "mestindio." Those were easy matters to resolve; but in human relations, the possibilities were endless. An individual of a mestizo and a mulatto became . . . what? Half white, one quarter black, one quarter "Indian"?

Well, the Spanish were not about to consider such a person "half" white. A mulatto who married a white person? Is this individual "white" by virtue of being three-quarters white, one-quarter black?

So what emerged was a very complicated caste system in which any black blood kept pushing you down in the pecking order. One drop of black blood was enough to push your rank beneath that of mestizo. The Spaniards did in the seventeenth and eighteenth centuries what the Germans did in this century, except that the Germans substituted "black" with "Jew."

Thus, the structure of colonial society was a complicated one. The professions were exclusively reserved for Europeans and criollos. Mestizos could own neither horses nor guns. Neither could the mestindios. Blacks were almost exclusively slaves. "Indians" and mestindios could be enslaved, although there were restrictions that varied from place to place and time to time. Free Indians living on communal lands were exempt from taxation—technically, for this was not always respected. Mestizos were free to move up the economic and social ladder without pushing their luck: Whites were doctors, but mestizos could be medical assistants; whites were plantation and hacienda owners, but mestizos could be their foremen, supervising Indians and blacks; whites owned the horses, but mestizos could drive carriages.

In such a society, the incentive was clearly to disguise black ancestry. This is precisely what happened. Over time, as the colonial era progressed, the word "mestizo" came to mean "absence of African blood." A child born of a black father and an "Indian" mother could pass off as "Indian" rather than mestindio. Blacks, if they couldn't "pass" as "Indians," could at least pretend to be mestindios, thereby increasing their opportunities in life. That the indigenous peoples of Mexico consisted of over fifty ethnicities presented the Spaniards with a dizzying array of possibilities. If in Mexico City a person who "looked" black insisted that he or she was, for example, a Chamula, who would be the wiser? The Spaniard in Mexico City probably never saw a Chamula in his life, and, more likely than not, unless he suspected the individual of being a runaway slave, it didn't matter to him.

The great incentive in colonial Mexico was to claim European blood, European credentials, European ancestry of any kind, however slight that might be. If nothing else, the majority of the blacks in Mexico knew they would "disappear." There were very few black women, and their children would by necessity be mestindios. The agony of enslavement must have been equaled by the hopeless realization of their impending racial extinction. As the colonial period continued, as the inevitable "disappearance" of blacks into the general gene pool of Mexico continued, a few communities of runaway slaves began to emerge. Veracruz, as the most important port of entry into colonial Mexico on the Gulf of Mexico, saw the arrival of the blacks. In the hills of the state by the same name, small and isolated communities of blacks grew, hidden from view, forgotten by the rest of Mexico.

In Mexico itself, however, the colonization continued, even as the colonial era came to an end. In the structure of New Spain, the economic and social incentives were such that "Europeanization" was richly rewarded. Indeed, the effect of this incentive system is evident even today. In Mexico City where colonial power was concentrated, the "Indian" peoples adopted Spanish surnames in the same way in which American blacks adopted English surnames. Everyone wanted to claim a single drop of European blood to make that great social leap from "Indian" to "mestizo." But this was only in the big colonial centers, where the structure of urban society gave rise to opportunities to the ambitious and where people were free to forget their past and start anew. The farther one moves away from Mexico City and other colonial centers, the less the effect. In Oaxaca, for example, most "Indian" people have two names—one in Spanish, the other in their native language. And most cities and streets have two names also. Farther south, in Yucatan, the Mayas couldn't have cared less about the Europeans, kept their own names; and today, of over one hundred municipalities in that state, only seven are named in Spanish.

In the corridors of power—in Mexico City, Cuernavaca, Puebla, Guadalajara, Veracruz, Monterrey—the Europeanization of Mexico continued with great enthusiasm, however, as did the quest for status. When the colonial era ended, Mexico—which was a polyglot nation of many dozens of indigenous peoples speaking easily a hundred languages, with distinct ethnic and cultural histories—fell into chaos. No one group constituted a majority that could keep the country out of anarchy. In the half century that followed Mexico's liberation from Spain, there were dozens of so-called "republics"—at times several claiming simultaneously to be the legal government. This inability to establish a consensus on anything proved devastating: A northern province split away and became the Republic of Texas; Mexico stumbled into a disastrous war with the United States which lost a third of its territory; and Mexico defaulted on its debts to the European powers, resulting in an invasion, after which the French Army installed an Austrian archduke as emperor.

The Mexicans knew they were held in contempt by the Europeans. As the Europeans prepared to invade Mexico, the *Times* of London characterized the Mexicans as "cross-bred, demoralized, blood-thirsty castes."

Mexico, which was in fact a geographic expression, was equally alarmed by the civil war in the United States: Thousands of American blacks sought freedom from slavery by fleeing to Mexico. Ships from American ports, like New Orleans, brought an influx of American blacks.

In the face of an invasion by the French, British, and Spanish armies, securing the borders was not a high priority—and the underground railroad had some depots scattered throughout Mexico. The installation of Maximilian as Emperor of Mexico, however, changed priorities once again: Mexico could redeem itself. The Empress Carlota, a Victorian romantic at heart, complained the Mexicans were "too Europeanized," by which she meant corrupt. She idealized the "Indian" masses of Mexico, whose "simple" beauty lay in their inner strength.

The days of the Mexican Empire were numbered, however. The United States, outraged at what it perceived as an open violation of the Monroe Doctrine and its civil war concluded, began to send arms to Benito Juarez, the President of Mexico who had been removed from power by the Europeans. Emperor Maximilian responded by making Matthew Fontaine Maury, an officer in the Confederate Navy, the Imperial Commissioner on Immigration. Thousands of fliers were distributed throughout the American South and an exodus of Southerners, who fancied themselves the "chivalric" defenders of civilization, emigrated to Mexico. The likes of Generals Edmund Kirby-Smith, John Magruder, and Jubal Early were joined by thousands of other American chivalrics, including the former governors of Louisiana and Missouri. They established Carlota Colony near the city of Cordoba, not far from the port of Veracruz, and dreamed of continuing their familiar way of life—including black slavery—in Mexico under the protection of Emperor Maximilian.

The American president, Andrew Johnson, was not disposed to tolerate any of that. Mexico, chaotic as it may be, provided sanctuary to American blacks escaping the Confederate South, and he was not prepared to let the Confederate elite use Mexico to stage an invasion at some future point. General Sheridan was ordered to have his men patrol the Rio Grande, and all immigration from the port of New Orleans was suspended.

The consequences of these events created dire repercussions for blacks. The historical factors that made it advantageous to deny black ancestry was all the more important now that European nobility ruled the land. High society of Mexico City was flattered that a Hapsburg, heir to the Austrian throne, had acquiesced and come from his castle in Miramar, near Trieste on the Adriatic Sea, to save them. That runaway American slaves were using Mexico was alarming; not since the eighteenth century had there been black immigration to Mexico.

Mexican fears were transparent. In late 1866 it was evident that the Mexican Empire was doomed. Empress Carlota had returned to Europe to seek military support from Napoleon III, and went mad. The Mexican emperor shipped his personal possessions back to his castle in late October. Rumors spread throughout Mexico City. One was that if the emperor fell, complete anarchy would follow when Benito Juarez returned to power. The other rumor, more frightening than the first, was that the United States was preparing to send in its army to make Mexico into a black colony ruled from Washington. Mexicans were more horrified by the latter prospect than by the former. Anarchy, Mexicans believed, was preferable to blacks.

The United States' transforming Mexico into a black colony was never a possibility, but the fear it struck in the hearts of Mexicans reveals the anxiety that Mexicans felt about blacks. Throughout their entire history, Mexicans have denied the existence of blacks. There were more "mestindios" in Mexico than there were "mestizos." There were more "mestindios" than there were whites. As city after city fell to troops loyal to Benito Juarez, the Mexican Empire disintegrated. Emperor Maximilian was captured in the city of Queretero and was executed. Benito Juarez was able to establish authority over Mexico. The imagined fears of a black "occupation" of Mexico waned.

So where are the blacks in Mexico? Where is their influence? Where have they gone? Where is their only legacy? Where, or where, did they all go?

They have vanished into the gene pool of Mexico. Denied their humanity and reduced to becoming property to be owned and disposed of by the Spanish rulers of colonial Mexico, blacks were the workhorses of New Spain. Bought as slaves from other Europeans, Cubans, or Africans, they were brought to a strange land, a land in which they were feared by the indigenous people. The children they fathered were mestindios, and for all practical purposes, "mestizos."

Robert Haskett observes that "when challenged, members of the [Native American] ruling group were quick to defend their material habits. . . . In 1714 don Melchor [a Native American governor] defended himself from charges that he had illegally been dressing as a Spaniard, for there were laws on the books, rarely enforced as far as the [Native American] elite were concerned, that prohibited indigenous people from doing so."[7] Don Melchor adopted more than European dress, however. He came to embrace the European contempt for blacks, thousands of which were being imported to address the chronic labor shortage in New Spain. They were reprehensible, he believed, a conviction that quickly spread among the Native Americans, who feared the Africans. The blacks and mulattos, don Melchor complained to the Spaniards, "run away . . . and become nothing but fugitives and thieves."[8] This is a far cry from the initial welcome that the first blacks in Mexico received. The blacks that accompanied Cortés were thought to be "soiled gods" and were held in reverence. In little more than a century, they descended to the lowest level of colonial society.

This is curious indeed. The common wisdom is that it was "Indians" who were held in contempt, occupying the lowest place on the totem pole, so to speak, of Spanish America. Perhaps in some places they were, but as far as colonial Mexico was concerned it was African slaves who were without worth, beings held in contempt by peoples who were themselves held in contempt by their European masters.

Mexico, struggling for centuries to deny its black ancestry, struggles with its emotions about blacks today. In Mexico, myths are commonplace about blacks, stories of sexual violence, of blacks being black of God's punishment, of being savage. Mexicans tell the most offensive jokes about blacks, and harbor the most irrational fears.

In the Valley of Mexico and in other colonial centers of power, the mixing of the races—encouraged by the Spanish—and made inevitable by the absence of black women, resulted in a miscegenation of sorts: white, black, and "Indian." The anger of the "Indians" was not so much that they were enslaved by the Spaniards—they had been enslaved under more cruel conditions by the Aztecs—but rather that their "purity" was defiled by miscegenation. It was a calamity for them, and they agonized over this unfortunate fate, fearing that they were damned to eternal hell now that the blood of Cain ran through their veins. The Mexican fear of being defiled by "black blood" still echoes today. To say that someone has "sangre negra"—that is, "black blood"—is to say that he or she is an evil creature capable of the most heinous acts.

During the time of Emperor Maximilian, in salons throughout Mexico City, behind closed doors, in private, white Mexicans discussed in hushed voices their "mistake": The native races were made more "barbarous" by "black blood." Late in the nineteenth century when Darwinism give rise to social Darwinism, Mexicans had "scientific" proof to support their arguments.

Mexico has forgotten its African heritage. In *Christopher Unborn*, Carlos Fuentes writes about a protagonist who is an unborn child in his mother's womb. Right before he is born, he forgets everything—he forgets the novel he has been telling the reader—and the novel ends. In Mexico there is a collective amnesia about African heritage. In Veracruz, the principal port of entry for blacks (although all the ports, from Acapulco to Tampico, served in the slave trade)—hence, a high concentration of

black slaves and, in time, some runaway black communities emerged—
there are many people of African ancestry. In fact, the term for people
from Veracruz is "jarocho," comparable to people from the state of Maine
being known as "downeasters." But "jarocho" was a colonial designation
for an individual born of a black and "Indian." Mexicans have forgotten
the origin of the word, because it serves the national myth.

Look around Mexico. Blacks have completely vanished. The only trace,
the only evidence left of African heritage is a saint. Throughout Mexico,
San Martin de Porres is revered. He is black. The cult of San Martin,
introduced to appease the slaves, to give them hope, lives on. Perhaps it
is because of shame, perhaps it is unconscious guilt, perhaps it is tradition.
But whatever the reason, it is ironic that a nation that despises blacks prays
to a black man, unaware of the significance of his presence.

The cultural bias against blacks is more than a theoretical consideration.
One quiet afternoon in the town of San Cristobal de las Casas, while
hosting a visiting colleague from New York who is black, two Native
American women—Chamula ladies—approached us as they were walking
from the opposite side of the road. They looked up and saw me. There was
no response, at first. Then their eyes moved and their gazes froze on my
friend. They became startled, it was clear to see. They stopped instantly.
After a pregnant pause, one Chamula lady made the sign of the cross. Her
companion also crossed herself before both ladies hurried to the other side
of the street.

They have seen a "Mandingo," a strictly local colloquial word for
"devil" or demon," which has its origin in the African slave trade.
Mandingo is a place in Africa from which slaves were exported to Mexico.
That this word has found its way to the Chiapas highlands is testament to
the missions of the Catholic Church in the New World. These Chamula
ladies don't know any better, and are scared. The devastating fact of life
here, however, is that these incidents are not relegated to simple people,
for, to a large extent, it is a continuation of the propaganda created to serve
the interests of the Mexican State, which is spread as incomplete truths by
apologists like Octavio Paz.

In one of the oldest cities in Mexico, there were a good number of slaves.
The exact number is difficult to determine because historical records are
scarce. In this city, the church of Santa Lucia was built exclusively for
blacks and mulattos. I have been told stories of how the Maya Indians
feared blacks. I have been told of Maya women who preferred to commit
suicide rather than bear children fathered by a black. This was common
in the nineteenth century. Santa Lucia is four blocks north of the main
plaza, where the cathedral reserved for whites stands.

Santa Lucia is a simple church. A sign on the iron gates announces an English-language Saturday service, for tourists who want to attend mass. Beneath the cobblestones in the courtyard of the church lies what once was a cemetery for the city's black and mulatto populations. No sign marks the spot. Pave over a cemetery with cobblestones and a history vanishes.

Mexico is haunted by its denial of its African heritage. Mexico is bewitched by irrational, racist views about blacks. Its haunted soul, almost bordering on guilt, betrays an insidious past. Mexicans would like to think of themselves as mestizos, all too eager to deny African ancestry. Throughout the century, and to this day, it is customary for Mexicans to compile lists tracing their lineage back to Spain. Oftentimes observers mistake this as an affront to the "Indian" heritage of Mexico. It is not. In practical terms, only in the past few years, with spectacular breakthroughs in archaeology and epigraphy, have the lineages of the ruling indigenous dynasties come to light. Only now are most "Indians" literate. Mexicans don't affect being "European," by compiling such lists, but rather they strive to assure themselves that they have no "black blood" in their veins.

The lingering ideas about blacks and the historical prejudices represent a formidable problem as contact between Mexicans and Americans increase. On several occasions when I have hosted black friends in Mexico and I have shown them about, it is astounding how many Mexicans will simply stare in disbelief. In small "Indian" towns, women will cross themselves and hurry to the other side of the street. In the bars and restaurants of even sophisticated resorts, it is not difficult to find Mexicans staring discreetly at black patrons, their only opportunity beyond American television broadcasts.

The troubled Mexican conscience, fearful of blacks, uncomfortable with its past, gives way to denial. In the creation of Mexico there are no blacks. Almost entirely by will, Mexico has erased its African past, a heritage that made Mexico possible: Without the labor of black slaves, without their genes, precious minerals would not have been mined, cities would not have been built, New Spain would not have provided the wealth that it did to Europe.

It is regrettable to report that the effectiveness of African-American executives is diminished in the Mexican cultural context, which is incredibly racist in nature. American firms establishing a presence, or expanding operations, in Mexico must be sensitive to the management challenges and limits imposed by this Mexican reality. If there is any silver lining to the ominous cloud over Mexico, it is that racism such as this constitutes a damning indictment of the moral bankruptcy of Mexican fascism that has been so pervasive in this century and that NAFTA hopes to ameliorate.

NOTES

1. Richard Rodriguez, *Days of Obligation: An Argument with My Mexican Father* (New York: Viking Penguin, 1992), p. 13.

2. Ibid., p. 8.

3. Ibid., p. 13.

4. Basil Davidson, *The African Slave Trade* (Boston: Little, Brown & Company, 1980), p. 63.

5. Ibid., p. 128.

6. Ibid., p. 121.

7. Robert Haskett, "Indigenous Rulers: Nahua Mediation of Spanish Socio-Political 'Evangelism' in Early Cuernavaca" (unpublished paper, 1994), p. 16.

8. Quoted in ibid., p. 16.

12

A Question of Corruption

No discussion of doing business in Mexico is complete without a discussion of corruption. The U.S. Foreign Corrupt Practices Act prohibits Americans from paying bribes overseas. As such, there is often a conflict, in view of the fact that Mexico is plagued by great renown as being among the most corrupt societies in the world. While it is true, however, that "gratificaciones," or "tips," are still the norm to have one's letters delivered, or garbage collected, or be on one's way after being pulled over by a policeman, in the business community this is less frequent. Of course, there is still the problem of officials who use the awarding of public contracts as opportunities for personal gain; this is less the case than in the past.

Nevertheless, because of the continuing issue of corruption, this discussion is presented to help American executives understand how, at times, Mexicans exaggerate the extent of the problem and what they mean by "corrupción." The reason that they do this is that Mexicans prefer to believe the worst about themselves—about themselves and about their societies—as a way of confirming their insecurities. In a convoluted act of repudiating the domination that they suffer at the hands of their ruling party, Mexicans wish to portray a devastating portrait of their system as a way of coping with the oppression that perfect hegemonies inflict. It would be easier to reform their political institutions, but a masochistic tendency is characteristic of Catholicism, and Mexicans are nothing if not good Catholics.

For the sake of argument, however, in this chapter instead of arguing the Mexican positions—that Mexico is corrupt—I will focus the discussion on the relative nature of the alleged corruption and on how, in fact, Mexico is no more corrupt than the other countries that compose North America, Inc.

In the eighties, it seemed, one could tell spring had arrived in Washington, D.C., by two events. The first was the Cherry Blossom Festival. The other was Senator Jesse Helms' annual accusation on the Senate floor that the government of Mexico is guilty of corruption. Regarding corruption, Richard Rodriguez says that "Mexico does not deny any of it—well, some—but Mexico has a more graceful sense of universal corruption."[1] That the government of Mexico is corrupt hardly seems noteworthy enough to warrant taking up time on the Senate floor of the U.S. Congress. That the government of Mexico is corrupt is inevitable for three reasons.

The first reason stems from the paternalistic structure of Mexican society. Where there are no free elections, public officials are not accountable to the alleged constituencies that they supposedly serve. Where there is no democracy, then, loyalty is given to the bureaucracy that is responsible for one's position. The ruling party, which runs the country as Big Daddy at some Southern plantation, dispenses positions among its members at its discretion.

In this most peculiar political arrangement, the role of elections are puzzling. Mexico realizes that just about everywhere in the world there are elections—but do elections have a place in a paternalistic society still characterized by patrimonialistic elements? If a household with two adults and three children held free elections to decide whether to have vegetables or ice cream for dinner, what would the point be?

The Mexican government assumes that the Mexican people are adult children incapable of taking care of themselves. Elections therefore puzzle. The Mexican government holds elections because other countries do, but the Mexican government sees little point to them. (That democracy is the struggle to hold public officials accountable to the people whom they serve is a notion that escapes the Mexican mind.) Thus, Mexican elections become a vehicle by which the ruling party legitimizes its existence— before the international community.

All too often, however, dessert is reserved for the ruling party's followers and cronies, a way of dispensing patronage. In such a system, then, it is inevitable that corruption will prevail. According to Octavio Paz, "Within the Mexican state . . . the body of technocrats and administrators, the professional bureaucracy, shares the privileges and risks of public administration with the friends, intimates and favorites of the current president, and with the friends, intimates and favorites of the current ministers."[2] If the ruling party is able to manipulate elections like enormous *fiestas*, it will be able to ensure that the paternalistic system will endure—a system in which "conflict of interest" and "ethics" never intrude in the nation's public life.

The second reason stems from the nature of *malinchismo*. Ever eager to believe the worst of their countrymen, Mexicans exaggerate the corruption that in fact exists. Mexicans *want* to believe the worst of their government, of their society, of their nation.

Consider the following Mexican joke.

[A] grandmother . . . tells her grandson to separate the lobsters they have caught into dark ones and light ones. The dark ones (representing Mexicans) should go in the basket without the lid, she says. The light ones (representing Americans) have to be put in the basket with the lid. "Why, *abuelita* [*grandma*]?" asks the boy. Because the light ones are smart, says the grandma. When one figures how to get out of the basket, it will help the others until all have escaped. "But what about the dark ones?" asks the boy. With them, there will be no problem, the grandma says. As soon as the first dark one tries to get out, all the others will try to pull him down.[3]

Such black humor betrays a lack of faith—but is also an act of resistance to the imposition of a "Mexican" label, an affirmation of regional, indigenous identities. Therefore, Mexicans exaggerate their depravity, the degree to which corrupt officials are plundering.

The third reason, however, is the most captivating. When compared to the United States, Mexico naturally appears corrupt. But is this perception a reflection of reality or a reflection of America's denial of its own corruption?

Mexico comes across more corrupt than it actually is because the United States indulges in a body of double-speak that glosses over corruption. American denial, of course, is easily understood in the exacting demands that emerged at the conclusion of World War II: In a bipolar world, roles had to be assigned and acted out. The role that America played from the conclusion of World War II to the collapse of the Soviet Union necessitated a body of language that denied the possibility of American corruption.

Mexico, where corruption is confessed by every citizen, on the other hand, appears beyond hope of redemption. There can be no doubt that there's a great deal of corruption in Mexico, but Americans, such as Senator Helms, presume that there is a great deal more than there actually exists. Mexicans call "corruption" many things that Americans do not.

In Mexico there are three kinds of corruption: bribery, fraud, and abuse. Bribery (*mordidas*) is what you pay a police officer who pulls you over for no reason. Fraud (*fraude*) is what you pay indirectly, as when the telephone company is ripped off by its directors and rates have to be raised to cover the loss. Abuse (*abuso*) is what happens when an individual uses his position for personal gain. These three broad categories are collectively known as "corruption." No one shies away from using the word, and Mexicans make no effort to deny the truth from themselves or the world.

In contrast, to Americans "corruption" is a frightening word, a word that denotes an evil, a word many Americans find unspeakable. "Corruption" is therefore seldom used by Americans when describing what happens in the United States.

This has not always been so. At the turn of the century, Americans openly discussed the rampant corruption in the United States. Today, in contrast, there is a great effort to deny that corruption exists at all. As Americans would have the world believe, corruption only occurs in foreign countries. The evil of corruption, a moral depravity somewhere overseas, is not to be found within the shores of the United States.

The idea that corruption is a foreign evil is a recent—but widespread—notion. Thus, Americans avoid the use of the word "corruption" through euphemisms and metaphors. Semantic games are often employed by the media, officials, and private citizens alike. "Wrongdoing," by far the most popular metaphor, is followed by "compromised," "bankrupt," and the euphemisms "poor judgment," "improper behavior," "questionable ethics," and "no contest."

These semantic somersaults are a conscious act. Speaking of the labor movement in the forties and fifties, David Brenner, for example, warns that "corrupt" is a dangerous word to use, and that perhaps "morally bankrupt" is better.

The *New York Times* reported that a Pentagon consultant—the thirteenth within a two-month period—pleaded guilty to "bribery, wire fraud, and conspiracy." But he didn't plead guilty to corruption. That same edition reported that a major defense contractor had been accused of "overbilling" the government by tens of millions of dollars. The contractor wasn't accused of "corruption," however.

The linguistic aversion to the word "corruption" in American vernacular intrigues. This is, after all, a far cry from America in the late nineteenth century. Mark Twain complained that "it was impossible to save the Great Republic. She was rotten to the heart."

He was not alone. One hears echoes of the short-lived yuppies in Walt Whitman's lamentation that "never was there, perhaps, more hollowness at heart than at present." Whitman also foreshadowed the current Wall Street scandals when he warned that "the depravity of the business classes of our country is not less than has been supposed, but infinitely greater." Ambrose Bierce, another writer of the era, putting it more bluntly, so despised "the corrupt beast" that his country had become that he left for Mexico where he could find "a few honest folk with whom I can spend the rest of my days." And he left, never to return.

Rotten to the heart? Depraved? Corrupt? The United States of America?

The reluctance of Americans today to use the word "corruption" offers insights into the psyche of a nation. The semantic somersaults used to disguise "corruption" must be understood in the broader context of America's self-image. The America of the eighteenth century was one in which a young boy, when confronted by his father, would look his father straight in the eyes and say, "I cannot tell a lie, sir; I cut down the cherry tree." The America of the twentieth century, however, is one in which that same boy would reply, "I cannot tell a lie, sir; I plead 'No Contest.' "

How is it that Mark Twain's Corruptionville, more commonly referred to as Philadelphia, achieved a remarkable transformation? When did this national catharsis take place? How did America eliminate "corruption" from its vocabulary?

The answer lies in the development of America's self-image in this century. The excesses and decadence that gave rise to widespread corruption in the United States at the end of the Grant administration were spiritually exhausting. The "Gilded Age" worried commentators who opposed the young nation's newfound infatuation with materialism. An era in which men like Jim Fisk, Boss Tweed, and Oakes Ames were admired and scandals (from Crédit Mobilier to Pomeroy) characterized American public life undermined the nation's future. These images, however, constituted the framework within which America saw itself. And, like Caliban, America was horrified by its own reflection in the mirror.

Without redemption, critics argued, America would be lost. The opportunity for redemption came during the Spanish-American War. The United States, a rapidly developing nation, seized on the idealism of war to begin a process of cleansing. The emergence of America at the conclusion of the war as a regional power in the Western Hemisphere coincided with the mounting of antagonisms in Europe, which eventually culminated in the outbreak of war. Woodrow Wilson, building on the new-found temperance of Americans, called for an effort to make "the world safe for democracy." This splendid idealism offered Americans the raw material from which to fashion a self-image. The nation, growing more important economically, had now abandoned isolationism and, as entry into World War I demonstrated, it was prepared to participate actively in the community of nations. Like a patient who sweats out a fever in the night, so did America cleanse its body of corruption.

America's international image of a developing whiz-kid nation responsible for saving democracy gave Americans great confidence. It was not until World War II, however, when the Europeans effectively blew themselves up, that the United States emerged as a world leader. The Soviet Union also emerged as a major power, thanks to nuclear physics more than anything else.

A world dominated by two major countries, each with nuclear arsenals, resulted in a balance of terror that necessitated a bipolar framework; America wore a White Hat and the Soviets did not. The nuclear nations became antagonistic superpowers, each the other's archenemy. This reality established parameters for the fashioning of self-images for both the United States and the Soviet Union. America saw itself so innocently. Consider the television shows of the period—from *I Love Lucy* to *Father Knows Best* to *Leave it to Beaver*. America was a world without segregation, poverty, social injustice, or racism. Lucy never wondered about the Korean War or nuclear proliferation; it never occurred to Beaver to ask his parents why the U.S. overthrew governments in Guatemala or installed puppets in Iran; Ozzie and Harriet didn't seem to notice the race riots, the execution of the Rosenbergs, or America's growing military presence in Southeast Asia.

America, however, did notice the Soviet Union. American fears of its reckless archenemy, risking nuclear war in Berlin, then in Cuba, precipitated an official vocabulary by which Americans could define themselves and create a notion of self. Thus, "evil empires" were possible, "propaganda offensives" inevitable, and "institutionalized terror" (also known as "nuclear deterrent") necessary. American missiles, after all, were the peacekeepers. Soviet missiles were not.

There is no room for corruption in this kind of America, is there? In contrast, Mexico has a tremendous absorptive ability to take in all the corruption imaginable. But as Octavio Paz observes, "The issue is less one of immorality than of the unconscious operation of another set of morals: in the patrimonial regime the frontiers between public and private spheres, family and state are rather vague and fluctuating."[4]

In Mexico, an American businessman who is originally from New York City, insists that "corruption" indicates a systematic, institutionalized evil, whereas "wrongdoing" only indicts an individual and not the system. Thus, while individual Americans may be corrupt, there is no institutional corruption in the United States.

But if this is so, why do Americans go to such lengths to absolve individuals of responsibility for their actions? Instead of saying that a former White House aide is the "victim" of a drinking problem responsible for his "lapses in judgment" in his lobbying efforts, why not say that he was a corrupt influence peddler? Instead of allowing the head of a major Wall Street firm to plead "no contest" to charges of bribery, kickbacks, and mail fraud, why not admit that he's a corrupt bum?

Are we also to believe that the Teamsters Union is not corrupt, just burdened by a few "wrongdoers" here and there? Are we to believe there is no pattern of corruption within the military-industrial complex, just a funny rash of "billing errors"? Are we to believe that there is no institutional framework for fraud within New York's construction business, just a most creative "profit-sharing" plan?

"We don't use the word 'corruption' in this country," another American in Mexico on business offers, "and you're forcing your linguistics on American English."

But if this is the case, then how come American reporters in Mexico prefer to send stories over the wire that are phrased, "Mexico's Attorney General charged so-and-so with corruption," instead of, "Mexico's Attorney General charged so-and-so with wrongdoing"? Reread the morning paper and substitute the word "corruption" for "wrongdoing" and see what image of America emerges then.

The antagonism inherent in a bipolar world makes it clear that (apart from organized crime, which exists only in the "underworld") there can be no corruption in America. It's not possible to wear a White Hat and also do wrong; the Lone Ranger was pure. And like television adventure shows, a world dominated by opposing superpowers requires scripts to move the action along. America was thus cast in the role of Luke Skywalker, and the Soviet Union was Darth Vader. These images, these roles, I submit, define how Americans see themselves and see others. Of course, "corruption" is a dangerous word under these circumstances; it upsets the protagonist's adversaries.

But these roles depend on two things: that no other player enters the scene and that the vocabulary by which the players understand their parts remains unchanged. If either the script's structure is altered or a player starts changing his role, the drama is upset. The Soviet Union could not be virtuous anymore than the United States could be capable of corruption.

Then along arrived Mikhail Gorbachev, who unilaterally changed the Soviet Union's script. Free elections in an evil empire? It appears that the keepers of a bipolar world, such as Jeane Kirkpatrick, who so easily dismissed Gorbachev's overtures as public relations ploys, were wrong.

Mikhail Gorbachev—and his successor, Boris Yeltsin—indeed, has sported a White Hat. This metamorphose also threatens the way in which Americans define their role in the world.

The language by which the Soviets understand their national identity has changed indeed. "Democracy," "market forces," "glasnost" are now slogans of former Soviets. America, too, is characterized by a new vocabulary. The "most extensive criminal securities fraud inquiry ever undertaken by the Federal Government," "a former employee ... is accusing the company in a lawsuit of deliberately overcharging the Pentagon," and "government files detailing ... murders, car bombings, political scheming" are phrases lifted from newspapers, days apart. Somehow, the Lone Ranger's hat has become scuffed.

The word "corruption" must find its place in American life in the same way in which "democracy" is heard on the streets of Moscow. Pretended American innocence was fine when an archenemy loomed over the horizon; but in a multipolar world, where the rival superpower is not inherently evil, language must become more honest and Caliban must stare, however painful, into that mirror. "Corruption" is, indeed, a dangerous word; it violates the language of a bipolar world.

The semantic games that Americans play today are designed to preserve an antagonistic struggle in the balance of terror that has become all too familiar in the postwar era. The world, to Americans, must be distinct opposites: good versus evil, freedom versus tyranny, us versus them. Nowhere was that more evident than in the McCarthy hearings (itself a form of corruption). And American foreign policy, as the conflicts in Central America underscore, has also been defined in an East-West context. How Americans redefine themselves—as the United States, its stature diminished, accepts the inevitability of a multipolar world—will be interesting to see. No longer the defender of the wild, wild West, what will the Lone Ranger do?

The reason why Mexico appears to be more corrupt than the United States is that Mexicans, in their enthusiasm to affirm their own identities, are not afraid of calling a thing by its proper name. That White House aide who peddled influence would in Mexico be called a "corrupt" person, not an "alcoholic." That businessman whose company stole millions from its clients would also be considered a "corrupt" person, not a "defendant" who pleaded "no contest." That congressman who entered into an unusual publishing agreement is guilty of "corruption," not "poor judgment."

If Mexico appears corrupt to Americans, it is because Mexicans take perverse pleasure in confessing their nation's shortcomings. If Mexico appears corrupt to Americans, it is because corruption in America is sophisticated, whereas in Mexico it is crude.

I have encountered corruption while driving to the resort of Acapulco. I was forced to pull over because some soldiers had set up a road block. One Mexican soldier—but a mere teenage boy—came over and said their truck was out of gas. I made the mistake of saying, "So?" Then another soldier came over and told me to get out. Two others approached, one of them opening my gas tank and proceeding to steal my fuel. Then they drove off. I had to walk four miles to the nearest gas station, get some gas, and hitch a ride back to my car. I'm not sure what category of corruption this comes under—abuse of authority or a bribe paid in the form of gasoline—but I was the victim of corruption, rather crude corruption at that.

I have also, however, been the victim of corruption in the United States. It was so subtle and sophisticated, I was completely unaware of it. My home in California is serviced by Pacific Bell, a subsidiary of Pacific Telesis. For a time in the eighties, Pacific Bell had been adding services and features to its customers. Since all utility bills are paid without great scrutiny, it was not until I read in a newspaper that the state of California had sued Pacific Bell for "overbilling" customers that I suspected something was wrong. The company claimed that "aggressive marketing" was the reason why customers were signed up for services—call waiting, call forwarding, regional discount plans, and so on—without their knowledge. The state ordered the company to reimburse customers who had been billed for services not requested. I received a letter from Pacific Bell stating that they owed me "more than an apology"; in my case it turned out that, over a nine-month period, I had been "overbilled" several hundred dollars.

There are institutional factors that contribute to Mexican corruption that are inherent in paternalism itself and in the iron cage that Weber denounced. These include the absence of free elections; the lack of an independent judiciary; and benefits, instead of salaries, for public workers. A "perfect hegemony" is corruption. Justice is routinely bought. It is ridiculous to expect police officers who are paid $90 a month to be of the highest calibre—or honest.

But these are also problems the world over, including the United States. Political scandals—PAC money, lecture fees, conflicts of interest, and campaign contributions—corrupt government at all levels. While judges are seldom corrupt, justice depends on one's attorney; a million-dollar lawyer can get you sentenced, at worst, to a "minimum security" country club, but a public defender can get you on death row. It is not surprising that the largest source of theft in corporate America comes from underpaid and ill-trained security guards.

What differentiates America is that an independent judiciary conducts investigations and prosecutes the "wrongdoers." Mexican corruption would be greatly reduced if law enforcement officers were better paid and the courts were not subservient to the interests of the ruling party. But it is important to see things in their true perspective.

Mark Twain believed that "everything which has happened once must happen again and again and again" for eternity. This cyclical view of history coincides with Mesoamerican thinking that still holds power over the minds of people in Mexico. There is hope that the excesses of Mexico under Luis Echeverría and José López Portillo have subsided. Scandals, thefts, and "wrongdoing" under Miguel de la Madrid were significantly reduced from previous levels, and under Carlos Salinas de Gortari additional progress was made, despite Senator Helms' denunciations to the contrary.

According to Octavio Paz, "The Mexican excels at the dissimulation of his passions and himself. He is afraid of others' looks and therefore he withdraws, contracts, becomes a shadow, a phantasm, an echo. Instead of walking, he glides; instead of stating, he hints; instead of replying, he mumbles; instead of complaining, he smiles."[5] It is also reassuring to know that Mexico has not always been corrupt, Octavio Paz's rationalizations notwithstanding. In the fifties, the government of Mexico was recognized throughout the world as efficient and honest. The International Monetary Fund had such confidence in the Mexican peso, for instance, that it was stockpiled as a reserve currency. But Mexicans, like the Europeans, are cynics at heart. Americans, in contrast, are optimistic, perhaps naïvely so.

This blind faith is due, in part, to the White Hat syndrome: making the world safe for democracy, saving it from fascism, and keeping the communists at bay. But this American mythology must reform itself in the wake of present-day realities.

Mexico, too, must learn that it is not as corrupt as it would like to think itself to be. Oh, to be sure, there are scoundrels who can compete with the best of them. Consider Carlos Hank González, a former school teacher who, in his career as a civil servant, has managed to accumulate a family fortune estimated by *Forbes* magazine to exceed $1.3 billion in U.S. currency. The audacity astounds in its vulgarity, as does the passivity of the Mexican nation. The lament of Emperor Maximilian comes to mind about the nothingness of the Mexican character that finds Mexicans helpless in the face of such bandit raids.

But this is the exception. The international debt crisis, after all, was really caused by mismanagement and stupidity more so than by corruption. This is difficult for Mexicans to accept because any idiot can screw things up, but corruption, if nothing else, requires a certain amount of cleverness and ingenuity.

Mexicans would rather be evil than be fools. Mexicans would rather forgive and let human frailties and the giving in to temptations be tolerated. It is never too late for redemption, for forgiveness, Mexico argues. Then again, Mexico does not require that the loot be returned as a requisite for being pardoned. Perhaps it should. Then its benevolence would appear just and not merely an excuse for public officials to plunder the national treasury.

But even those nations fortunate enough to enjoy authentic democracy cannot escape corruption. Consider recent American history. Under the Reagan administration, the Department of Housing and Urban Development, known as HUD, festered with rampant wrongdoing. According to published newspaper accounts, a congressional investigation uncovered misappropriations that exceeded $8 billion. Such a figure is almost unimaginable. To understand it, think of it this way: The amount of money misappropriated at HUD each day of the Reagan administration every week of every month of every year for eight years was over $2,700,000.

Mexico cannot hope to rival this kind of corruption, nor should it.

NOTES

1. Richard Rodriguez, *Days of Obligation: An Argument with My Mexican Father* (New York: Viking Penguin, 1992), p. 90.

2. Octavio Paz, *The Labyrinth of Solitude: Life and Thought in Mexico* (New York: Grove Press, 1961), p. 388.

3. Patrick Oster, *The Mexicans* (New York: Harper & Row, 1989), p. 219.

4. Paz, *Labyrinth of Solitude*, p. 397.

5. Ibid., pp. 42–43.

Epilogue

Mexico and Russia both experienced revolutions which concluded in 1917 and were founded on utopian principles of socialism and weightless, liquid dreams. The Bolshevik Revolution in Russia established the Soviet State, which then embarked on a communist program that abolished private property, as well as human rights and hopes. The Mexican Revolution, which in fact was a civil war, resulted in the creation of an authoritarian state with a mixed economy (more socialist than capitalist) and with mixed records on respecting human freedoms. These sister revolutions transformed their respective countries and—being the absorbing concurrent social experiments on opposite sides of the globe that they are—invite comparison. It is only instructive to check in every now and then and take note of observations that offer insights into the progress of these experiments. Both revolutions, after all, failed miserably; those fabulous Bolshevik boys wreaked havoc and destruction, as did Mexico's own band of Frito Banditos.

The implementation of NAFTA heralds the final conclusion of the Mexican Revolution, and Mexico is now embarked on a race against time to make up for lost decades. Ernesto Zedillo, who will deliver Mexico to the twenty-first century, confronts enormous challenges as the authoritarian hegemony that characterizes the political economy of the Mexican nation-state is dismantled. NAFTA constitutes a blueprint for the systematic surrender of the Mexican economy. There is, however, no blueprint for the transformation of Mexico into a democracy. Herein lies the greatest risks to corporate America, for there is always the danger of self-destruction, as witnessed in some of the republics of the former Soviet Union.

The future proves promising for North America, Inc., and in fact, as

the economies of North America restructure and grow . . . NAFTA will make North American firms more competitive in world markets and thus better able to take advantage of the increased trade opportunities created by the prospective Uruguay Round Reforms. . . . One should see the NAFTA . . . as an integral part of a national competitiveness strategy, one that complements domestic economic reforms designed to improve productivity and promote the ability of local industries to compete more effectively against foreign suppliers at home and in world markets.[1]

One should see NAFTA, in other words, as the beginning of North America, Inc., and the beginning of the end of Mexico. What Mexico forgot to consider, after all, is that in this world, despite wishful thinking, one-third of anything will always be the bottom third. In the North American trading bloc envisioned by NAFTA, the United States, Canada and Mexico may be equals, but some will be more equal than others.

Mexico is embarking on NAFTA in an alarming manner. The Emperor Maximilian lamented that Mexico was "ruled by men who had never had responsibility and did not understand it." Critics of NAFTA point out how this surrender of sovereignty has enormous implications for the idea of the nation-state, in much the same way in which the European Community constitutes an integration of historic proportions. For her protestations to the contrary, Mexico has freely chosen to surrender her sovereignty and to become a vassal state of the United States and Canada. But an integration among equals is one thing, and the wholesale incorporation of Mexico into North America is another. For a nation of people who profess the desire to assert their sovereignty and to be free, there is something ominous and tragic about Mexico's complete surrender to the will and interests of the United States and Canada.

The unquestioning enthusiasm with which Mexico is embracing all things American has within it the potential for significant social consequences as various groups within Mexican society compete for rank in the changing ranks of status. There are forces at work, most notably the hard-core leftist elements within the ruling party and the disenfranchised half of Mexico's population, that stand to lose status in the new paradigm of Mexican society. At the same time, those who stand to benefit from the age of free trade, too, have lingering doubts and, as Mexicans have always been throughout history, remain insecure about who they are and their place in the world. At a time when Mexico is striving to become a modern democracy and have a rational economy, there is fear, for servitude of one kind or another is all that the Mexicans have ever known. I am reminded of Octavio Paz's reflection: "The arrival of the Spaniard seemed a liberation to the people under Aztec rule. The various city-states allied themselves with the conquistadores or watched with indifference—if not with pleasure—the fall of each of their rivals, especially that of the most powerful, [Mexico City.]"[2]

The final irony, then, is that for corporate America, the Mexican impulse to serve offers unexpected opportunities. I was speaking with a Mexican friend who is a businessman. In the early nineties he bought a Dairy Queen franchise. I asked him how it was going. It was going great, he told me. It was like no other way of doing business, he told me. Everything had been taken care of for him—from the equipment to the floor tiles, from the ice cream to the cash register tape. All he had to do was open for business and report back on the day's sales. He pushed a button and the cash register, which is really a computer, spit out all kinds of information. He faxed this to people in the United States who later faxed him back an analysis, which was really a set of instructions. It was all easy, he told me, because all the thinking was done for him. Once he put up the initial investment, he explained, everything was taken care of. All he had to do, he told me with delight, was exactly what he was told.

In many ways, what could please corporate America more?

NOTES

1. Gary Clyde Hufbauer and Jeffrey J. Schott, *NAFTA: An Assessment* (Washington, D.C.: Institute for International Economics, 1993), p. 116.

2. Octavio Paz, *The Labyrinth of Solitude: Life and Thought in Mexico* (New York: Grove Press, 1961), p. 93.

Appendix I
Mexican Trade Offices in the United States

California
8484 Wilshire Boulevard
Suite 808
Beverly Hills, CA 90211
213/655-6421

Florida

New World Tower
100 N. Biscayne Boulevard
Suite 1601
Miami, FL 33132
305/372-9929

Georgia

229 Peachtree Street, N.E.
Suite 917
Atlanta, GA 30343
404/522-5373

Illinois

225 N. Michigan Avenue
Suite 708
Chicago, IL 60601
312/856-0316

New York

150 East 58th Street
17th Floor
New York, NY 10155
212/826-2916

Texas

2777 Stemmons Freeway
Suite 1622
Dallas, TX 75207
214/688-4096

Washington

Plaza 600, 600 and Stewart Street
Suite 703
Seattle, WA 98101
206/441-2833

Washington, D.C.

Embassy of Mexico
1911 Pennsylvania Avenue, N.W.
7th Floor
Washington, DC 20006
202/728-1700

Appendix II
Mexican Trade Organizations

Industry Associations

Asociación de Fabricantes de la Cerveza
(Beer Manufacturing National Chamber)
Avenida Horacio No. 1556, Colonia Chapultepec Morales
11570, Mexico, D.F.

Asociación de Ingenieros de Minas, Metalurgistas y Geologos
de Mexico, A.C.
(Mining Engineers, Metallurgists and Geologists Association)
Tacuba No. 5-19 B,
Apartado Postal 1260
06000, Mexico, D.F.

Asociación Mexicana de Agencias de Publicidad
(Advertising Agency Association)
Plaza Carlos J. Finlay No. 6, 4o Piso
06500, Mexico, D.F.

Asociación Mexicana de Caminos
(Mexican Road Association)
Río Tiber No. 103, 2o Piso
06500, Mexico, D.F.

Asociación Mexicana de Criadores de Ganado Suizo
(Mexican Association of Swiss Cattle Breeders)
Andalucia No. 162
03400, Mexico, D.F.

Asociación Mexicana de Distribuidores de Gas Licuado y
Empresas Conexas, A.C.
(Mexican Association of Gas Distributors)
Filadelfia No. 119, 1er Piso, Colonia Nápoles
Mexico, D.F.

Asociación Mexicana de Fabricantes de Válvulas
(Valves Manufacturers National Association)
Copérnico No. 47, Colonia Anzures
11590, Mexico, D.F.

Asociación Mexicana de Hoteles y Moteles de la República, A.C.
(Mexican Hotel and Motel Association)
Hamburgo No. 108-104
06600, Mexico, D.F.

Asociación Mexicana de la Industria Automotriza, A.C.
(Automotive Industry Association)
Ensenada No. 90
06100, Mexico, D.F.

Asociación Mexicana de Restaurantes
(Mexican Restaurant Association)
Torcuato Tasso No. 325-103
11560, Mexico, D.F.

Asociación Nacional de Fabricantes de Aparatos Domésticos
(Household Appliance National Association)
Zacatecas No. 155, Colonia Roma
06067, Mexico, D.F.

Asociación Nacional de Fabricantes de Medicamentos
(Pharmaceutical Manufacturers National Association)
Eugenia No. 13-601
03810, Mexico, D.F.

Asociación Nacional de Fabricantes de Pinturas y Tintas
(Paint and Ink Manufacturers National Association)
Gabriel Mancera No. 309
03100, Mexico, D.F.

Asociación Nacional de Fabricantes de Tableros de Madera, A.C.
(Lumber Manufacturers National Association)
Acapulco No. 35-501
06700, Mexico, D.F.

Asociación National Hotelera
(National Hotel Association)
Edison No. 84, 2o Piso, Colonia Tabacalera
Mexico, D.F.

Asociación Nacional de la Industria del Café
(Coffee Industry National Association)
Avenida Insurgentes Sur No. 682
03100, Mexico, D.F.

Asociación Nacional de la Industria Química
(Chemical Industry National Association)
Avenida Providencia No. 1118
03100, Mexico, D.F.

Asociación Nacional de Industrias de Plástico, A.C.
(Plastic Industry National Association)
Doctor Vertiz No. 546
03500, Mexico, D.F.

Asociación Nacional de Productores de Aguas Envasadas
(Bottled Water Producers National Association)
Paseo de la Reforma No. 195-301
06500, Mexico, D.F.

Asociación Nacional de Vitivinicultores, A.C.
(National Association of Grape Growers and Wine Producers)
Calzada de Tlalpan No. 3515
04650, Mexico, D.F.

Industry Chambers of Commerce

Camara Minera de Mexico
(Mining Chamber of Mexico)
Sierra Vertientes No. 369, Colonia Lomas de Chapultepec
11000, Mexico, D.F.

Camara Nacional del Aerotransporte
(Air Transport National Chamber)
Paseo de la Reforma No. 76, 17o Piso
06600, Mexico, D.F.

Camara Nacional de Cemento (Canacem)
(Cement National Chamber)
Leibnitz No. 77
11590, Mexico, D.F.

Camara Nacional de Hospitales
(Hospital National Chamber)
Vito Alessio Robles No. 23, 6o Piso
01030, Mexico, D.F.

Camara Nacional de la Industria de Aceites, Grasa y Jabones
(Oil, Grease and Soap Industry National Chamber)
Melchor Ocampo No. 193, Torre A, Colonia Veronica Anzures
11300, Mexico, D.F.

Camara Nacional de Industria de Artes Gráficas
(Graphic Arts Industry National Chamber)
Avenida Río Churubusco No. 428, 2o Piso, Colonia Del
Carmen Coyoacan
04100, Mexico, D.F.

Camara Nacional de la Industria Azucarera y Alcoholera
(Sugar and Alcohol Industry National Chamber)
Río Niagara No. 11, Colonia Cuauhtemoc
06500, Mexico, D.F.

Camara Nacional de la Industria del Calzado
(Shoe Industry National Chamber)
Durango No. 24S, 12o Piso
06700, Mexico, D.F.

Camara Nacional de la Industria Cinematográfica
(Cinematography Industry National Chamber)
Gen. Anaya No. 198
04210, Mexico, D.F.

Camara Nacional de la Industria de la Construcción
(Construction Industry National Chamber)
Periférico Sur No. 4839
14010, Mexico, D.F.

Camara Nacional de la Industria de la Curtiduría
(Tannery Industry National Chamber)
Tehuantepec No. 255, 1o Piso
06760, Mexico, D.F.

Camara Nacional de la Industria Electrónica y de
Comunicaciones Eléctricas
(Electronic and Electronic Communications National Chamber)
Guanajuato No. 65
06700, Mexico, D.F.

Camara Nacional de la Industria del Embellecimiento Físico
(Physical Fitness Industry National Chamber)
Salamanca No. 5
06700, Mexico, D.F.

Camara Nacional de la Industria Farmaceutica
(Pharmaceutical Industry National Chamber)
Avenida Cuauhtemoc No. 1481, Colonia Santa Cruz Atoyac
03380, Mexico, D.F.

Camara Nacional de la Industria del Hierro y del Acero
(Iron and Steel Industry National Chamber)
Amores No. 338, Colonia Del Valle
03199, Mexico, D.F.

Camara Nacional de la Industria Hulera
(Rubber Industry National Chamber)
Manuel María Contreras No. 133-115
06500, Mexico, D.F.

Camara Nacional de la Industria Maderera y Similares
(Lumber and Related Products Industry National Chamber)
Santander No. 15-301
03920, Mexico, D.F.

Camara Nacional de la Industria Panificadora
(Bakery Industry National Chamber)
Doctor Liceaga No. 96
06620, Mexico, D.F.

Camara Nacional de la Industria de la Pesca
(Fishing Industry National Chamber)
Manuel María Contreras No. 133, Colonia Cuauhtemoc
06500, Mexico, D.F.

Camara Nacional de la Industria de la Platería y la Joyería
(Silver and Jewelry Industry National Chamber)
Reynosa No. 13
06100, Mexico, D.F.

Camara Nacional de la Industria de Radio y T.V.
(Radio and T.V. Industry National Chamber)
Horacio No. 1013
11550, Mexico, D.F.

Camara Nacional de la Industria Textile
(Textile Industry National Chamber)
Plionio No. 20, Esquina Horacio
11560, Mexico, D.F.

Camara Nacional de la Industria del Vestido
(Garment Industry National Chamber)
Tolsa No. 54
06040, Mexico, D.F.

Camara Nacional de las Industrias de la Celulosa y el Papel
(Cellulose and Paper Industries National Chamber)
Priv. de San Isidro No. 30, Colonia Reforma Social
11650, Mexico, D.F.

Camara Nacional de Industrias de la Leche
(Milk Products Industry National Chamber)
Benjamin Franklin No. 134
11800, Mexico, D.F.

Camara Nacional de las Industrias de la Silvicultura
(Forest Products and Derivatives Industries National Chamber)
Baja California No. 225, Edificio A, 12o Piso
06170, Mexico, D.F.

Camara Nacional de las Manufacturas Eléctricas (Caname)
(Electric Manufacturers National Chamber)
Ibsen No. 13
11560, Mexico, D.F.

Camara Nacional de Transportes y Comunicaciones
(Transportation and Comunication National Chamber)
Pachuca No. 158-Bis
06140, Mexico, D.F.

National Associations

Asociación Mexicana de Bancos
(Mexican Bank Association)
Lázaro Cárdenas No. 2, 9o Piso
06079, Mexico, D.F.

Asociación Nacional de Importadores y Exportadores de
la República Mexicana
(National Association of Importers and Exporters of
the Mexican Republic)
Monterrey No. 130, Colonia Roma
06700, Mexico, D.F.

Camara Nacional de Comercio de la Ciudad de México
(Mexico City National Chamber of Commerce)
Paseo de la Reforma No. 43, 3er Piso
06048, Mexico, D.F.

Camara Nacional de la Industria de la Transformación
(Canacintra)
(Manufacturing Industry National Chamber)
Avenida San Antonio No. 256
03849, Mexico, D.F.

Confederación de Camaras Industriales de los Estados Unidos
Mexicanos (Concamin)
(Confederation of the National Chambers of Industry)
Manuel María Contreras No. 133, 8o Piso
06500, Mexico, D.F.

Confederación de Camaras Nacionales de Comercio (Concanaco)
(Confederation of National Chambers of Commerce)
Balderas No. 144, 3er Piso
06079, Mexico, D.F.

Consejo Coordinador Empresarial (CCE)
(Businessmen's Coordinating Council)
Homero 527–6o Piso
11570, Mexico, D.F.

Selected Bibliography

PRIMARY SOURCES ON THE
CONQUEST OF MEXICO

Anales de Mexico y Tlateloco. Preserved at the National Museum of Anthropology, Mexico City.

Anonymous Manuscripts of Tlateloco (1528). Preserved at the National Library of Paris. Facsimile edition published by Ernst Mengin in *Corpus Codicum Americanorum Medii Aevi.* Vol. 2. Copenhagen, 1945.

Atlas o Codice de Duran. In *Historia de las Indias de la Nueva España e Islas de Tierra Firme,* by Fray Diego de Duran, Porrúa, Mexico, 1968.

Cantares Mexicanos (collection of Mexican Native American songs). Sixteenth-century manuscript preserved at the National Library of Mexico. Facsimile reproduction published by Antonio Peñafiel. Oficina Tipográfica de la Secretaría de Fomento, Mexico, 1904.

Chimalpain Quauhtlehuanitzin, Francisco de San Anton Munon. *Sixième et Septième Relations* (1258–1612). Translated by Remi Simeon. Maisoneuve et Ch. Leclerc, Paris, 1889.

Codice Aubin. Edited and Translated by Ch. E. Dibble. Chimalytac, Madrid, 1963.

Codice Florentino. 3 vols. Facsimile edition published by the Mexican government, Mexico, 1979.

Codice Ramirez. "Relación del origen de los indios que habitan esta Nueva España segun sus historias." Editorial Leyenda, Mexico, 1944.

Ixtlilxochitl, Fernando de Alva. *Obras Historicas.* 2 vols. Mexico: National University, 1975–1977.

Lienzo de Tlaxcala. Antigüedades mexicanas. Published by Junta Colombina de
    Mexico en el IV Centenario del Descubrimiento de América. 2 vols.
    Oficina de la Secretaría de Fomento, Mexico, 1892.
Muñoz Camargo, Diego. *Historia de Tlaxcala*. Mexico, 1892.
Portillo, Miguel Leon, ed. *The Broken Spears: The Aztec Account of the Conquest
    of Mexico*. Boston: Beacon Press, 1990.
Sahagún, Fray Bernardino de. *Florentine Codex: General History of the Things
    of New Spain*. Translated from Nahuatl into English by Arthur J. O.
    Anderson and Charles E. Dibble. 12 vols. Santa Fe, N.M.: School of
    American Research and the University of Utah, 1950–1982.
Tezozomoc, F. Alvarado. *Crónica mexicana*. Edited by Vigil. Mexico: Editorial
    Leyenda, 1944.

OTHER REFERENCES

Bergsten, C. Fred, Thomas Horst and Theodore Horst. *American Multinationals
    and American Interests*. Washington, D.C.: Brookings Institution, 1978.
Custine, Marquis de. *Empire of the Czar: A Journey through Eternal Russia*. New
    York: Doubleday, 1989.
Davidson, Basil. *The African Slave Trade*. Boston: Little, Brown & Company, 1980.
Didion, Joan. *Miami*. New York: Simon & Schuster, 1987.
Drucker, Peter F. *Technology, Management and Society*. New York: Heinemann,
    1970.
———. *Managing in Turbulent Times*. London: Heinemann, 1980.
Economic Strategy Institute. *NAFTA: Making it Better*. Washington, D.C.: ESI,
    1992.
Faux, Jeff, and William Spriggs. *U.S. Jobs and the Mexico Trade Proposal*.
    Washington, D.C.: Economic Policy Institute, 1991.
Fuentes, Carlos. *Christopher Unborn*. New York: Random House, 1990.
Galbraith, John Kenneth. *The New Industrial State*. Harmondsworth, England:
    Penguin Books, 1968.
———. *Economics in Perspective: A Critical History*. Boston: Houghton Mifflin,
    1987.
Ginzberg, Eli, and George Vojta. *Beyond Human Scale: The Large Corporation
    at Risk*. New York: Basic Books, 1968.
Hamilton-Paterson, James. *The Great Deep: The Sea and Its Thresholds*. New
    York: Random House, 1992.
Haskett, Robert. *Indigenous Rulers: An Ethnohistory of Town Government in
    Colonial Cuernavaca*. Albuquerque: The University of New Mexico
    Press, 1991.
———. "Indigenous Rulers: Nahua Mediation of Spanish Socio-Political
    'Evangelism' in Early Cuernavaca." Unpublished paper. 1994.
Hufbauer, Gary Clyde, and Jeffrey J. Schott. *NAFTA: An Assessment*. Washington,
    D.C.: Institute for International Economics, 1993.

McKinsey & Company. *Service Sector Productivity.* Washington, D.C.: McKinsey & Company, 1992.

Mayer, J. P. *Max Weber and German Political Thought.* London: Faber and Faber, 1979.

Meadows, Dennis, et al. *The Limits of Growth.* New York: Universe Books, 1972.

Organization for Economic Cooperation and Development. *Financing and External Debt of Developing Countries: 1990 Survey.* Paris: OECD, 1991.

Osmond, Neville. "Top Management: Its Tasks, Roles and Skills." *Journal of Business Policy* (Winter 1971).

Oster, Patrick. *The Mexicans.* New York: Harper & Row, 1989.

Paz, Octavio. *The Labyrinth of Solitude: Life and Thought in Mexico.* New York: Grove Press, 1961.

———. "The Philanthropic Ogre." *Dissent* (Winter 1979).

Porter, Michael E. *Competitive Strategy: Techniques for Analyzing Industries and Competitors.* New York: The Free Press, 1985.

Rich, Jan Gilbreath. "Planning the Border's Future: The Mexican-US Integrated Border Environment Plan." U.S.–Mexico Occasional Paper No. 1. Austin: LBJ School of Public Affairs, University of Texas at Austin, 1992.

Rieff, David. *The Exile: Cuba in the Heart of Miami.* New York: Simon & Schuster, 1993.

Rodriguez, Richard. *Days of Obligation: An Argument with My Mexican Father.* New York: Viking Penguin, 1992.

Sahagún, Fray Bernardino de. *Conquest of New Spain, 1585 Revision.* Translated by Howard F. Cline and edited by S. L. Cline. Salt Lake City: University of Utah Press, 1989.

Shiells, Clinton, and Robert C. Shelburne. "A Summary of 'Industrial Effects of a Free Trade Agreement between Mexico and the USA' by the Inter-industry Economic Research Fund, Inc." In U.S. International Trade Commission, *Economy-wide Modeling of the Economic Implications of a FTA with Mexico and a NAFTA with Canada and Mexico.* Washington, D.C.: USITC Publication 2508, 1992.

Smith, Gene. *Maximilian and Carlota: A Tale of Romance and Tragedy.* New York: William Morrow, 1973.

Tillich, Paul. *A History of Christian Thought: From Its Judaic and Hellenistic Origins to Existentialism.* New York: Simon & Schuster, 1968.

Whalen, John. "The North American Free Trade Agreement, the Liberalization of the Mexican Trucking Industry, and the Removal of Obstacles to the Free Flow of Goods via Truck Between the United States and Mexico." Unpublished paper. Georgetown University Graduate School of Foreign Service, 1992.

Wriston, Walter. *Risk and Other Four Letter Words.* New York: Harper & Row, 1986.

Yip, George. *Barriers to Entry: A Corporate Strategy Perspective.* Lexington, Mass.: Lexington Books, 1981.

Index

ABOUT THE AUTHOR

LOUIS E.V. NEVAER is director of Political Analysis at International Credit Monitor, a consulting firm specializing in political risk assessments, of which he is cofounder. He has extensive experience in overseas work, and has worked as a consultant to foreign governments, international firms, and nonprofit organizations.